A Ride Through
**AMERICA'S
ENDURING HISTORY**
with the Gun

FIRST
FREEDOM

★

DAVID
HARSANYI

THRESHOLD EDITIONS

New York London Toronto Sydney New Delhi

Threshold Editions
An Imprint of Simon & Schuster, Inc.
1230 Avenue of the Americas
New York, NY 10020

First Threshold Editions hardcover edition October 2018

THRESHOLD EDITIONS and colophon are trademarks of
Simon & Schuster, Inc.

For information about special discounts for bulk purchases,
please contact Simon & Schuster Special Sales at 1-866-506-1949
or business@simonandschuster.com.

The Simon & Schuster Speakers Bureau can bring authors to your
live event. For more information, or to book an event, contact the
Simon & Schuster Speakers Bureau at 1-866-248-3049 or visit
our website at www.simonspeakers.com.

Interior design by Lewelin Polanco

Manufactured in the United States of America

10 9 8 7 6 5 4 3 2 1

Library of Congress Cataloging-in-Publication Data

Names: Harsanyi, David, author.
 Title: First freedom : a ride through America's enduring history with the gun, from
the Revolution to today / David Harsanyi.
 Description: New York : Threshold Editions, [2018] | Includes bibliographical
references and index. |
 Identifiers: LCCN 2018014025 (print) | LCCN 2018015929 (ebook) | ISBN
9781501174025 (eBook) | ISBN 9781501174001 (hardcover : alk. paper)
 Subjects: LCSH: Firearms—United States—History. | Firearms industry and trade—
United States—History. | United States. Army—Firearms—History. | Firearms
ownership—United States—History. | United States. Constitution. 2nd Amendment.
 Classification: LCC TS533.2 (ebook) | LCC TS533.2 .H37 2018 (print) | DDC
338.4/768340973—dc23
 CRLC record available at https://lccn.loc.gov/2018014025

ISBN 978-1-5011-7400-1
ISBN 978-1-5011-7402-5 (ebook)

To those who serve

The Struggle on Concord Bridge

CONTENTS

PART III
MODERNITY

"Without sulfur and saltpeter . . . there can be no freedom."
—Eighteenth-century German-American saying

PROLOGUE

★

FROM PREY TO PREDATOR

"You come against me with sword and spear and javelin, but I come against you in the name of the Lord Almighty, the God of the armies of Israel, whom you have defied."

—David to the Philistine

A samurai shooting
an early firearm in
the mid-1600s

The future king of Israel wasn't entirely forthcoming. After all, in addition to the blessing of the Lord Almighty—or, perhaps because of it—David was also in possession of a major technological advantage. By the time he faced the Philistine giant in the Valley of Elah, the sling had emerged as one of the most potent projectile weapons of the ancient world. The meager sword was no match for David. Not when he was armed with a missile launcher that held a stopping power equivalent to a small-caliber bullet. If for some reason Goliath had been unacquainted with the sling's capability, he would soon learn, as would millions of others in the coming millennia, that superior size meant little when facing superior firepower.

Inventing and perfecting weapons that could kill others from afar was a concern nearly as old as human existence itself. From almost the beginning men had been throwing things at each other. Lethal things—projectiles that could slice through his enemy's skin, pierce through his armor, burn his foes, and, ultimately, blow them up. David's weapon was a mere blip in an arms race that spans tens of thousands of years, from rocks, spears, slingshots, bows and arrows, javelins, catapults, and cannons, to the predominant guns of American colonial life, the musket and rifle, and, finally, the automatic weapon.

To hit Goliath square in the forehead, David had been incredibly proficient with his weapon. As a shepherd protecting his flock from predators and thieves, David, who was also likely a soldier, had an intuitive understanding of his release point—a skill mastered only through years of experience. Attaining proficiency with a handheld missile launcher was no mere hobby for a man of his era or those of any another. It was a means of survival. For most of history, in fact, men lived their entire lives under the unremitting threat of violence.

Despite the tendency in contemporary culture to envision prehistoric man meandering on breezy plains with fellow villagers or cohabitating in serene villages, most humans pursued a policy of proactive martial violence against other members of their species. Man has habitually been in a state of war. Evidence of this bellicose disposition is strewn across the ancient and prehistoric world. "Peaceful pre-state societies were very rare; warfare between them was very frequent and most adult men in such groups saw combat repeatedly in a lifetime," Lawrence H. Keeley, an anthropologist at the University of Illinois at Chicago, recently observed.[1] Early man had an astronomically high chance of being killed by the ax, spear, stone, fist, or arrow. According to Keeley, around 65 percent of tribes engaged in perpetual warfare, and 87 percent fought in a battle at least once a year.[2]

In this environment, a human could best defend himself by creating space between himself and his enemy. Man probably developed "ranged weapons"—arms that could hit targets at distances greater than hand-to-hand combat—around 71,000 years ago in Africa. Not only did the ranged weapons hold a significant advantage by lowering the risk of injury, but, as the historian Alfred W. Crosby has pointed out, it transformed those who used them from "prey to predator."[3]

The first ranged weapons were probably made of long, thin blades of stone that were blunted on one edge and then glued into slots that were carved in wood or bone, creating a light arm that could hurl projectiles.[4] The sling itself has been in use for around 10,000 years, if not longer. Ancient warriors and hunters typically made their pouches from animal hides and used hair or sinews to make a cord. The earliest ammunition, the kind of smooth stones that David relied on to slay the giant, were abundant around the many streams, lakes, and rivers that humans first gathered around to form their societies.

The equipment David used to smite Goliath was certainly not new to the Jews, who had exploited slingers to expand their small kingdom—and would continue to do so in the coming century. Archaeologists have found slings in Egypt dating to around the time of David. The ability to fire projectiles in an arching trajectory over the walls to strike defenders was a significant upgrade in ancient warfare, which typically pitted men against each other in feats of strength, making it indispensable for armies well into the Iron Age.

As effective as the sling was, however, for most of human history one weapon ruled them all. The earliest evidence of bows and arrows date back to 20,000 BC, in cave paintings in La Valltorta Gorge, Spain, in which hunters are depicted aiming their bows at game with arrows jutting out of their hides. Sometime over the subsequent thousand years, we began to see feathers added to improve aim and flight, and flint points bound by sinew to add deadliness. Man would figure out ways to make their projectiles increasingly lethal, from daubing arrows in poison to dipping them in excrement to cause infections.

Holmegaard bows, found in the bogs of northern Europe and made from single pieces of wood, have been dated to 9,000 BC and were long, stiff weapons that used the outer limbs as levers; their efficiency was comparable to today's high-performance bows. To put such bows and arrows in perspective, it's fair to say that in terms of range, accuracy, and rapidity, these were preferable to most early guns. As we'll see, even after hundreds of years of propelling objects with gunpowder in Europe, the bow was still the weapon of choice.[5] "In 1595, by order of the Privy Council, the

English armed services abandoned the longbow and fought with muskets for the next two centuries and more," noted the American historian Edmund S. Morgan. "Nobody is sure why."[6]

The next step in range warfare was, naturally, trying to light your enemies on fire from afar. As with many discoveries of the ancient world, we will never have a firm date or definitive names attached to the discovery of gunpowder, but at some point between the years 600 and 900 CE, Chinese alchemists searching for an elixir for immortality combined saltpeter, sulfur, and charcoal and inadvertently stumbled upon a man-made recipe that would cause more premature death than any other mixture in history.

In the eleventh-century Song dynasty book called the *Wujing Zongyao*, a Chinese military compendium of techniques for war, the unknown author mentions incendiary bombs being thrown by siege engineers on catapults, as well as fire lances, which shot flames and debris out of bamboo tubes attached to spears and can probably be considered the first "guns" ever invented. An abundance of bamboo offered a convenient cylindrical container to stuff gunpowder into, making it easy to create fireworks. Innovators with deadly intent figured out that a larger amount of gunpowder could launch broken porcelain and various other fragments at people they didn't like. Soon the military appropriated the idea and began replacing wood with metal tubes and pottery with a fatal mix of flames and shrapnel.

These firearms would get a lot bigger before they got small again. By the early 1300s, the Chinese were constructing heavy bronze handheld cannons that were about a foot long. Then they made iron barrels with two-foot stocks and stuffed them with stone, metal, and other debris to spray at their enemies. The weapons continued to grow until two-man teams were needed to lug them around. The Chinese also gave their devices wonderfully descriptive names like "Heaven-Shaking Thunder-Crash Bomb," "Dropping-from-Heaven Bomb," "Match-for-Ten-Thousand-Enemies Bomb," and "Bandit-Burning Vision-Confusing Magic Fire-Ball." One particularly nasty device was dubbed a "Bone-Burning and Bruising Fire Oil Magic Bomb." But, in truth, the Chinese had not realized the full potential of the formula they had invented. Others, however, would.

By the end of the thirteenth century, the invading Mongols procured Chinese gunpowder knowledge and applied it to their own siege-making efforts. Through a policy of aggressive expansionism, the Mongolians would export the idea of gunpowder across Asia. The knowledge was soon being used on the Indian subcontinent, where gunpowder was integrated into siege warfare by the end of the 1300s. Some modern Indian historians argue that gunpowder was one of the major contributing factors that accelerated the formation of states in southern Asia in the fifteenth century, playing a defining role in the region for centuries.[7] The Japanese, who already boasted some of the best metalsmiths in Asia, were also quick adapters of the new technology.

By 1200 we see nebulous, and perhaps far-fetched, references to cannons and handguns in Europe. Many historians dispute the veracity of these early accounts. But the first documented case of gunpowder being used in a war in Europe can be found in a statement from Bishop Albertus Magnus from 1280: he describes cannons at the Siege of Seville, a more-than-yearlong Reconquista effort led by forces of Ferdinand III. As was quite often the case in medieval European conflicts, famine and disease, rather than gunpowder or any other weaponry, finally brought down the city. Other sources retroactively claim that Europeans had encountered gunpowder and various firearms in the Battle of Mohi in 1241, a decisive Mongol victory against the Christian kingdom in Hungary. According to Arab historian Ahmad al-Hassan, Muslim Mamluks had employed the "first cannon in history" against Mongols in the southeastern Galilee during the Battle of Ain Jalut in 1260.

What we are more certain about is that in 1346 the ill-fated Genoese mercenaries fighting for Philip VI in the muddy fields of northern France during the Hundred Years' War would come under fire from England's Edward III's armies at Crécy, facing two of the most important advances in warfare in hundreds of years: the deadly longbow *and* the cannon. The battle is often referred to as "the beginning of the end of chivalry" due to the armies' focus on peasant infantry and the decline of the mounted knight in European warfare. The role of the cannon in the victory has long been debated by historians, though recent archaeological digs in the area confirm that some rudimentary guns had helped the English.[8]

In the coming century, the longbow became one of the most devastating weapons of European war. Some suggest that trained archers of Edward III's armies could reach as far as four hundred yards. The gun, on the other hand, still had a way to go. The cannon used in Crécy was probably a *pot-de-fer*. As the French name suggests, these weapons were quite literally a big iron pot packed with gunpowder. An iron arrow-like bolt was inserted through the narrow opening at the top and a slow-burning fuse was lit with a linstock through a hole in the side. We know what this primitive cannon probably looked like because of an illustration included in a manuscript, *De notabilibus, sapientiis et prudentiis regum* (*Concerning the Majesty, Wisdom, and Prudence of Kings*), written by Walter de Milemete, which was presented to Edward III on his accession to the throne of England in 1326.[9] De Milemete's portrait, the first of any European gun, was offered without accompanying text or explanation, which leads historians to believe it was known to the British before defeating the larger army of French and Genoese led by Philip VI of France at Crécy.

This was not a precision weapon by any stretch of the imagination, although armies made various alterations with leather straps and weights to help aim it. It's unlikely these cannons inflicted any significant casualties. The dominant weaponry of war was still the lance, bow, and sword. It is more likely that the cannon created a psychological advantage, a horrifying noise and smoke that incited both confusion and fear in the enemy. As Giovanni Villani, a chronicler of the time, described the guns at Crécy: "They made a noise like thunder and caused much loss in men and horses."[10]

Others had been playing with this deadly idea as well. In 1338, the French used the *pot-de-fer* and fire bolts with iron feathers against the English near Southampton.[11] The castle of Burg Eltz, in Rheinland-Pfalz, Germany, holds surviving examples of these iron arrows that date back to circa 1332. In 1350, Petrarch, the famous chronicler of his age, claimed that cannons on the battlefield were "as common and familiar as other kinds of arms."[12] By 1375, the French were firing hundred-pound stone balls at the English, and Ottomans used cannons at the Battle of Kosovo in 1389. By the end of the fourteenth century every European arsenal had some form of weapon using gunpowder.

To whatever extent cannons lost or won battles, by the fifteenth century Europeans were quickly mastering gunpowder and fabricating weapons that would make lethal use of it. Big artillery became the most coveted kind of gun, as it could break through walls and end sieges. As the years progressed, not only did cannons become more fearsome, they became more durable and less likely to blow up. Gunmakers dispensed with pots and began to construct large bars of iron that they manipulated into cylinders like barrels. As the hot iron tubes were put together, they cooled and shrank around crossbars, making them stiffer, with the ability to project larger ammunition.[13] The musket would soon be born.

The first European "handgonnes" were essentially miniature cannons designed to be held by hand or attached to a pole for use by individual soldiers. These earliest firearms probably had barrels made of iron with wooden handles. Since the gunpowder had tremendous recoil, infantrymen attached the small cannons to poles that they stuck in the ground. The guns were fired from fixed positions. In *Bellifortis* (*Strong in War*, 1405), the continent's first fully illustrated manual of military technology, there is a picture of a gun being fired in this manner. Not long ago, archaeologists discovered fragments of metal propulsion weapons, evidence of the use of firearms in the 1461 Battle of Towton, in Yorkshire, northern England, one of the bloodiest ever fought on English soil. On the battlefield fragments of shattered guns were unearthed, suggesting close fighting in volleys of gunfire that was more dangerous than ever.[14]

By 1468, military illustrations show infantry discharging guns in much the same way later muskets or rifles were fired.[15] The guns were loaded exactly like full-size cannons, with holes drilled in the backs, or breeches. The differentiation between handguns and cannons was soon evident, with the former often featuring metal barrels and rudimentary stocks.

For our story it is important to note that the proliferation of black-powder weapons also opened the door to another movement in Europe: the populist revolt. Many factors fueled the democratized use of handheld guns. The recipe and process for making effective gunpowder were widely known by the fifteenth century. Nearly anyone could make it. The weapon itself was an effective tool that could be employed with very little training. The cost of a gun was far less than a crossbow, much less the armor of a knight. A simple working handgun could be constructed by a middling blacksmith if he put his mind to it. All he needed to do to create one was to flatten some iron and then roll it into a tube, drill a pan and touchhole into it, and make some kind of hammer or match.

By the early fifteenth century, locally made handheld guns were the weapon of choice of the peasant Hussites who rebelled against the Holy

Roman Empire. They would not be the last people to use this populist weapon as a means of societal upheaval. In fact, by the fifteenth century guns had become commonplace in nearly every European kingdom— among the military and among the people. The efficacy of the gun lay in its mobility, power, and affordability. It could easily be taken to war and to sea. It could soon be bought and built by the common man, the soldier, the explorer, the apostate, and the colonizer.

PART I

★

NEW WORLDS

First Blow for Liberty

1

★

FIRST CONTACT

"I had come with no other intention than to make war."

—Samuel de Champlain[1]

Musketeer from
Jacob de Gheyn's
*Wapenhandelinge
van Roers*, 1608

On the muggy summer afternoon of July 30, 1609, an army of Huron and Algonquian warriors readied to face off against the mighty Iroquois on the southern shores of what would later be known as Lake Champlain. The Iroquois force, numbering somewhere around two hundred Mohawks, had emerged from the wilderness and marched toward their enemies behind three ostentatiously garbed chiefs festooned in high plumes of red and blue feathers and equally colorful robes. These fighters had prepared to battle their longtime foes armed with weapons they had used for centuries: bows and arrows, tomahawks, and clubs and other blunt instruments. What the Iroquois could not have known was that the Huron had recently made a new ally, a French explorer named Samuel de Champlain. And as the two armies began to move toward each other, the man who would be known as the founder of New France was hiding in the brush, holding a weapon that would soon redefine life on their continent forever.

Until Champlain introduced the musket to Indian warfare, guns had virtually no impact in North America. On his first voyage to the New World in 1492, Columbus's three ships probably carried only a single firearm among them, the clumsy and heavy hand cannon. Although the name might conjure up thoughts of Dirty Harry's famous Magnum revolver, his gun was nothing more than a small mortar mounted on a pole. As it turned out, its most devastating feature was the loud boom it created when fired, a noise that led many natives to believe the Spanish could conjure thunder.

Which is not to say firearms hadn't been used at all by the first explorers. The earliest known gunshot victim in the Americas is a five-hundred-year-old Inca man found in a mass grave in Peru.[2] In 2004, while excavating hundreds of mummies and other bodies in the suburbs of Lima, archaeologists discovered a man who they believe was killed by a musket during an uprising against the invading Spaniards in 1536. Yet, while the swift and devastating defeat of the native populations of South America by the explorers and warlords was contingent on numerous technical advantages, firearms were far from the most important one. Almost all of the Inca bodies uncovered near Lima bear signs of violent hacking and tearing caused by the advantage of iron technology: weapons like swords and lances. Only a single body presented any evidence consistent with a shooting victim. It's not surprising that the first conquistadors, hard-boiled veteran soldiers and mercenaries searching for gold, used horses and the far more reliable crossbows in their conquests. Cortés's entire bloody subjugation of the Aztecs in the 1520s was accomplished with a mere five hundred soldiers who carried only twelve guns among them.[3]

With the ability to pierce armor and take down heavy cavalry from close range, the musket fired that day had in many ways revolutionized European warfare. What was a devastating weapon in the pitched battles of Europe, however, often became useless in the unpredictable environments of the New World. The gun, weighing fifteen to twenty pounds, was unwieldy in sparse or chaotic skirmishes. Its barrel usually had to be placed on a forked stand to be fired. It could be easily spotted at night. Since these guns were all handcrafted from iron, it was still expensive or unfeasible to maintain in a place lacking blacksmiths and raw material.

Throughout the late sixteenth and early seventeenth centuries, firearms had been upgraded. The shapes of the stocks became narrower and started to resemble those on modern rifles. Inventors created and improved "locks" that allowed shooters to pull triggers and ignite the gunpowder rather than lighting the propellant with linstocks. These changes sparked a technological revolution that improved both the precision and the deadliness of the gun. Gradually, the musket began to supplant the crossbow as the projectile weapon of choice in Europe and America. This evolution would help make the North American continent inhabitable for the newcomers and often have a devastating impact on the people who were already living on it.

It was one of these weapons that Champlain aimed at his new enemy by the lake that day. The explorer, who had spearheaded the French efforts to establish colonies along the St. Lawrence River, was an expert musketeer who fully understood the power potential of the gun. Unlike the British, the French were less concerned with the long-term colonization of America and more interested in creating economic hubs for the exchange of furs and other goods. With this mission in mind, Champlain's diplomatic acumen served him well. He quickly cemented trading ties with the Montagnais, the Algonquian, the Huron, and other local tribes. Some of the deals he made were predicated on the promise that France would not do business with the hated Iroquois—in particular, the promise not to arm their hated rivals with European weapons. That promise soon grew, and the great European power joined in a military alliance against the Five Nations (later six).

In the summer of 1609, Champlain gathered a handful of soldiers and headed south from Canada to what is now upstate New York. Along the way, he coaxed a number of local Indians to his cause. In one colorful scene, Champlain encountered two chiefs, Algonquian and Huron, who demanded the Frenchman fire his harquebus before engaging in negotiations. When Champlain obliged, the dozens of Indians who had gathered shouted appreciation and promised to provide even more warriors for the cause. Often, when Native Americans heard a musket for the first time, it was the noise and smoke of these curious contraptions that impressed them the most. That was about to change.

When evenly matched Huron and Iroquois met on the shores of Lake Champlain, the sides participated in conventional North American combat, exchanging hails of arrows and defending themselves with tree-trunk ramparts. That was before Champlain stepped into the fray. His gleaming armor and alien appearance so shocked the Iroquois warriors that they stopped momentarily and stared in bewilderment. As they did so, the French explorer and his two European cohorts aimed their harquebuses at the Iroquois line and fired. As the plumes of smoke drifted upward, two of the chiefs had already fallen to the ground dead, and a third would be critically wounded. "As I was loading again," Champlain noted, "one of my companions fired a shot from the woods, which astonished them anew to such a degree that, seeing their chiefs dead, they lost courage and took to flight, abandoning their camp and fort, and fleeing into the woods, whither I pursued them, killing still more of them."[4] The battle was over.

This moment had wide-ranging consequences. As France's involvement in the tribal conflicts against the Iroquois would soon illustrate, the gun didn't change merely how Europeans interacted with Indians but how Indians interacted with each other. The desire for firearms became a dominant concern of tribal leaders beginning in the late seventeenth century. For the Iroquois confederacy, the new reality meant ramping up the fur trade and becoming a proxy in the European wars of North America.

And as intra-Indian conflict modernized, it became consequently more devastating, as the gun exacerbated long-standing animosities and ultimately led to the devastation of the Huron by the Iroquois, who would be armed by the British and Dutch. The Iroquois ended up decimating many other tribes, with their influence ranging from the Ohio River Valley to modern Wisconsin, South Carolina, and into Canada. With the emergence of the gun, the way locals hunted, fought wars, defended their homes, and interacted with others was dramatically altered.

For the French it meant conquest. Champlain's book *The Voyages of 1613* features the only surviving contemporary likeness of the explorer, a self-flattering drawing titled *"Deffaite des Yroquois au Lac de Champlain."* It depicts Champlain, unflustered in his armor, standing between two Indian armies, steadily aiming his heavy harquebus despite the barrage of arrows flying around him. The drawing relays the kind of fearlessness that was expected of the seventeenth-century musketeer. Keeping your wits about you in the midst of combat is indispensable for the soldier, but, as we'll see, hardly simple.

The harquebus Champlain aimed at the unsuspecting Iroquois was one of the widely used smoothbore "matchlock" muskets of the time. Since there was no mass production of weapons yet, every musket was somewhat unique, although the apparatus all worked basically the same.

The harquebus was a long, heavy gun that often required a fork rest. On the outside where the butt met the barrel was the gun's "lock." (The device that allowed the gun to fire was called the lock because, as the theory goes, the early mechanisms resembled door locks.) Attached to the lock was a forked holder known as a serpentine that held the fuse, or "match." The match was a long braided cord that was sometimes soaked in a solution of saltpeter that burned slowly at around four to five inches an hour. The serpentine was attached on the inside of the lock to a lever called the "sear." The trigger acted through the sear, pushing the lighted match in an arc toward the flashpan that contained the priming powder. The match ignited the powder in the pan, which in turn set off the charge in the barrel through a small hole in the pan that led to the interior of the barrel and fired the gun.

Although, mechanically speaking, the matchlock utilized a relatively simple design—one that had probably been around in one form or another for two hundred years—the loading and shooting of the gun was a dangerously long and clumsy process. What the Iroquois at Lake Champlain didn't understand after facing the first volley from the French guns was that they probably could have turned around and slaughtered their new European enemies with relative ease once the barrage had been fired.

The first firearms in North America could be powerful and overwhelming, but they could also be frustratingly ineffective. Imagine the scene a musketeer like Champlain might encounter: standing in the center of dense foliage or on a sand-strewn beach, facing hostile Indians, a shooter would first have to remove his match from the serpentine so that it would not accidentally ignite the powder for the next round. (Unintentional bursts of fire were a perpetual fear of the musketeer. In September of the same year, a stray match ignited John Smith's powder bag, setting off an explosion that lit the Jamestown colony founder's clothing ablaze, badly burning him.)[5] Champlain had probably first opened a smaller flask, containing a finer grain of gunpowder, with which he filled his flash pan. He then blew away any loose powder to avoid unwanted ignition and closed the pan. Next, holding the match with one hand, he pried open a cylinder containing his charge powder and poured the contents down the barrel with his other hand. After this was accomplished, Champlain grabbed a lead ball and a wad from a pouch on his belt and forced all these elements down the barrel of his weapon with a long rammer that was typically attached to his barrel. (Champlain claims to have loaded four balls into his musket before firing his fateful shots at the Iroquois chiefs.)

The simplicity of the musket design allowed it to fire a variety of ammunition. Most often the ammunition for a musket was a round ball of lead, a malleable metal. Round balls were intentionally loose fitting in the smooth barrel so that they could quickly be loaded even after the inside of the barrel had been fouled by numerous previous shots.

Once all the preparations were completed, the cinder at the end of the match once again needed to be blown to ensure striking the pan would ignite the powder. Sometimes the priming powder flashed without igniting the main charge; the phrase "flash in the pan" originated from this frustrating event. Then again, sometimes the fuse went out completely, which was why the musketeer burned his fuse at both ends. If the fire was properly lit, the match would be returned to the serpentine and adjusted to ensure it hit the pan properly. It was only then that Champlain could take his aim, shoot, and, of course, pray that his firearm did not misfire (a regular occurrence) and hit its intended target (a rare one). If wind happened to be blowing, the shooter had to contend with sparks and fire flying back into his face. Perhaps in the least hazardous conditions the best-trained musketeer might be able to reload within forty seconds. For the shooter those seconds probably seemed like an eternity as he wondered whether a poison-tipped arrow or hatchet might find its intended target.

Along with the clunky loading, there were other drawbacks to the matchlock gun that put the Europeans who first explored and colonized America in constant mortal danger. Since one never knew when they might need one's musket, a fire was kept lit as a way to light matches, which in turn meant the newcomers made themselves more susceptible to ambushes by Indians or their European adversaries. Then again, oftentimes the elements could make it impossible to keep the matches lit anyway.

Why, then, with all these numerous drawbacks, would firearms be more instrumental in transforming Native American society than any other item brought to the New World by the Europeans? Well, as it had done for the Europeans who first encountered it, the guns' sheer energy and noise created a psychological advantage that natives admired, feared, and wanted to emulate. "The Iroquois were much astonished that two men should have been killed so quickly . . . ," Champlain later wrote, "although they were provided with shields made of cotton thread woven together and wood, which were proof against their arrows. This frightened them greatly."[6]

Unlike arrows, if a harquebus hit its target, as the French explorer's gun did that day, it was likely to create a shockingly bloody and deadly result. Even from close ranges, arrows often merely wounded their intended targets. Champlain's shot went right through the cotton and wood shields carried by the Indian chiefs to repel the arrows of their enemy. If one of the primary purposes of a weapon was to inflict the most damage and fear possible, even an awkward gun was an invaluable tool. What the Indians of the Northeast did not yet know, however, was that the booming firearm they had encountered would soon be antiquated technology. The new guns the Europeans carried would be more dangerous and more enduring—as would the ideology they brought with them.

2

★

PILGRIM'S PROGRESS

"Loud over field and forest the cannon's roar . . ."

—Longfellow

Samoset comes "boldly" into Plymouth settlement

On the second night exploring the area around Plymouth Bay for a suitable spot to begin building their permanent settlement, a group of hungry, scurvy-ridden Pilgrims were awakened by harrowing shrieks emanating from the woods outside their camp. It was, as Governor William Bradford later described it, a "hideous and great cry" that reminded him of "a company of wolves or such like wild beasts." And as a traumatized scout ran toward the camp from the woods yelling, "They are men! Indians! Indians!" feathered arrows—most of them over a yard long—rained down on the newcomers, who would fortify themselves as best as they could behind makeshift barricades and peek out to try to discern who was attacking them.[1]

These radical Puritans hadn't landed on Cape Cod in December 1620 looking for trouble. Rather, they were looking to escape it. For that matter, despite fashionable thinking in many quarters of contemporary American life, neither the first English, German, Dutch, nor Scandinavians who journeyed to North America landed with the goal of conquering, displacing, or subjugating the locals. They had yet to imagine themselves expanding thousands of miles westward; in fact, most of these early colonizers had no idea who or what was beyond the wilderness right outside their settlement. More often than not, they were prepared to farm, trade, and proselytize, viewing their story in sweeping biblical terms. Rarely did the first settlers initiate violence.

Which is not to say that the newcomers didn't contemplate the prospect of hostility in this new land. To avoid disagreeable incidents, the Pilgrims had hired a stout and ginger-haired English officer named Myles Standish, who had befriended the group and their pastor, John Robinson, while stationed in the Netherlands. With him they brought a small armory and plenty of muskets. These guns, as it turned out, probably saved their lives on the beach that early morning. As the arrows fell around them, the English lit their matches and shot their muskets into the trees until Standish could organize a concerted defense and an escape. Judging from the noise, the Pilgrims guessed that there were around thirty or forty Indians (perhaps Wampanoags, though we can't say for certain). Soon the locals retreated back into the unknown. By the time it was all over, it seems that the Europeans were just as horrified by the shrieking of the Indians as the Indians were by the racket the muskets produced.[2]

This first short and bloodless battle with the native population helped instill an urgency into the newcomers as surely as it did the Indians. Danger loomed in the wilderness. Once a colony was established—after a hastily written document of self-governance was produced—Standish quickly organized the militia to secure it. The Pilgrims needed to concern themselves with the potential threat of not only local Indians, whose intentions were still uncertain, but also well-armed Old World antagonists like the French and Dutch who had stakes in lands not far from them. To deal with this menace, the Pilgrims relied on more than just handheld firearms.

They had brought some dangerous firepower: wheeled cannons—one, a 1,200-pounder that could shoot a 3.5-pound cannonball—and placed them in a two-story fort overlooking the harbor.[3]

Without any formal military protection, necessity drove Americans, from the Pilgrims forward, to rely on militias even more than their relatives in England. As the historian Daniel J. Boorstin once noted, "In America the profession of arms was being dissolved into communities of citizen soldiers—not through force of dogma, but through force of circumstances."[4] These circumstances spurred the evolution of independent units that would one day have a profound effect on the prospects of a new nation.

While the Christian nonconformists may have been escaping King James's repressive policies back home, self-defense was predicated on secular traditions they had brought with them from the European continent. One of the most important and consequential was civil defense. The idea was not unique to the newcomers, even if it would take on more urgency and importance in North America. In early fifteenth-century England, most male citizens were already trained to serve in a military reserve and knew how to use a musket. From the ages of sixteen to sixty, reservists gathered in town squares across England four or five times each year and local military leaders inspected their weaponry and equipment—which they most often personally owned. The Pilgrims reproduced this tradition in their own towns.[5] Local officers were tasked with training blacksmiths, farmers, and carpenters from every locality in New England to use their pikes and muskets against possible threats against their families and livelihood. A 1650 militia statute in Connecticut, for instance, dictated that "all persons that are above the age of sixteene yeares except magistrates and church officials shall beare arms."[6] This commitment to self-defense most often meant that the head of the household was obligated to buy arms for the eldest son or a servant, who would then serve in the local militia.

Many colonies treated the idea of traveling to church and other public meetings with a weapon as a civic duty, although a number of colonial municipalities could also fine men who did not own and carry weapons. In early Virginia, one law required that men not "go . . . abroad without a sufficient partie well armed" or to "worke in the ground without their arms . . ."[7]

By 1639, Governor John Winthrop was already commenting on the Plymouth Colony's two "skillful" regiments of militia. Though certainly not anywhere as skilled as a trained European army, most of the New

Englanders took their jobs seriously. A couple of years later Winthrop assessed that "about 1200 men were exercised in most sorts of land service; yet it was observed that there was no man drunk, though there was plenty of wine and strong beer in town, not an oath sworn, no quarrel, nor any hurt done."[8] By the end of the seventeenth century, nearly every colonial town featured some kind of requirement impelling white inhabitants to bear arms (slaves, free slaves, indentured servants, and Catholics were typically prohibited from owning them) to protect their communities from external threats—and, on occasion, from internal perils.

By the time these new inhabitants of North America had established towns, the guns they carried had become even more lethal and accurate. In fact, by the time the Pilgrims had befriended their Wampanoag neighbors and invited them over for a famous three-day feast, gun technology was already rapidly changing on the European continent. The matchlock was being supplanted by "flintlocks," "doglocks," and "wheellocks," and by 1675 the old gun would virtually disappear in North America.

In the NRA National Firearms Museum in the Washington suburb of Fairfax, Virginia, sits a glass enclosure holding the purported musket of John Alden, a twenty-year-old passenger on the *Mayflower* voyage. "The *Mayflower* Gun," a beautiful and intricate "wheellock" carbine, is purported to be the only remaining piece of physical evidence left from the first permanent settlement of Europeans in New England.

As the story goes, Alden, gun in hand, was one of the first *Mayflower* passengers to set foot on New England soil. Perhaps. What we do know for certain is that Alden was the crew's cooper, responsible for maintaining all of the ship's barrels. His union with *Mayflower* passenger Priscilla Mullins is alleged to have produced more descendants than any other Pilgrim family.[9] Along with Plymouth's military commander Myles Standish, the couple were immortalized in the popular nineteenth-century Longfellow poem "The Courtship of Miles Standish."

Alden's gun, discovered in a cubby during the 1924 restoration of his family's home in Massachusetts, wasn't standard for settlers of the time. Its sophisticated mechanism was superior to most models used by those who landed in Massachusetts—certainly the matchlocks used to ward off the first Indian attack. The firearm was likely the most expensive item Alden

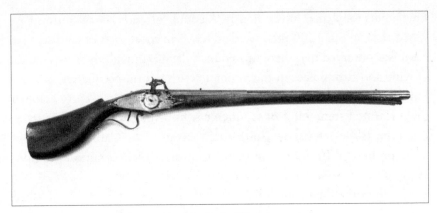

Mayflower Gun

owned, and he probably took great care to keep it clean and polished, rarely using it. It would be the sort of exotic weapon that an English seaman, typically an officer, might have procured from a sea merchant or mercenary at port rather than a local gunsmith.

More importantly, the *Mayflower* Gun heralded the soon-to-be predominant flintlock models, which eliminated many of the matchlock's disadvantages and helped the settlers use guns in more effective ways. No need to worry about keeping fires or cinders lit or burning oneself. In the case of the *Mayflower* Gun, a rotating steel wheel created sparks, much like a modern cigarette lighters, igniting the gunpowder in a pan, which flashed and ignited the main charge in the firearm's barrel and then fired.

The wheellock had probably been invented in Germany in the early 1500s, but it would take a century for the speedier ignition system—often called the "snaphaunce"—to be used throughout Europe. The expense of owning one of these guns inhibited widespread military adaptation, much less ownership by the common man. It was most often a gun of the gentleman and the officer. John Smith of the ill-fated Jamestown colony owned a German- or French-made snaphaunce.[10] Smith used this pistol in his fight with the Powhatan, which famously necessitated his supposed rescue by the princess Pocahontas. Although most of the guns in Jamestown were still matchlocks, an early wheellock pistol with a brass barrel, iron lock plate, and wooden fishtail was found by archaeologists at James Fort;[11] much to the consternation of its owner, one imagines, it had been lost down the shaft of the well.

There has long been debate about the origins of the "pistol" itself. Even the etymology has been disputed, with some historians making the case that the word came from Czech or Spanish. Others argued that the inventor of the pistol was Camillo Vitelli, who had created the weapon in Pistoia, Italy, and thus the town of origin left the name.[12] As with many forms of technology, the most likely answer is that numerous engineers had been playing around with the idea of shortening the barrel of a gun at around the same time. What we do know is that many of the first pistols—often made at nearly right angles—were heavy and clumsy, and fired large ammunition.

It was the smoothbore "flintlock" musket, however, that would become the most prevalent gun in North America from its first appearance shortly after the *Mayflower*'s arrival until the Civil War. The flintlock mechanism was safer than the matchlock and cheaper than the wheellock. The idea that made it work was simple and elegant.

The flint, a hard rock that had been part of human technology since the Stone Age, struck the iron or steel "frizzen." The force and friction of that downward motion produced sparks. At the same time the hammer's blow would snap the frizzen back to expose the gunpowder in the pan and ignite the gunpowder. When the pan's gunpowder ignited, it flashed through a small hole in the side of the barrel to ignite the gunpowder inside the barrel.

The first flintlock guns were likely developed in France in the early 1600s by the brothers Marin and Jean le Bourgeoys, gunsmiths of King Louis III.[13] Initially more expensive and complicated to construct than the simple matchlock, it took decades for the technology to be universally applied. As we'll see, throughout history military leadership would be slow in adopting new technology—or, to be more precise, it was reluctant to move on from what it already knew. The flintlock was no different. It was only during the French victory at the Battle of Steinkirk in 1692, when British generals noticed their soldiers dropping matchlock muskets and picking up the flintlocks of the fallen enemy soldiers, that they realized wholesale change was needed.[14]

Once it was adopted by Europeans, though, it was taken up by Americans and transformed, improved, mythologized, and embedded in the everyday lives of people across the continent. By that time the advanced locks had proliferated to English and North American gunmakers and would soon become the mechanism for the first guns manufactured by the United States and a tool of necessity.

With a large number of people living scattered and away from denser population centers, newcomers found themselves more reliant on firearms for hunting and protection from unfriendly Indians. The *Mayflower* Gun's primary purpose, if and when it was used, was probably to hunt deer, turkey, grouse, and other birds that fed the new colonists.

In Europe, hunting was typically reserved for the well-bred. That was not to be the case in the colonies. Samuel Johnson once remarked that "hunting was the labor of the savages of North America, but the amusement of the gentleman of England."[15] The wealthy looked upon common men who hunted as lazy and potentially unmanageable. Those who chased around small animals were, as *The Laws of England Concerning the Game of Hunting, Hawking, Fishing and Fowling, &c.* (1727) explained, "very bad Christians . . . of little or no Worth . . . loose, idle, disorderly and dissolute Persons" who would, inevitably, use their weapons for criminal acts.[16]

Yet one reason the common man in England could not enjoy hunting as the American "savage" did was that nobility had banned men from participating in the practice either for survival or sport. In the centuries before the *Mayflower* landed at Plymouth Rock, the English aristocracy enacted a number of decrees limiting the ability of the average man to hunt for food. Ostensibly these laws were aimed at preserving game, and to some extent that was true. But as William Holdsworth, the noted nineteenth-century historian of English law, explained, such bans were also for "prevention of popular insurrections and resistance to the government, by disarming the bulk of the people; which last is a reason oftener meant than avowed by the makers of forest or game laws."[17]

Perhaps in England, where land was in high demand, such positions could be rationalized and insurrections averted. In America, not only would hunting be a necessity; it would soon evolve into a source of recreation for the common man due to the abundant wildlife. Within a few years municipal governments in New England were passing laws regulating hunting, not to limit use of guns, as some modern historians argue, but rather to protect private property from the numerous guns of sports hunters. In the vast lands of the New World, these laws would be nearly impossible to enforce.

Hunting, not war, was the main use of the gun in early America. By the turn of the century, Indian reliance on European firearms for stalking prey was also growing. As Native Americans gradually adopted the apparatuses, they became increasingly adept at fixing and maintaining the weapons—even, occasionally, making their own ammunition. However, Indians were never able to manufacture and craft iron, and this doomed their hold on the land.

Bradford had worried that selling Indians guns was sinful, and perhaps that losing technological superiority over the native population could be a dangerous proposition over the long term. Yet the lure of trade was often stronger than the need for safety. The settlers of New England so regularly traded guns—often hiring Indians to do beaver and food hunting—that the British Crown was forced to issue a law prohibiting it: "In trucking or trading with the Indians no man shall give them from any commodity of theirs, silver or gold, or any weapons of war, either guns or gunpowder, nor sword, not any other Munition, which might come to be used against ourselves."[18] As the British soon learned, controlling the colonists across a vast sea was no easy task, and the gun trade continued unabated. More consequentially, the gun proliferated among the colonists, and the newcomers soon started devising technology that outshined anything they were doing in Europe.

In 1681, another influx of pacifist immigrants, much like the Pilgrims, sought to escape the perpetual violence and quarreling of Europe. At first the German Quakers and Swiss Mennonites found North America to be only marginally more hospitable than their homelands. Considered heretics by the Puritans of New England, their books were burned, their property was confiscated, and some were expelled from their homes. In the early 1660s, four Quakers were hanged on Boston Common for alleged crimes against the budding Massachusetts Bay Colony. The violence stopped only after King Charles II stepped in to demand an end to incidents of intolerance.

It was the same King Charles II who, twenty years later, handed over an immense piece of his North American landholdings to the Quaker William Penn as a means of satisfying a debt he owed Penn's father. This property encompassed much of present-day Pennsylvania and parts of

Delaware. Penn, who had become a Quaker in 1666 and was briefly imprisoned for this apostasy, harbored quixotic plans for his new land. His first journey to the New World included an armada of twenty-three ships containing plenty of well-to-do Quakers from London and Bristol, along with many others seeking refuge from around Europe.

Penn's intent was to create not merely a safe space for his coreligionists but a "tolerance settlement" that was to be a haven for persecuted Christian sects of Europe that would be "void of Sword or Staff, Drum or Musket, Tumult or Violence."[19] Penn had planned for densely populated cities to be surrounded by idyllic farming communities that fed them. This was not to be. Thousands were drawn to the promise of fertile land, and that freedom lay inland. New immigrants continued to make their way westward into the vast expanses of America, a habit that continued unabated for the next 150 years or so.

These settlers needed the proper weapons and tools to survive. It was a group of Quakers and Mennonites from the Krefeld region of the Rhineland who would help build the first recorded German settlement in the English colonies, naming it, appropriately enough, Germantown.[20] In the coming decades, tens of thousands of Germanic people streamed through Philadelphia and settled the vast colony, quickly outpacing mere subsistence farming to make Pennsylvania "the Bread Colony," exporting fur, fruit, livestock, and grain (wheat, corn, rye, oats, and barley). Penn's "holy experiment" was to become one of the cultural and political centers of American life and the birthplace of the Constitution.[21]

It was in this historical current that a young man named Martin Meylin was swept up when he left his home in Zurich, Switzerland, in 1710. Along with about a dozen fellow Mennonites, Meylin ended up in the German-speaking area of Lancaster County, Pennsylvania. Though setting up in a town teeming with pacifists, Meylin would be credited with being the first great American gunmaker and inventor of the Pennsylvania long rifle—which was to become known as the Kentucky long rifle ("Kentucky," in those days, being anything in the wilderness west of Lancaster). Meylin's small cobblestone cabin still stands off a two-lane road in Lancaster. Local schools are named after him. Plaques have been erected in his honor. State politicians have even written legislation commemorating his contribution to American life. The gun sparked a revolution in gun technology.

The problem with Meylin's story, like with so many others in the early history of the gun, is that it seems to be predicated on lore rather than tangible historical evidence. Although a "Martin Mylin" (the spelling would vary over the years) was one of the German-speaking Mennonites to emigrate to Lancaster County in the early 1700s, little else can conclusively be said about the man. In fact, there were likely two Martin Meylins, father and son, both blacksmiths, who emigrated to North America at roughly the same time. There are also two surviving early specimens of Pennsylvania long rifles that have the stamp "MM" on them. One of these rifles is currently held by the Lancaster County Historical Society and dates to the 1740s. It is inscribed "Martin Meillin Germantaun 1705." Which raises the obvious question: How did Martin Meylin (or Mylin, or Meillin) construct a rifle in Germantown in 1705 if he emigrated to America five years later, in 1710?[22]

Rather than get bogged down in the debate over the veracity of Meylin's tale, it's probably the case, as we have seen elsewhere, that numerous inventors and blacksmiths engineered the Kentucky rifle over a period of decades. In early colonial times, new inventions were a collective effort developed by communities and driven by necessity.

What's indisputable is that the invention created by these German-speaking immigrants like Meylin and their children changed the way Americans hunted, fought, and explored. Captain John Dillin, author of

Kentucky rifle

a popular book about the Kentucky rifle in the 1920s, would claim that the gun "changed the whole course of world history; made possible the settlement of a continent; and ultimately freed our country of foreign domination. Light in weight; graceful in line; economical in consumption of powder and lead; fatally precise; distinctly American; it sprang into immediate popularity; and for a hundred years was a model often slightly varied but never radically changed."[23]

Dillin was not wrong. It's true that few American inventions were as adored and idealized in our history as the long rifle. Dillin's sentimentalized telling of the Kentucky rifle's story is laden with patriotic imagery for good reason. The invention involved reengineered and reimagined Old World technology and was adapted to the rigors and uniqueness of frontier life. For the first two hundred years of colonial life, the gun was an extension of European efforts in technology, design, and purpose. With the Kentucky rifle, the American colonialists, perhaps for the first time, had created a weapon of their own, specifically designed for their unique lives.

Lancaster would become the center of gun innovation for more than a century. The settlement the Meylins helped establish in the 1700s quickly grew to become one of North America's first real inland cities. (It was the capital of the United States for a single day in September 1777, after the Continental Congress was forced to flee the British in Philadelphia.) The town stood within reasonable distance of the coastal ports but was also a gateway to the unexplored continent that would lure millions in the coming centuries. With nearby iron ore and plentiful lumber and abundant serviceable farmland, it was the perfect location for the invention of the American rifle.

Inasmuch as men like Meylin were not merely dissenting Christians but pacifists as well, it can be safely assumed that most were disinclined to pick up gunsmithing as a means of war and violence. But the fact was that firearms played an essential role in the everyday lives of most families in America, even of those eschewing violence. All of which makes the story of the American rifle even more improbable.

The first German gunsmiths of Pennsylvania produced traditional Jäger rifles. These guns, expensive and often ornate, were short, easy-to-carry, large-ammunition flintlock guns built to be quickly reloaded so that the carrier could hunt big game in dense German forests. The rifle—the word derived from the German *riffeln*, meaning to cut grooves—was first developed in Europe as a sporting weapon for noblemen to hunt with more precision. Meylin almost certainly knew of this technique before arriving in Lancaster. The invention of gun barrels with spiral grooves on the interior is often credited to a Viennese gunmaker named Gaspard Kollner, but it probably first originated among a number of blacksmiths in southern Germany and Switzerland. By 1520, Nuremberg gunmakers were proficient in the technology.[24] The physics of spinning propulsion as a means of improving aim was known to weapons makers for thousands of years—ever since feathers were placed on arrows to make them spin.

As we'll see, muskets of early America were smoothbore weapons, and ammunition was fired at relatively low velocity. Moreover, the musket ball, which fit loosely when loaded down the muzzle, would bounce off the inside of the barrel when fired, making the final landing place unpredictable. The rifle Meylin and other gunsmiths made, on the other hand, immediately offered shooters decent accuracy at 150 or more yards—or a hundred more than an average musket. Soon the Americans were figuring out ways to improve on that distance. While the German Jäger rifle barrel length was typically around 35 inches, the American model grew to upward of 48 inches—sometimes longer. The longer barrel increased the distance between the rear and front sights, giving the shooter a better bead on his target. With its elegant elongated design, a rifle typically weighed only around nine pounds: much lighter than a musket and therefore much easier to carry. The bore size, or "caliber"—which represents the diameter of the barrel—was reduced to save on powder and lead. The .45-caliber long rifle could deliver three times the number of shots from the same amount of powder that was used in the typically .75-caliber musket. These improvements made hunting for game—the most important use of the gun at this time—much more successful.[25]

There were downsides to the weapon, of course, as the American revolutionaries would soon learn. For starters, rifles were incredibly difficult to load. Fitting a projectile that fit the bore tightly enough to engage the rifling sometimes required hammering it all the way down the barrel. This was fine for a frontiersman who was hunting deer, but it created a perilous situation for a soldier. Another disadvantage of rifled weapons was that the black powder burned dirty and the grooves gunked up with residue after a few shots. This fouling often made loading impossible until the barrel was cleaned with a damp swab.

At least at the start, the rifle was also expensive. The rifling technique was unknown outside Germany and this small part of North America, meaning that specialized gunsmiths were required to design, produce, and fix them. It was metalwork, and woodwork, and mechanical work. These blacksmiths used specialized equipment to cut the grooves and other equipment to ensure the barrel was straight. In the pre-industrial age, building a gun was a job that required technically demanding precision. Not only did any imperfection in the mechanisms mean that the gun might fail to work, but such defects could potentially maim or kill the user. The work of the eighteenth-century gunmaker was also physically demanding. "From a flat bar of soft iron, hand forged into a gun barrel; laboriously bored and rifled with crude tools; fitted with a stock hewn from a maple tree in the neighboring forest; and supplied with a lock hammered to shape on the anvil; an unknown smith, in a shop long since silent," John Dillin noted.

The manipulation of Old World ideas for frontier needs was indicative of the kind of adaptive engineering that would mark American gunmaking in the coming years. The imagination and techniques mastered by Meylin and others like him offered the thousands of incoming settlers and explorers the opportunity to continue to push into the wilderness of the Cumberland Mountains and surrounding areas. The newcomers relied on the long rifle primarily for hunting. Soon, though, this unique colonial invention would be called to help forge a new nation.

3

★

POWDER ALARM

*"War! war! war! was the cry, and it was pronounced in a tone which
would have done honor to the oratory of a Briton or a Roman."*

—John Adams[1]

The Method of Refining Salt-Petre, illustrated by Paul Revere

In the predawn hours of September 1, 1774, a battalion of British regulars rowed thirteen boats three miles up the Mystic River, marching to the Provincial Powder House located in what is today's Somerville. The soldiers had been deployed by Major General Thomas Gage, the British commander in chief of North America, who had reasoned that preemptively getting hold of as much black powder as possible would help defuse the potential insurgency brewing among the colonialists. According to British law, every town in Massachusetts could legally use the regional magazine to house their gunpowder. As tensions mounted, numerous towns began withdrawing their allotted amounts as a precautionary measure against British confiscation, including from the Boston magazine. In turn, fearing that militias would forcefully raid the Crown's supply, Gage began planning ways to secure the powder for safekeeping.

Both of these fears were well warranted.

The cone-shaped, stone-cobbled structure the powder was stored in, which still stands today, was first erected in the early 1700s as a windmill. If the British soldiers had bothered gazing up at the building's roof as they marched up the hill, they would have noticed one of Benjamin Franklin's famous lightning rods—and for good reason. The building had been converted into a gunpowder magazine only after local Bostonians protested that such dangerous munition should not be stored near their homes.

Unlike modern powder, the black powder of the late eighteenth century was hazardous and highly volatile. A number of major European cities, including London, had experienced devastating fires due to accidental explosions in inner-city powder houses. Early Americans did not pass laws limiting gun ownership, but they were not above nudging citizens into protecting cities from hoarders of gunpowder. One typical late eighteenth-century regulation in New Hampshire, for example, offered that gunpowder "greatly endanger[ed] the lives and properties of the inhabitants thereof in case of fire; which danger might be prevented . . . the owners of such powder [were required] to deposit the same in the magazine provided by said town for that purpose . . ."[2]

It was not surprising, then, that the British soldiers who arrived in the dark early hours that morning were forced to wait until full daybreak before removing the bounty lest they blow up the storehouse with their torches or a random spark. By mid-morning, however, Gage's men had surreptitiously removed 250 barrels of gunpowder from the public storehouse and rowed back to Boston. At the same time a small detachment of soldiers wound their way through the town of Cambridge to collect two additional field pieces from the local armory. All the items were transferred and stored in the British fort on Castle Island in Boston Harbor.

While the mission itself had been a success, the long-term prospects of confiscating powder would have disastrous consequences for the British. The people of Boston were already agitated by the possibility of the occupiers attempting to disarm them. Once evidence emerged that there had been a conspiracy to do so, the threat of violence loomed.

A few days before Gage sent troops to the Provincial Powder House, William Brattle, a wealthy Bostonian who had long played both sides of the Tory-Patriot debate, hatched an idea. Whether he was eager to avoid violence or simply a Loyalist at heart, we can't know, but Brattle penned a letter to Gage warning him that it was conceivable American plotters might steal gunpowder and bolster the strength of local militias. He went on to offer, in great detail, information about the contents of the munitions that were housed in the magazine—and then gave Gage the keys.

Gage, either by accident or for some undetermined political reason, dropped Brattle's letter from his pocket in the streets of Boston. It was fortuitously recovered by an American patriot and published in the city's newspapers the day after the raid on the Provincial Powder House, infuriating the local population. Brattle, whose life was now in danger, escaped the city, claiming that Gage had demanded an inventory of the magazine and the key. Whatever the case, the inflammatory news spread quickly throughout the region. "This," wrote Abigail Adams to her husband John, who was in Philadelphia at the time, "has so enraged and exasperated the people that there is great apprehension of an immediate rupture."[3]

Soon wild rumors about British atrocities against colonial townsmen also began spreading: war had broken out, militiamen were being gunned down, and the British were bombarding Boston with their warships. One visiting Irish merchant staying in a tavern around thirty miles outside Boston recalled being woken in the middle of the night by a violent banging at the front door. Agitated voices outside told a dramatic tale of powder being taken with "six men killed & all the people between there & Boston arming & marching down to the Relief of their Brethren at Boston." The merchant added that he had never seen anything like it, with "fifty men collected at the Tavern, tho' now deep in night; equipping themselves & sending off Posts every Way to the neighboring Towns."[4]

It wasn't long before thousands of these New Englanders clustered in large groups across the region, many of them moving toward Boston. A reported 4,000 headed toward Cambridge's Tory Row, the name given to Brattle Street where Loyalists lived. In towns around Boston, locals quickly took control of the militia from the Crown.[5] The reaction was widespread and impressive and portentous. And as the reality of the situation hit Gage, he wisely abandoned a plan to confiscate gunpowder that was housed forty miles away in Worcester. Once the colonists began to learn that the accounts of British carnage had been merely gossip, the situation decompressed.

Why all the drama over gunpowder? To understand the colonists' concerns, we have to jump ahead for a moment. It's important to remember that the dearth of black powder would be one of the persistent anxieties of colonial leaders before and during the war. Finding it, buying it, and producing it would be a constant headache. One of the first topics taken up by the Second Continental Congress, in fact, was gunpowder shortage.

When war broke out, the shortage fears of revolutionary leaders was felt immediately. The nascent militia-army at the Battle of Bunker Hill had been unable to repel British advances because lack of gunpowder had inhibited the militia from properly training with cannons before the war. Ultimately, this meant hand-to-hand combat and retreat. The carnage that was inflicted on the British by Colonel William Prescott's men in redoubt on Breed's Hill, one of the first battles of the war, was even more impressive when we consider the small amount of gunpowder available to the Americans. The British general Sir Henry Clinton noted in his diary that day, "A few more such victories would have shortly put an end to British dominion in America."[6] Yet, by the end of the battle, colonialists had so little powder left that they were forced to wait until Welsh grenadiers, who made their methodical and deadly march up the hill in spite of massive casualties, were within thirty feet before shooting to ensure that they did not waste a grain. Had the rebels been in possession of more gunpowder, the battle—and perhaps the trajectory of the war—might have had a very different outcome.

According to an inventory commission by George Washington a few months after Bunker Hill, the Americans possessed less than forty tons of black powder.[7] Some of the cache would supply troops who had surrounded the British in Boston, and much of the rest was taken by Benedict Arnold, then a highly regarded general, who participated in the attack on Fort Ticonderoga in upstate New York. When Washington reviewed the situation on August 3, 1775, he found there wasn't enough powder for each of his men to carry half a pound each. And there was almost none left for his cannons.⁸ By the end of the first nine months of war, practically all the gunpowder had been used up. "Our want of powder is inconceivable. A daily waste and no supply administers a gloomy prospect," Washington wrote in December 1775.⁹ If General William Howe, who arrived in the middle of the Siege of Boston, had known about the shortage of supplies, he might have been able to burst out of Boston and end the Revolution right there.

In many ways the run on powder was the true start of the Revolution. This was the moment that American leaders made their first concerted efforts to marshal military forces to stop the British. Although the Americans were driven by idealistic beliefs, protecting the powder was a practical concern. There was, need it be said, no way to defend your beliefs in natural law, the right to self-defense, or personal liberty without the ability to pour powder into your musket.

How was it that the American colonies, a place with vast natural resources, teeming with firearms, and populated by an individualistic population that already prided themselves on self-reliance and innovation, could find itself in such a predicament? It's complicated. Although modern Americans do not concern themselves with shortages of weapons, much less gunpowder, it's worth understanding how the substance found its way to colonialists at the dawn of war.

Incendiary substances had been utilized in warfare going back to at least the ninth century BC. Perhaps the most mysterious of the early flammable weapons was developed in the seventh century by the Byzantines. "Greek fire" was used to protect Constantinople from Arab siege. While we still don't know for certain the formula for Greek fire, it was likely a base of distilled petroleum—with saltpeter added to intensify combustibility, according to some sources. The solution was said to have stuck to whatever it hit, incendiary or not, and water could not extinguish it. The mix, delivered in packages launched by catapults or slung by soldiers, would burn the hulls of ships and have disastrous consequences for those attempting to jump overboard.¹⁰

By the mid-1200s, all mention of Greek fire comes to an abrupt end. It's possible that the formula, known only to the upper stratum of the Byzantium leadership, was lost in a palace upheaval and forgotten. Or, more likely, a more effective alternative had already come along to replace it, because, by the 1300s, we know that Muslims were already using their own incendiary devices against Christians in the Holy Land. It was a brew that had come to them by way of Asia. And until the middle of the nineteenth century, gunpowder remained man's only known chemical explosive.

It was the Chinese Taoists, keenly interested in purification and chemical amalgams, who had been studying saltpeter (potassium nitrate), a substance formed by the decomposition of organic matter. All three of the ingredients that make up gunpowder had been used in medicinal combinations with varying levels of success over those years. This new grayish powder these experimenters cooked up did something that man had never seen before: it didn't just burn; it blew up.

The invention of gunpowder was based on empirical observation, trial and error, and luck. Its inventors knew nothing about the chemical qualities or underlying science of explosions or propulsion. How does black powder work? Fire is a chemical reaction that is contingent on the presence of three things: oxygen, fuel, and heat. Simply put, sulfur and charcoal act as the fuel, and the saltpeter as the oxidizer. When saltpeter decomposes at high temperature, it provides the oxygen for the reaction. This means that gunpowder doesn't need to be exposed to air to burn. This is why smothering fireworks won't stop them from exploding and why the mixture would work in a metal tube.

Gunpowder typically consists of 75 percent saltpeter, 15 percent charcoal, and 10 percent sulfur. When lit, it emits 40 percent gas and 60 percent solid, in the form of smoke and residue. If you put gunpowder in a confined space, the pent-up gas will look for ways to escape and in the process propel objects that get in its way: ammunition like bullets or pottery or stones. The explosion produces a flash, white smoke, a sulfurous odor, and a loud bang. As millions of soldiers would be able to attest in the coming centuries, it is an assault on all the senses. Quality gunpowder later consisted of various other components that improved both combustibility and reliability, but the basics had been discovered. And whoever it was that first figured out how to propel objects using this powder had changed history in incalculable ways.

The Europeans took this technology and adapted it most successfully for war. We will never know with any certainty when the West was first introduced to gunpowder. It's possible that various weak forms of the concoction had been employed by professional magicians conjuring colorful smoke and noise for their audiences for centuries without understanding its potency. Whatever the case, early European gunpowder was at best erratic, weak, and unreliable. And unlike the Chinese, Europeans had a far more difficult time finding the needed ingredient, saltpeter, an organic component that occurs naturally only in unique conditions where the environment animates development of the necessary bacteria. Moreover, there are two kinds of saltpeter: one is calcium nitrate, the other potassium nitrate. The former is more abundant, usually found on manure, but makes a bad-quality gunpowder, as it absorbs water more easily. And a moist gunpowder is useless.[11]

So Europeans had to figure out ways to manipulate nature to meet their needs. The first saltpeter "plantations" were opened in Frankfurt in the 1380s, but they would soon be found throughout Europe. The process entailed dumping straw, leaves, and barnyard garbage into a pit or cellar and then marinating the entire mix with urine for a year. This repugnant blend was then dug up, strained, washed, and boiled to make saltpeter.[12] Nearly anyone looking to make some extra money, and willing to live with the inhospitable stench that the cocktail produced, could brew some homegrown saltpeter.

As the need for the powder grew, entire mass-producing plantations began to pop up to supply the busy armies of Europe. At first, the powder itself was created by simply grinding up the three ingredients and mixing them together. This method was sometimes dangerous and often fruitless. Even if the combination was proportioned properly, if packed too tightly, it would fizzle and if packed too loosely, the components would separate and make the concoction useless. Soon gunpowder makers began mixing the components with water to create a slurry that was set on sheets to dry. When the saltpeter dissolved into the water, it would enter the porous charcoal component of the mixture, making separation less likely.

The resulting hard cake was more resistant to moisture, would last far longer in storage, burn more quickly, and increase the ballistic power of weapons. Europeans utilized crushing devices to grind the ingredients into uniform grain sizes that helped shooters calibrate gunpowder to their weapons. Early musketeers, for example, often used medium-grain gunpowder to shoot and fine-grain gunpowder to prime their guns. Cannoneers, on the other hand, used large-grain powder, which took longer to ignite. A more standardized process made production more stable and provided big advances in quality control.

Despite the improvements, gunpowder remained a perishable commodity in the best of circumstances, spoiled by dampness and clumping, or by agitation that turned grains to dust. The wooden barrels in which it was stored and shipped contributed to the problem. The saltpeter in the powder dried out the staves, opening seams and allowing moisture to penetrate. It was not uncommon that more powder was spoiled than was used.

This is what gunpowder looked like to the would-be revolutionaries in North America: often dangerous, often ineffective, often difficult to procure, but always a necessity. During the French and Indian War of the 1750s, a number of frontier entrepreneurs began running low-production mills, but none of them survived long. Once hostilities against the French ended, the British dissuaded colonists from trading or making black powder, closely controlling its manufacturing and importation. Not that they needed to apply much pressure, since the British imported low-cost high-quality product to the colonies, rendering inefficient operations economically impractical. British gunpowder was cheap and it was good. The problem was that the colonists had to rely on their soon-to-be enemies to sell it to them.

Before the Revolution broke out, there was really only one consequential producer of gunpowder in North America, the water-powered mill in Frankford Creek, north of Philadelphia. Oswald Eve, a prosperous English-born Quaker, had opened the mill only a few months before King George III banned exportation of gunpowder to the colonies in 1774. The place became something of a tourist attraction, as colonists visited to catch a peek of how gunpowder was made, often hoping to take back the secret of making it themselves.[13]

The Provincial Congress in Watertown had asked the silversmith Paul Revere to visit the mill in 1774, for "in Philadelphia powder mills are Erected and the manufacturing of powder is carried on with Considerable dispatch and advantage."[14] Revere anticipated replicating the operation in Massachusetts, but Eve was less than helpful when the two met, perhaps realizing that facilitating a competing mill was bad for business. That didn't stop the perceptive Revere from taking a good look around and sending detailed sketches to Sam Adams. A plant in Canton, Massachusetts, was soon opened. It would produce a modest quantity of powder—that is, before it blew up in 1779.

The Americans also experimented with state-owned and-operated mills. In February 1776, with congressional approval, Pennsylvania began plans for the operation of mills that produced about a ton of powder weekly. By April 1776, the nascent government had built a gunpowder mill and a gun factory (added in December 1776) on the outskirts of Philadelphia. At its peak, the site was producing approximately two tons of gunpowder each week, and hundreds of locks for Continental muskets. Threatened by advancing British forces in late 1777, the majority of the military stores and supplies were removed from the site under orders from George Washington and moved inland to Lancaster County, the capital of American gunsmithing. Days later a detachment of Hessian Field Jäger Corps and British light infantry destroyed the buildings and remaining military stores.[15]

American military leaders often groused about not only the lack of gunpowder but also its inferior quality. Washington sarcastically noted that "there must be roguery or gross ignorance" in colonial powder-making efforts. In truth, it's unlikely to have been either corruption or stupidity. Unlike Europeans, who had been producing gunpowder for centuries, colonialists had little tradition in the craft, and it showed. Without the quality Indian saltpeter the British used, American powder was sure to remain inferior. Before the war, most saltpeter was procured from the limestone caves in Virginia, Georgia, Tennessee, and Kentucky.[16] This would not be nearly enough.

To assist production, the Americans established depots in New York and Philadelphia for the collection of saltpeter and sulfur. In January 1776, the Pennsylvania Committee of Safety placed ads in Philadelphia newspapers announcing that "such persons as are willing to erect Powder Mills in this Province, within fifty Miles distance of this City, are desired to apply to the Committee of Safety, who will lend them Money, on Security, if required, for that purpose, and give them other Encouragement."[17] It received six proposals from Americans willing to build mills. Very little came of the projects.

A *Royal American Magazine* piece in 1774 (illustrated by Revere) offered a step-by-step process of powder production at home. In the piece, the author claimed that saltpeter was "an effluvia of animal bodies. Pigeon houses, stables, and barns, but especially old walls, are full of it."[18] The Second Continental Congress, which also recruited French experts to teach Americans homebrew production methods, promised to buy up all saltpeter at half a dollar per pound. And once hostilities had begun, committees of safety in nearly every colony offered fiscal incentives to spur the production of saltpeter and pamphlets offering detailed instructions on its fabrication in hopes of spurring a local saltpeter industry. Yet this method could be an arduous process that yielded only small amounts of subpar saltpeter.

Another way of obtaining gunpowder was to take it by force. The race for gunpowder propelled the other major colonial player toward open rebellion and would soon precipitate the start of the war. This was the reason Gage sent the men to the Provincial Powder House. "No Quantity, however Small, is beneath notice," wrote George Washington from Cambridge in 1775.[19] Even before Washington put out the call, local municipalities had taken it upon themselves to secure as much as they could, resorting to violence when necessary. Four months before Revere would make his famous "midnight ride," he had journeyed to Portsmouth, New Hampshire, to warn locals that two regiments of British were on their way via sea to collect the gunpowder and munitions held in Fort William and Mary. The fort, situated on Great Island, at the mouth of the harbor, was guarded by a mere handful of British soldiers.

The reaction, which portended trouble for the British, was overwhelming. Led by John Langdon, a staunch revolutionary and later politician, hundreds took to beating drums and chanting on the street of the town, menacing the stronghold across the bay. The province's chief justice, Theodore Atkinson Sr., confronted the crowd, warning them that "they were going about an Unlawfull Act to take away the Powder out of his Majestys Fort, and that it was the highest Act of Treason and Rebellion They could possibly commit."

Undaunted by the stark threat, groups of men numbering over four hundred launched boats into the Piscataqua River to obtain the booty. Captain John Cochran, the British commander, refused to hand over the cache and ordered his half-dozen soldiers "not to flinch on pain of death but to defend the fort to the last extremity."[20] At his command, they fired their muskets and three cannons at the patriots who had just landed, all of their shots missing their marks. The Americans immediately swamped the ramparts and took the garrison. "I did all in my power to defend the fort," an unconvincing Cochran would later tell an inquiry into the event. The Americans had held the British soldiers prisoner for an hour and a half, Cochran later wrote to the governor of New Hampshire, "but all my efforts could not avail against so great a number."[21] So, on December 14, 1774, four months before any shots were fired in Lexington, the colonialists relieved the British garrison of around 10,000 pounds of powder. A plaque would be affixed to the fort, soon renamed Fort Constitution, declaring it the location of the "first victory of the American Revolution."[22] It wasn't quite Bunker Hill, but similar raids followed across the colonies.

In the end, neither confiscation nor domestic production would be enough to properly supply Washington's army. American gunpowder production would never take off due to a confluence of issues: inflation, reliance on imported ingredients, the accidental destruction of the few mills that did exist in North America, and then the purposeful destruction of other mills by the British.[23] In the end, around 90 percent of the gunpowder used by the revolutionaries was imported, with most of it finding its way to the Americas through the French colonies of the West Indies. Eager to harm their archenemy, the French became the primary source of ammunition. The French had struggled with many of the same problems the Americans did—namely, finding a source of quality saltpeter. Starting in 1775, Antoine-Laurent Lavoisier, one of the leading chemists of the European "Chemical Revolution" of the day, would become director of France's Gunpowder Administration and transform the nation not only into a self-sufficient gunpowder producer but an exporter of the much-needed chemical compound. Lavoisier recruited top chemists to develop procedures to help him increase both productivity and purity. Soon the Committee of Secret Correspondence, established by the Second Continental Congress to build relationships with friendly Europeans, was sending ships to France's Mediterranean ports; they would bring back ten tons of powder per voyage and help save the Revolution.

All that was to come later. Right now, as the British were preemptively attempting to disarm the populace, patriot leaders were more convinced than ever that it was imperative to secure gunpowder and weapons—and to do it quickly. While the so-called Powder Alarm had failed to blow up into open, widespread conflict, it was—inadvertently, perhaps—a dry run of the colonial warning system. The next time American militias were called on to repel British confiscatory measures, they would be better armed, more organized, more rapidly deployed, and much more dangerous.

4

★

"FIRE!"

"Once committed to what they regarded as a just and necessary war, these sons of Puritans hardened their hearts and became the most implacable of foes."

—David Hackett Fischer

The Battle of Lexington

The uniforms of the men in the twenty-one companies of British grenadiers and light infantry who marched through the fields and forests of Middlesex County, Massachusetts, were still soggy. Their journey had begun the night before when they had been crammed into naval barges at Boston Common and when they disembarked in the dark of midnight near Cambridge into three feet of water. Nevertheless, they almost immediately proceeded on an eighteen-mile march toward the town of Concord, where they were to confiscate a cache of weapons and munitions. To do so, these irritated and weary British soldiers would be forced to pass through another American hamlet called Lexington.

It was there, on April 19, 1775, in the triangular common at the center of town, that seven hundred British soldiers encountered seventy or so American militiamen. Most of the locals who showed up that day did so with muskets that had either been brought to the continent by the British military during the French and Indian War or were approximations of British guns that had been assembled by local blacksmiths. The preponderance of these muskets had been used for hunting deer or in militia drills, but little else. Some of the colonists had brought along a handful of homemade musket balls, assuming any interaction would end peacefully. Others, however, had brought hats filled with lead balls and flints, and were prepared for war.

Once the Americans were alerted to the British advance, the militiamen scrambled to load their flintlocks and assemble into rudimentary military lines, two deep, just as they had practiced many times in drills. Facing the tight military columns of battle-tested redcoats was a wholly different experience, to say the least. Adrenaline, anger, and fear mingled to create a combustible situation as the two asymmetrical forces steadied themselves. Civilians, perhaps as many as eighty or ninety, peered from the surrounding houses and buildings as the Americans and British faced off less than one hundred yards apart—a distance that was close enough to kill but too far to take any real aim. Other colonists surely jumped onto horses to warn other towns of what was transpiring.

"Disperse you Rebels—damn you. Throw down your Arms and disperse!" a British commander reportedly yelled at the rabble.[1] Local American captain John Parker first instructed his men, "Stand your ground. Don't fire unless fired upon. But if they want to have a war, let it begin here." The British soldiers began their battle chants of "Huzzah!" as their officers screamed at the Americans to lay down their arms. Once the locals began to contemplate their odds, the bluster on the colonial side began to subside. Parker, considering the situation, reportedly ordered his men to go home. Some did, some did not, and some did so very slowly. John Robins, one of the militiamen, later wrote that it was in the midst of this confusion that a British officer gave the order to fire.[2]

Thus began what is considered the first battle in United States history. One can imagine that the well-trained British line of musketeers had little problem unloading their deadly volleys of lead balls into a small rabble of militiamen, some of whom didn't even bother to reload their muskets. The British, in fact, fired a number of volleys into the rebels before order was restored in Lexington that day. When the black smoke finally cleared, eight Americans lay dead and nine had been wounded. Only one British soldier was hurt in this first round of shooting.

With this seemingly straightforward victory in hand, the redcoats then marched onward to Concord, where, after four hours of searching, they found very little of worth. But unbeknownst to the British, by the time they were prepared for the long march back to Boston, a few thousand American Minutemen—militiamen known for their ability to rapidly assemble and deploy for battle—were gathering.

The conflict in North America might have become inevitable the day the British fleet first sailed into Boston Harbor with its occupying army in 1768. Or perhaps it had become inevitable the day the Pilgrims first set their feet on the ground around Plymouth Bay. But however one views the underlying causes behind the violent confrontation that pitted the British against their subjects in North America, it was the policy of gun and powder confiscation that sealed the deal.

In September 1768, when rumors of an impending occupation by British troops first hit Boston, hundreds of musket-carrying Bostonians turned up at Faneuil Hall to pass resolutions protecting their claim to self-rule. Moreover, if the right to self-defense had been good enough for the Britons, they argued, it would be good enough for them:

> Whereas, by an Act of Parliament, of the first of King William and Queen Mary, it is declared, that the Subjects being Protestants, may have Arms for their Defence; it is the Opinion of this town, that the said Declaration is founded in Nature, Reason and sound Policy, and is well adapted for the necessary Defence of the Community.[3]

That same year an editorial in the *Boston Gazette*, the most influential newspaper in the colonies at the time, counting Sam Adams and Paul Revere among its contributors, noted that nothing was "more grievous to the people" than "that the inhabitants of this Province are to be disarmed."[4]

This is why one of the persistent calls of Boston patriots in these years was the vital role of self-defense. "For it is certainly beyond human art and sophistry, to prove the British subjects, to whom the privilege of possessing arms is expressly recognized by the bill of Rights," wrote Sam Adams, referring to the British codification of rights. As many of the colonists saw it, the aim of the British, no matter what justification they offered, was that of an invading army attempting to leave the inhabitants defenseless beneath their rule.

There would be no way back after December 16, 1773, when Americans dressed as Indians, and probably led by the ardent Samuel Adams, boarded three British ships in Boston Harbor and threw 342 chests of tea overboard. In reaction, the Coercive Acts of 1774—what colonialists referred to as the Intolerable Acts—were enacted to punish rebellious New Englanders for this destruction of property. The acts effectively closed the port of Boston to trade, suspended colonial self-government, and coerced locals to house and quarter British troops on demand, sometimes in their private residences. Additionally, there was a ban on the import of gunpowder and arms to America, decreeing that all supplies be secured for the Crown.

The king had ordered General Thomas Gage to "repel all force and violence by every means within his reach." And so he tried, despite his misgivings. Married to an American heiress, the aristocratic Gage was well acquainted with colonial life. Gage had fought alongside General Edward Braddock in his disastrous 1755 campaign to clear the French from the Ohio Valley. It had been Gage, in fact, whose rearguard actions allowed thousands of American and British soldiers, including his soon-to-be nemesis George Washington, to elude capture. Hard-liners back home saw the hardworking Gage as a man out of his element dealing with the quick-witted radicals. He was "too honest," one observer noted, "to deal with men who from their cradles had been educated in the wily arts of chicane."[5]

These men of chicanery soon pushed even further. In February 1774, the British appropriated 13,000 musket cartridges from a military store near Boston, abusing the Americans who were tasked with guarding it. At night "a party of officers, heated with liquor committed excesses in the streets and attacked the Providence coach. These insults irritated and inflamed the people," one nineteenth-century historian wrote.[6] When, in late 1774, Tory legislators in Boston proposed disarming the city, they backed off after an uproar among the people. In October, the Massachusetts Provincial Congress, with John Hancock acting as its president, adopted a resolution that condemned the military occupation of Boston and called on private citizens to arm themselves and engage in military drills.

Other intrusions tested colonial patience as well. The British hadn't learned their lesson after the near-disastrous Powder Alarm. In early 1775, British regulars marched out of Boston to make their way to Salem and Jamaica Plain, south of town, inflicting relatively small damage as they searched for munitions. Dr. Joseph Warren warned with his typical bluster that "it is the opinion of many, that had they marched eight or ten miles, and attempted to destroy any magazines, or abuse the people, not a man of them would have returned to Boston."[7]

Few among the British high command believed the colonialists possessed the will or ability to follow through on their threats. A notion calcified among some British that the inherent disposition of the American soldier was cowardly and lazy. "The Americans are in general the dirtiest, the most contemptible, cowardly dogs that you can conceive," wrote Colonel James Wolfe in a dispatch during the French and Indian War.[8] "There is no depending upon them in action. They fall down dead in their own dirt and desert battalions, officers and all."[9] General Braddock had thought the Americans under his command of a "Slothfull and Languid Disposition," rendering them "very unfit for Military Service."[10] As tensions rose, the British governor of Georgia, Henry Ellis, assured England that the colonists were a "poor species of fighting men" given to "a want of bravery." Another colonel remarked that the American soldier was "an effeminate thing, very unfit for and very impatient of war."[11] An MP thought that "good bleeding" would "bring those Bible-faced Yankees to their senses."[12]

So, after the Americans had acted up again during the Powder Alarm, William Legge, 2nd Earl of Dartmouth, secretary of state for the colonies, suggested to General Gage that he should contemplate disarming all of New England. At the time, it was assumed by many of the British that the rebelliousness was a factional problem contained in Boston. The jumpy but prescient general, who knew well of the widespread use and ownership of firearms in colonial America, responded that the only way to do so was by massive force. "Your Lordships Idea of disarming certain Provinces, would doubtless be consistent with Prudence and Safety; but it neither is nor has been practicable, without having recourse to Force and being Masters of the Country," Gage wrote.[13] This interaction was made public in the House of Commons, and soon Benjamin Franklin was disseminating it among the patriots to great effect.[14]

It wasn't the first time Gage, who better comprehended the size and scope of the problem than most, had cautioned that he would need a substantial army to quell the upstart locals. Back in 1765 the general had written his superiors amplifying the fact that "nothing but a very considerable Military force" would allow him "to grasp control of the American situation."[15] In November 1774, Gage again wrote home requesting an additional 20,000 troops to secure the British presence in North America. This was larger than the standing peacetime army of all of Great Britain at the time.

Gage's superiors sent him four hundred auxiliary marines.

European powers were not used to being out-armed by their subjects. One of the problems for the British was that New England was teeming with weapons at the dawn of the revolution. "The Colonists were the greatest weapon-using people of that epoch in the world. Everywhere the gun was more abundant than the tool," wrote historian Charles Winthrop Sawyer about colonial times.[16] For the most part, the muskets were older, bought through trade from Britain and other European powers, or made by local blacksmiths to resemble those guns. But a good musket, properly cared for, could be operational for many decades.

In 1774, Richard Price, the Welsh philosopher and intellectual who championed the American cause in Britain during the Revolution, pointed out that in the colonies "every inhabitant has in his house (as part of his furniture) a book on law and government, to enable him to understand his civil rights; a musket to enable him to defend these rights; and a Bible to enable him to understand and practice his religion."[17] In that same year, an Englishman visiting New England wrote home that there "is not a Man born in America that does not Understand the Use of Firearms and that well . . . It is almost the First thing they Purchase and take to all the New Settlements and in the cities you scarcely find a Lad of 12 years that does not go a Gunning."[18]

There have been sporadic attempts by politically motivated historians—most notably by the now-discredited Michael A. Bellesiles[19]—to embrace a history that comports with political antagonism toward the Second Amendment. These revisionists have argued that it wasn't until the mid-nineteenth century, with the rise of industrial manufacturing and affordable weapons, that American "gun culture" became pervasive. Yet, in recent years, historians have examined probate inventories (appraised lists of assets after death) and contemporaneous accounts and come to the conclusion that there was widespread ownership of firearms in the colonial era.

Two professors at Northwestern University Law School, James Lindgren and Justin Lee Heather, for instance, found that guns were owned by 50 to 73 percent (depending on the county) of male estates in North America. To put this in some context, guns were more abundant in these homes than other common items of the time. In one itemized 1774 inventory of hundreds of estates, firearms were more common than books (62 percent); only 30 percent of these estates had any cash, only 25 percent owned Bibles, and only 14 percent owned swords or knives.[20]

Another study calculated that, among the wealthiest 10 percent of estates, around 74 percent featured at least one gun in the largest Virginia counties of the era. None of the other five items that were measured—tables, seating furniture, hoes (despite tobacco being the primary means of making a living), axes, and sharp knives—were as common as guns, which appear to have been present in 50 percent of estates overall. In another study of pre-revolutionary Maryland, probate records show that estates had more firearms (78 percent) than chairs (63 percent), hand mills (53 percent), books (40 percent), pictures and curtains (24 percent), chamber pots (22 percent), or personal ornaments (20 percent). Any deep dive into the probate inventories around the country lands on similar findings.[21]

The number of guns, valued and transferable commodities, owned by Americans was likely even higher than these records show. As we noted earlier, from the 1600s on, militia duty was common in the colonies. Men needed guns to perform this duty, and so weapons were handed from one relative, friend, or neighbor to another, without any record of the transfer. In some Virginia counties, firearms were not even subject to inheritance laws.[22]

Many poorer colonial Americans likely aspired to own muskets and pistols—or more of them—but did not have the means to do so. In the mid-1700s, a musket could cost around two pounds and four shillings, no small amount in those days. The firearms that were tallied in probate records were often in good condition, signaling that the firearms were important to households, that the armory was replenished, and that the weapons were cared for and used. Of the 87 percent of itemized male estates with guns listed, at least one gun was not listed as old or in poor working condition.[23]

Then as now, guns were more common in rural areas—which makes sense, when one considers that urban dwellers often rely on the protection of numbers and are insulated from frontier violence by professional soldiers and other law-keepers in their towns. Rural Americans, on the other hand, were often impelled not only to hunt for their own food but to repel unfriendly marauders and Indians. (Native Americans, by the way, were also armed by the mid-1700s. There are numerous contemporaneous accounts of tribal warriors fighting, raiding, and hunting with an array of muskets during this era. As we've noted, the British, French, and Spanish had been equipping and trading with Indian tribes for more than a century by the time the Revolutionary War broke out. Guns had become an essential factor in Indian life and conflict. The archaeological record shows that Indians not only possessed weapons for hunting and war but had some rudimentary knowledge of how to fix them and build new parts.)[24]

As a practical matter, then, the situation the British faced made confiscation nearly impossible. As a philosophical matter, it meant war. Whether it required repelling hostile Indians, the French, the Dutch, or ultimately the British, for America's founding generation self-defense was the principal manifestation of natural rights—universal and inalienable. Contemporary cynics might discount this kind of idealism, but the many letters and articles written by Americans in those days illustrate an unvarnished commitment to the principles that would soon be codified in the Constitution. Few were more stressed than the right to self-defense.

So war it would be. Five days after the Powder Alarm ended, the colonial leader Dr. Joseph Warren—a man who would be yelling, "By Heaven, I hope I shall die up to my knees in blood!" on Breed's Hill (he did)—introduced a draft of the Suffolk Resolves, named after the county he represented, which included Boston. Across Massachusetts, other county conventions drafted similar declarations of opposition to the Intolerable Acts, officially signaling that Americans were prepared to take up arms against the king.

Among other actions, the resolutions promised to boycott British imports, to ignore the Intolerable Acts until they were repealed, and to see those who had attempted to enforce them removed from their royal positions. The most consequential resolutions were the ninth through twelfth, which urged the colonies to raise their own militias, free of British control, and defend themselves through violence if necessary. For colonists who were already likely the richest and freest subjects in the British Empire, to make such a declaration was tantamount to sedition.

The mood of the people was bellicose, and Warren's warning came true soon enough. In April 1775, Gage received word that the colonists had a stockpile of munitions in Concord, a small town northwest of Boston. All year Gage had continued to confiscate black powder and seize colonial arms in an effort to undermine preemptively any organized colonial insurgency. Gage knew that the local committee of safety in Concord had made considerable deposits of powder and munitions in its military store and was determined to guard and then move it as quickly as possible. The general had already dispatched spies to the area to sketch local roads in anticipation of taking them.

The Americans, of course, had their own spies. On April 18, 1775, Dr. Warren was informed by a source inside the British high command that troops would march to acquire the gunpowder and muskets that night. It was then that the doctor famously dispatched the silversmith Paul Revere and, less famously, the tanner William Dawes Jr. (another rider, Dr. Samuel Prescott, soon joined them) to alert Americans of the arrival of the British soldiers. The first task of the messengers, who traveled on different routes toward Concord under moonlight, was to alert Samuel Adams and John Hancock that they were to be apprehended. The two revolutionaries went into hiding. Then the riders went on to alert the militias. When a local sergeant cautioned them against unnecessary noise, Revere prophetically rejoined, "You'll have noise enough here before long: the regulars are coming out."[25]

With an easy victory against the colonial militia seemingly in hand, the British who left Concord must have been confident in their ability to deal with rebels. Soon the real consequences of attempting to disarm a heavily armed and trained population would be upon them.

As we've seen, by the time of the Revolution, Americans had at least a century's worth of experience with militias in the Massachusetts Bay Colony, a tradition of local defense that began with the first Puritans and had its roots in England. Some of these militia units, armed initially with matchlocks and pikes, had been able to gather within half an hour of being warned to deal with Indian uprisings, wars with foreign powers like France, or even threats of local insurrection.

At first these militia units were called "Snowshoemen," as each was to "provide himself with a good pair of snowshoes, one pair of moggisons, and one hatchet" and be ready "to hold themselves to march on a moment's warning."[26] By the time of the French and Indian War, they began referring to themselves as the "Minutemen."

Each municipality would have to decide the size and consistency of the units. Membership was voluntary, but there was certainly communal pressure to participate. In some units there were no ranks and in others men voted for their leaders. They met in reserved fields outside their towns to conduct military exercises, which most often entailed shooting practice and very little else. Any trained solider witnessing these drills likely found the scene amateurish at best. "*It is a curious masquerade scene* to see grave sober citizens, barbers and tailors who never looked fierce before, strutting about in their Sunday wigs with muskets on their shoulders," one Englishman visiting Massachusetts in the early 1700s observed.[27]

It is true that militia would not be able to stand up to hardened military forces over an extended war. Yet, as the British learned outside Boston that day, there were a couple of things the militiamen did excel at: speed and marksmanship. During the extended march back to Boston, the strung-out British columns were continually stalked by militiamen who hid in the woods and behind fences, houses, and large rocks. By the time the British had gotten back to the safety of Boston and the naval support at Charlestown Neck, 273 of their troops had been killed or wounded, and thousands of Minutemen had been summoned.

The battle also taught Americans lessons about the limitations of guerrilla warfare. For one, without any centralized command or leadership, they would not be able to fight a war. Many of the local units stopped pursuing the retreating British once they left the vicinity of their hometowns.

Even open rebellion did not dissuade the British from their confiscation efforts. Three days after Lexington, Gage warned elected Bostonians that meetings amounted to "a large body of men in arms" and that there would be more bloodshed. A committee of locals met with Gage to work out a deal that allowed those who handed over their weapons to leave the besieged city. After debating the arrangement in Faneuil Hall, the Americans agreed. In the days ahead, colonial city dwellers—the ones who some modern historians tells us supposedly owned very few weapons—handed over another 1,778 muskets, 634 pistols, 973 bayonets, and 38 blunderbusses.[28]

Americans took up positions in Charlestown and Dorchester, surrounding the British in Boston and in full rebellion. Massachusetts fielded twelve regiments, Connecticut added a force of around 6,000 men, and within the week there was an army of 16,000. As the war dragged on, enthusiasm waned. Washington had predicted as much early on. "When Men are irritated, & the Passions inflamed, they fly hastily, and chearfully to Arms," he wrote John Hancock in September 1776, "but after the first emotions are over to expect, among such People as compose the bulk of an Army, that they are influenced by any other principles than those of Interest, is to look for what never did, & I fear never will happen; the Congress will deceive themselves therefore if they expect it."[29]

Soon the states had to entice prospective soldiers with cash, land, and various goods. Congress mandated that men who enlisted must sign on for three years or the duration of the conflict, whichever came first. General Washington had urged conscription, stating that "the Government must have recourse to coercive measures." In April 1777, Congress recommended a draft to the states and within a year most states were conscripting men.

Although Americans often struggled to maintain the kind of discipline necessary to excel at this brand of warfare, they invented and excelled at others. Those who believed in the dangers of colonial resistance rested their argument on the population's size and proficiency with guns, which even most skeptics admitted was superb. The Duke of Manchester, a moderate member of Parliament at the time of the Revolution, warned his countrymen to move forward judiciously, as Americans "had now three million of people, and most of them were trained in arms . . ." One correspondence from England, reported in the *Boston Evening Post* in late

1768, put it more bluntly, noting that "the total number of the militia, in the large province of New-England was likely to be in upwards of 150,000 men, who all have and use arms, not only in a regular, but in so particular a manner, as to be capable of shooting a Pimple off a man's nose without hurting him."[30]

This contention wasn't far from the truth.

5

★

THE FINEST MARKSMEN IN THE WORLD

"I never in my life saw better rifles (or men who shot better) than those made in America."

—British colonel George Hanger

Maryland Rifleman

On October 7, 1777, a child of Irish immigrants named Timothy Murphy perched in a sturdy tree on the edge of the Second Battle of Saratoga (also known as the Battle of Bemis Heights) and took in the scene around him. From the brush-covered hillside just beyond the battle, he was situated opposite the right flank of General John Burgoyne's army of red-coated British soldiers, who marched in the conventional formations of European battle. There, for the first time in history, a mere soldier was able to aim his gun—in Murphy's case, a unique double-barreled long rifle invented by German immigrants of Pennsylvania—and kill another man from around 350 yards. Not just any man, but a British brigadier general.

The twenty-six-year-old Murphy, who had grown up on a wilderness farm along the Susquehanna River in central Pennsylvania, enlisted in the Continental Army in 1775, serving in the Siege of Boston and the Battle of Long Island before making a name for himself sniping at the British in Westchester. A rifleman who could regularly hit a seven-inch target at 250 yards, Murphy was transferred to "Morgan's Kentucky Riflemen" in July 1777 and within a month joined five hundred of his brethren marching upstate to reinforce the Continental smoothbore musket troops opposing Burgoyne's invasion of northern New York. The British were hoping that General Howe's march up to Albany would effectively split New York, ending the war. By the time Murphy was heading toward Saratoga, the rifle companies had been turned into light infantrymen units that used the forested land to scout, pester, stalk, and confuse the British.

Henry Knox, the future secretary of war, would refer to Morgan's Kentucky Riflemen as "the most respectable body of Continental troops that were ever had."[1] In his 1856 book, *The Life of General Morgan of the Virginia Line of the Army of the United States,* James Graham writes, "After examining all the sources of information within my reach, I became convinced that few, if any, of the heroes of that day furnished larger contributions than he did to the glory of our arms, or surpassed him in the amount and value of their services."[2]

Whether or not that sort of exuberant praise is warranted, there is little argument that the leader of the riflemen, Daniel Morgan, was a uniquely American figure—brave, brash, and independent. Born in New Jersey, the sturdy and often belligerent Morgan was the sort of person contemporary Americans might consider an adrenaline junkie. After leaving his family at the age of sixteen in search of fortune, Morgan took various jobs in sawmills and farms in the Shenandoah Valley before settling in as a professional merchandise hauler making his trips back and forth from Virginia's mountains and bustling seaports. "The Great Wagon Road" opened Philadelphia and went through the great rifle center of Lancaster, down to Frederick, Maryland, and to Winchester, traversed the eastern and middle parts of the Valley of Virginia, and ended up at the Yadkin River in North Carolina.

As an independent wagoner, he was well acquainted with both the Kentucky rifle and the violence of frontier life. So it was not surprising that Morgan would take to soldiering quickly when war broke out between the French and English in 1756.[3] Using Winchester as his base, Morgan became a Virginia militia leader. Spurred by tales of Indian atrocities, some real and many others imagined, he headed to the frontier and Fort Edwards. A short time after his arrival the fort was attacked by a formidable army of French and their Indians allies. Morgan acquitted himself bravely, displaying the brand of leadership that would repulse the enemy, and as they retreated, Morgan is said to have yelled at the top of his voice, "Let us follow the red devils!"[4]

The defense of Fort Edwards brought Morgan to Washington's attention, and the two became lifelong friends. When the Revolution broke out and the call for riflemen arrived, Morgan was one of the first to answer, conducting shooting trials to build a regiment and anticipating the rise of the rifleman. Yet one of the ironies of American history is that while the Pennsylvania rifle would later be mythologized and beloved by so many, often credited for winning the Revolutionary War, in reality it was underutilized and misunderstood. In many ways, expectations were simply too high for the riflemen. Some leaders in the budding American rebellion believed the rifleman could counterbalance the imposing if thinly spread military of the world's reigning superpower.

John Hancock, president of the Second Continental Congress and the first signer of the Declaration of Independence, claimed that riflemen "were the finest marksmen in the world," and because they could shoot "their Rifle Guns at an amazing distance," the Continental forces should make extensive use of them.[5] The future president John Adams concurred, noting that the riflemen could fire their weapons with "great exactness to great distances."[6] Washington, no doubt recalling his days with Braddock in the French and Indian War, believed that the riflemen could become highly effective modern soldiers, perhaps even forming the core of the entire Continental Army. Colonel George Hanger would have similar dreams for the British forces. The thinking was both premature and unrealistic, as the rifle had yet to be tested in large-scale conventional warfare.

In one of its first acts in June 1775, Congress authorized the raising of six companies of "expert riflemen" with an enlistment period of one year. Soon hundreds of peculiar characters began emerging from the backwoods to take their places in the forefront of the uprising. The response in Pennsylvania's outer counties, where the most riflemen were based, was overwhelming. The colony's quota was increased from six to eight companies—and then from eight to twelve. In July, the *Virginia Gazette* reported that so many frontiersmen had volunteered for the colonial cause that shooting tests were needed to ensure the integrity of the regiments. Judges drew noses on a board with chalk and sixty men riddled the targets from 150 yards to test their aptitude.[7] This soon became common practice in the effort to recruit riflemen.

The colonists treated the new soldiers as celebrities. And as the frontiersmen marched to meet the English forces in Boston—some of them traversing five hundred miles before they could do so—people emerged from their homes and farms to gawk and cheer at these unusual men. In turn, the image-conscious riflemen were not above preening for the cheering locals. One witness described them as "painted like Indians" and another portrayed them as "remarkably stout and hardy men, many of them exceeding six feet in height. They are dressed in white frocks, or rifle-shirts, and round hats." Some of them carried Indian tomahawks. Others wore buckskin breeches. Many wore moccasins and were decked in ornately decorated outfits with porcupine quills. Believing the garments generated a psychological advantage as well as highlighting the egalitarian ethos of the colonial troops, Washington turned into a fan of the Indian-style garb and "rifle shirts." The general noted that the cheap and utilitarian wear might undermine any "Provincial distinctions which would lead to jealousy and distractions."[8]

Local eyewitnesses also marveled at the potential self-sufficiency of such a fighting force. How, one Marylander wondered, could the British possibly stop a thousand of the men who "want nothing to preserve their health and courage but water from the spring, with a little parched corn, with what they can easily procure in hunting; and who, wrapped in their blankets, in the damp of night, would choose the shade of a tree for their covering, and the earth for their bed"? The *Boston Gazette* saw them as "heartily disposed to prosecute, with the utmost Vigour, the Noble Cause in which they are engaged."[9]

The frontiersman was more particular about choosing the rifle he carried, one European commented, "than choosing his wife."[10] "A well grown boy at the age of twelve or thirteen years," one settler observed in the Valley of Virginia in the 1760s, "was furnished with a small rifle and shot-pouch. He then became a fort soldier, and had his port-hole assigned him. Hunting squirrels, turkeys and raccoons, soon made him expert in the use of his gun."[11] For most frontier families, there was no choice.

Although the ability of these men to survive in the wilderness of North America was impressive, nothing captivated the imagination of the locals more than a rifleman's exactitude with his weapon. While other armies soon endeavored to adopt the techniques of the American riflemen, nowhere in the world did anyone have a fixation on firearm accuracy quite like Americans. Their displays of shooting so impressed General Washington that he ordered a demonstration of their skill to a crowd that turned out in Cambridge. The men hit poles of seven-inch diameter from 200 yards without much effort—some from 250 yards. They did it lying on their backs and on their sides, and sometimes while in a quick march.

One onlooker later recounted how shooters set up clapboards "with a mark the size of a dollar" as a demonstration of their trick shooting. One young marksman picked up the target and held it in his hand while his brother "very coolly" shot it from some distance. The brothers then switched roles, one picking up his rifle and the other the clapboard, and they performed the trick again. It didn't end there. "But will you believe me, when I tell you that one of the men took the board, and placing it between his legs, stood with his back to the tree while another drove the centre," the astonished letter writer relayed.[12]

These public displays of accuracy only buttressed the mythology surrounding the rifleman, and the expectations. By the middle of August around 1,400 of them, decked out in their peculiar outfits, were facing the professional British Army in Boston. Soon, the colonial army pulled together 82 of the very best of these riflemen and began sniping at British lines. No European army had ever experienced anything quite like it. The American sharpshooters were able to exact a steady toll on the redcoats, targeting officers in particular.

Targeting individuals was a tactic largely unknown in European warfare, as marksmanship was neither practiced nor taught by the English.[13] One British soldier noted that the American riflemen "conceal themselves behind trees etc till an opportunity presents itself of taking a shot at our advance sentries, which done they immediately retreat. What an unfair method of carrying on a war!"[14] Soon, General Howe was writing back to England about "the terrible guns of the rebels" who not only terrorized sentries but, more barbarically, deliberately picked off officers. British general James Murray, in a letter detailing the fears of many English officers, did not merely point out the superb marksmanship but the ability of the riflemen to excel at guerrilla combat:

> The reason why so many officers fell is that there are amongst the provincial troops a number of enterprising marksmen, who with rifle guns, and I have been assured many of them at 150 yards, will hit a card nine times out of ten . . . [T]hough these people in fair action in open field would signify nothing, yet over breast works, or where they can have the advantage of a tree (or a rock) and that may have every 20 yards in this country, the destruction they make of officers is dreadful.[15]

The claim that North America had a tree every twenty yards might be only a slight exaggeration, yet the tactics of the American upstarts became a real concern for the British. To better comprehend what he was up against, General Howe successfully kidnapped one of these colonial snipers and his rifle; the American marksman was then sent to England to be exhibited and perform for crowds.[16] A London periodical described the soldier as "a Virginian, above six feet high, stout and well-proportioned . . . He can strike a mark with great certainty, at two hundred yards distance. He has a heavy provincial pronunciation, but otherwise speaks good English. The account he gives, is, that the troops in general are such kind of men as himself, tall and well-proportioned."[17]

It was Morgan's men who gave cover to smoothbore-carrying regulars in one of the most pivotal deployments of the American Revolution and perhaps the most important for the riflemen in Saratoga. Burgoyne, who in 1775 had noted that the chances of "untrained rabble"[18] beating a conventional European force were somewhere around "nil," marched down from Canada with a force of around 6,000 British, Hessians, Loyalists, and Indians, hoping to cut away New England along the Hudson River Valley and quickly put an end to the war. As Burgoyne's army descended into the dense forests of New York, sharpshooters who employed many of the same guerrilla tactics advanced to meet the Americans.

Burgoyne brought with him a number of Indian scouts and a sharp-shooter specifically trained in wilderness combat. Chosen "for their strength, ability and being expert at the firing of ball," their mission was "to act on the flanks of the advance brigade and reinforce by what number of Indians the General may think fit to employ." All of which likely offered Burgoyne a false sense of security as some 2,000 British troops—a third of Burgoyne's entire army—headed into the thick New York woods. The force was led by Brigadier General Simon Fraser, a Scottish aristocrat, his most capable subordinate.

When Benedict Arnold, then considered one of the finest generals in the Continental Army, noticed the British general marshaling his troops for a pushback, he called out to Morgan: "That man on the grey horse is a host unto himself and must be disposed of—direct the attention of some of the sharpshooters amongst your riflemen to him!"[19] Many recollections of the incident then have Morgan instructing Murphy, one of his finest marksmen, to shoot down that "gallant officer . . . General Fraser. I admire him, but it is necessary that he should die. Do your duty."[20]

This scene seems to inject a level of chivalry into the unconventional targeting of officers. Morgan, who never mentioned Murphy by name, would later offer a more down-to-earth reminiscence of the event in 1781: "Me and my boys," explained Morgan, were pinned down by British fire until "I saw that they were led by an officer in a grey horse—a devilish brave fellow." Then "says I to one of my best shots, says I, you get into that there tree, and single out him on the . . . horse. Dang it, 'twas no sooner said than done. On came the British again, with the grey horseman lead-ing; but his career was short enough this time."[21]

Murphy purportedly went about his duty, the first bullet missing its target and nicking Fraser's horse. His next shot missed as well, clipping the general's horse a second time. However, his third attempt was lethal, hit-ting Fraser, supposedly more than three hundred yards away, in the stom-ach. When the British forces saw Fraser fall from his horse and dragged off the battlefield, they broke ranks and the defense fell back in retreat. The tide of battle was reversed. Even Burgoyne admitted that the loss of Fraser "helped to turn the fate of the day." By the end of the battle, his

62nd Regiment was decimated. Of forty-eight artillerymen in one battery, Morgan's sharpshooters killed or wounded all but twelve. A British officer wrote, "The only shelter afforded to the troops was from those angles which faced the enemy as the others were so exposed that we had several men killed and wounded by the riflemen, who were posted in trees."

As before, the British were horrified by the targeting of their officers. Burgoyne wrote of the sudden deadly impact of the American riflemen: "The enemy had with their army great numbers of marksmen, armed with rifle-barrel pieces; these, during an engagement, hovered upon the flanks in small detachments, and were very expert in securing themselves, and in shifting their ground. In this action, many placed themselves in high trees in the rear of their own line, and there was seldom a minute's interval of smoke, in any part of our line without officers being taken off by a single shot."[22]

Ten days later, around 6,000 British troops surrendered to the Americans, saving the cause. Moreover, the colonial victory over Burgoyne in October 1777 changed the complexion of the war. As a military matter, it demonstrated that the Americans could beat a British field army. It illustrated that riflemen could be an important factor in battle, if deployed correctly. In political terms, it showed European powers that Americans could launch a formidable rebellion. The victory was used by American diplomats as leverage to cement the colonies' relationship with Louis XVI. The sides would sign a formal alliance by February 1778, and by June, France declared war on the British (with Spain and the Netherlands soon joining them). This widening of the war helped the Americans prevail by offering them naval support and ground troops needed to win the war.

Murphy continued to fight on the frontier and serve as a sharpshooter right through the end of the war, by which time he had accumulated forty-two confirmed kills.[23] For the American riflemen, underdogs in the war, guerrilla warfare was often a means of survival, and the targeting of officers was a means of evening the odds.

But their heyday was still to come.

One question emerges: Would the Revolution have been won more quickly if Washington had figured out how to better deploy his sharpshooters? Alternative histories are always frustratingly inconclusive, but there are many reasons why the rifle was not ready. For a new weapon to be effective in war, no matter how modern, there need to be policies dictating its broader use. In the end, the American Revolution was fought on late nineteenth-century European terms, which is to say in linear battle formation, often in open fields. And so smoothbore muskets were used by most regulars because they were far easier to load, and with lines of soldiers alternating volleys, they were far more effective in open battle.

Even if Washington had come up with more successful ways to deploy riflemen, the general would have found it difficult to make them a major component of his forces. For one thing, there was no industrial sector capable of mass-producing a new rifle. As it stood, every rifleman owned a unique weapon, each one the result of specialized work by blacksmiths and gunmakers. What they did produce was often of inferior quality and would break down easily in combat. The widespread manufacture of this new rifle necessitated the production of specialized parts and meant training gunsmiths around the country in new techniques.[24] This couldn't happen overnight.

When the rifle was deployed—which, as we've seen, was not often—it was hampered by a number of technical problems. For one, it took an excruciatingly long time to reload a rifle—often almost two minutes due to the difficulty of forcing the ball down a constricted, rifled bore. Moreover, the residue from the cheap, coarse gunpowder that was used during the war quickly fouled the grooved barrels, making the gun difficult to maintain. Speedy reloading was an obsession of late eighteenth-century armies, for a good reason.

Unlike modern-day snipers, colonial-era marksmen were in immediate danger after firing. No matter how hidden the shooter's position, no matter how pristine his aim, once the gun went off, a plume of smoke would rise and immediately betray his position. On numerous occasions American riflemen were tasked with fighting off bayonet-wielding British soldiers. For the most part, this contest did not go well for them. The lack of a bayonet rendered the riflemen even more vulnerable in pitched battles. In the Battle of Long Island, one Hessian remarked that "these frightful people deserve more pity than fear." In 1778, General Anthony Wayne, commander of the Pennsylvania Line, asked the state board of war to trade in rifles for muskets, because "I would almost as soon face an enemy with a good musket and bayonet without ammunition—as with ammunition with a bayonet." Colonel George Hanger, for instance, wrote of a skirmish with Morgan's riflemen: "Not one in four [riflemen] had time to fire and those that did had no time to reload again; the infantry not only dispersed them, but drove them for miles over the country."

The riflemen, it should also be mentioned, were often free spirits who were unable to function under the discipline of army life. "They do not boast so much of the Riflemen as heretofore," General Artemas Ward wrote to John Adams in October 1775. "Genl. Washington has said he wished they had never come. Genl. Lee has damned them and wished them all in Boston. Genl. Gates has said, if any capital movement was about to be made the Riflemen must be moved from this Camp."[25]

When the delegation from Maryland offered to raise more rifleman units in October 1776, the congressional secretary wrote that "if muskets were given them instead of rifles the service would be more benefitted" and if it were up to him he "would speedily reduce the number of rifles" and replace them with more manageable muskets, "[a]s they are more easily kept in order, can be fired oftener, and have the advantage of bayonets."

For these reasons, by 1778, Washington sent what was left of the rifle corps to missions on the frontier and disbanded the rest. By this time, the war board would not accept any new rifle regiments—and was looking to replace the ones they did have with muskets. As a result of Baron Friedrich Wilhelm von Steuben professionalizing the American forces during the spring of 1778, a wholly traditional European-style army came down from the hills of Valley Forge. He taught the manual of arms, platoon volley fire, and proper use of the bayonet to a musket-equipped army. The rifle's time had not yet come.

6

★

LIBERTY'S TEETH

I saw the plundering British bands,
Invade the fair Virginian lands.
I saw great WASHINGTON advance
With Americans and troops of France;
I saw the haughty Britons yield,
And stack their muskets on the field.

—Joseph Plumb Martin

The Death of General Mercer at the Battle of Princeton, January 3, 1777

Even as they were digging trenches in the Virginia soil, Joseph Plumb Martin and his men could make out two of the redoubts held by the British surrounding the fort at Yorktown. All the men were also aware that at some point soon their commander, Alexander Hamilton, would order the bloody march to seize the fortifications. "I mistrusted something extraordinary, serious or comical, was going forward," Martin later wrote, "but what I could not easily conjecture."[1] The situation soon became clear to them as the sun began to fall and Martin was ordered to move his detachment of colonial infantrymen beyond the trenches they had just built and lie down on the ground to await the signal for an attack on the fortification. General Washington had planned on taking a number of positions using the elements of surprise and darkness. Martin's troops quietly crawled to within around one hundred yards or less of the British carrying unloaded muskets, or "cold steel," only to be loaded once the battle began to limit the amount of noise. Once artillery began pounding the redoubts, Martin's men quickly rose to form lines and rushed toward the enemy, whom they could see in the moonlight.

It had been an arduous journey for Martin. Like many of his friends, the fifteen-year-old had enlisted in the Connecticut state militia after hearing about the exhilarating events in Lexington. After his six months of militia duty were up, Martin enlisted in the Continental Army and served seven more years fighting the British up and down the East Coast. By the time he'd reached his mid-twenties, Martin was a sergeant who had participated in the Battle of Brooklyn, the Battle of White Plains, the Siege of Fort Mifflin, the Battle of Monmouth, and the Siege of Yorktown. What makes Martin's story unique is that it was only in 1830, at the age of seventy, that he would publish a firsthand account of his time during the war, titled *A Narrative of Some of the Adventures, Dangers, and Sufferings of a Revolutionary Soldier; Interspersed with Anecdotes of Incidents That Occurred Within His Own Observation.* Although it almost certainly was embellished in places, the book was culled from journals Martin kept during the war, and it would offer insights into the everyday lives of the average soldier during the American Revolution.

Although Martin relays astonishing stories of colonial shooting competence—in one unlikely tale, a light infantryman snipes a British guard who was mocking him from over three hundred yards away—he never mentions the American rifle, because for most of the men who fought for American independence, there was no real sight for aiming, and any success in long-distance shooting was often luck. "A soldier's musket, if not exceedingly ill bored, will strike the figure of a man at 80 yards; it may even at 100," the British marksman George Hanger once noted, "but a soldier must be very unfortunate indeed who shall be wounded at 150 yards."[2]

On the battlefields, as Martin relays on numerous occasions, American and British soldiers met each other in two or three lines of musketeers. Right behind these lines was where the reserves marched, ready to step in the place of casualties. Martin and other infantrymen of the late eighteenth century were drilled in quick loading and firing, on command. These linear formations steadily moved to within an uncomfortable forty to fifty yards of the enemy and delivered volleys of musket balls in succession. While one fired, the other line busied themselves with reloading. The formations proceeded forward at intervals until the lines were close enough to charge with their bayonets and engage in hand-to-hand combat. Thus, the art of speedily loading was more vital than the art of aiming.

The guns the two major participants of the war fired at each other were remarkably similar—sometimes, in fact, the very same models. Since most of what the revolutionaries knew about warfare, and almost all of their military-grade equipment, had come from the British, it's unsurprising that the famous "Brown Bess," one of the most reliable and long-serving firearms in history, became one of the most prevalent weapons used by the American soldiers early in the war.

At various points in the early eighteenth century, the British had attempted to standardize musket parts to make it simpler to produce them and train armies to use and maintain them. In 1715, King George's

Brown Bess

government created the Board of Ordnance, which established the "system of manufacture" to set standards of production for weapons. The effort both reduced British dependence on foreign firearms makers and improved the quality and capacity of domestic musket manufacturing. This entailed developing a network of domestic contractors who supplied the government with musket parts, which were then delivered to gunmakers to assemble into finished muskets.

One outcome of this system was the Long Land Service musket, known alternatively as the King's musket, the Tower musket, and most famously, the Brown Bess. It was a flintlock, .75-caliber barrel-loading musket, and it became the standard firearm for British soldiers in 1722 and remained so for over a hundred years. The gun would be continuously tweaked over the next century—the British toyed with the length, locks, and material—but the basics remained the same: the Brown Bess was most often made of walnut stock, it had a banana-shaped lock plate (the elongated piece of metal serving as a mounting for the lock), and it used brass. The barrel was forty-six inches long, and the gun weighed a little more than ten pounds. Its flintlock mechanism was attached with just two screws. It was simple and trustworthy, and, most vitally, the parts were now easy to replace and produce.

Why the name "Brown Bess"? The etymology has been debated for a century, with a seemingly endless number of theories. Some claim the "Brown" in Brown Bess comes from the brown anti-rusting agent that was smeared on the metal. But the gun had its moniker long before the browning of the gun. Some claim that "Bess" came from the old harquebus, or that the gun's name derived from the German or Middle Dutch terms for "brown" and "barrel," or that it was due to the brown of the rifle stock; or perhaps "Bess" referred to Queen Elizabeth I. All of it seems unlikely. It was not unusual for men of the age—or any era, for that matter—to refer to their guns using women's names. One theory is that the word "gun" itself had been derived from the Norse woman's name "Gunnildr," which became "Gunna," which became "gonne." The word is used by Geoffrey Chaucer, who for a time served in the administration of Edward III, the victor at Crécy, perhaps the first battle using firearms in Europe. Chaucer wrote in 1384: "As swifte as pelet out of gonne, / Whan fire is in the poudre ronne."[3]

Whatever the source of the nickname, men like Martin needed to get their hands on many if they wished to succeed. Once war broke out,

American "committees of safety" had gone about the business of acquiring existing firearms by controlling local armories, but the colonists also purchased, and on occasion confiscated, Loyalist firearms. They would also engage in ongoing efforts to procure older Dutch, Spanish, and Prussian weapons, with only modest results at the start of the war.[4]

The muskets that were useful in hunting and personal defense were rarely durable enough for wartime conditions, and soldiers often complained about their weapons in the early years of the conflict. "The arms were in horrible condition, covered with rust, half of them without bayonets, many from which a single shot could not be fired . . . [M]uskets, carbines, fowling pieces and rifles were seen in the same company," wrote General von Steuben, the Prussian who had modernized the military tactics and brought a modicum of discipline to the Continental Army at Valley Forge in 1778.[5]

There would also be concerted efforts to create new muskets. There were perhaps a couple of thousand colonial gunsmiths working on the continent during the Revolutionary War, and not all of them ended up laboring for the cause of liberty. Many had been trained to repair British muskets, and so they might well be employed by the Crown. Although the British had relied on the raw materials found in the colonies to produce weapons for decades, they had prohibited any large-scale manufacturing facility for guns in the colonies, leaving Americans at a disadvantage.[6]

So blacksmiths supporting the colonial cause would be relegated to assembling a hodgepodge of mixed parts from antiquated muskets and various foreign guns. When ambitious craftsmen created usable firearms, they were often made to broadly feel, work, and look like the Brown Bess, although few could match its dependability. One such surviving firearm, purportedly used by a man from Wrentham, Massachusetts, featured an American-made stock using a Dutch lock, a French iron side plate, a British brass butt plate, and a Queen Anne ribbed pattern ramrod. American gunmakers avoided putting their names or insignias on the firearms so that there remained few clues that might lead to retribution should the American experiment be squashed by the British.

In March 1776, Silas Deane, a Connecticut delegate to the Continental Congress (who would later be accused of embezzling), left for France to press the Americans' need for arms, equipment, and financial aid against the British. Deane, with the help of the Marquis de Lafayette, assured the French that the colonists were interested in "total separation"—not that France needed a whole lot of prodding when given the chance to undermine British holdings in North America. It was not until 1778 that the French and British were officially at war. But in the meantime France continued to smuggle muskets, ammunition, tents, cannons, and other supplies to the colonies, many routed through the West Indies.

The best-known and most widely used of these firearms—and the one that Martin's men almost certainly held when charging the Yorktown redoubts—was a musket that not only helped win the war but became the template for American postwar arms. The Charleville musket was first introduced in 1717. A smoothbore, it used a smaller, .69-caliber barrel, making it a lighter gun—and a bit more accurate—than the Brown Bess.[7] Like the Brown Bess, it was the first gun the French army built with standard parts and to use standard ammunition to better facilitate production and repair. Also like the Brown Bess it was used into the mid-1800s until the flintlocks were replaced with percussions caps. (More on that later.) The gun was made in cities across France—Charleville, Saint-Étienne, and Maubeuge—but since most of the American arms had been produced in Charleville, the colonial soldiers simply started calling it by that name.[8] The Americans, as we'll see, would copy the contours of the Charleville when creating their first official muskets at the United States armory in Springfield, Massachusetts.

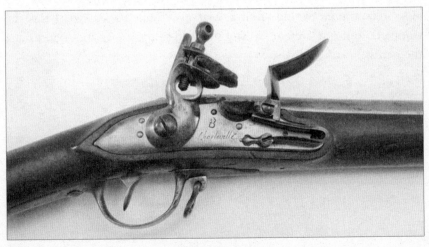

Charleville lock

While the men at Lexington fought with makeshift versions of the Brown Bess—though some had probably held locally produced unreliable muskets—by the time Martin's unit was crawling toward the British regulars and German mercenaries who fortified Yorktown, they were holding the most sophisticated and reliable muskets available in the world. In the two hundred years preceding the Siege of Yorktown, gun technology had made a number of impressive technological leaps. Along with developments in design and balance, at least three basic ignition systems had been invented during this period. The firearm had gone from being little more than a small, clumsy, loud cannon to a sleeker, lighter, considerably better-balanced gun that a man could shoot faster and farther, and with better and better accuracy. A weapon primarily deployed in sieges, as a way to rip through armor, or as a tool of psychological warfare was now the predominant weapon of combat.

As soon as Martin ordered his unit to charge the redoubt, the British fired their Brown Bess muskets and "seven or eight men belonging to the infantry were killed, and a number wounded." Once the Americans rallied and loaded their own Charlevilles and English muskets, they quickly outgunned the defenders in the fortification and Martin's war came to an end. By the end of the next day, Lieutenant General Charles Cornwallis and the British Army had surrendered to Washington. The British government was impelled to negotiate an end to the conflict that had broken out near Boston seven years earlier between trained redcoats and American militia.

"The next day we were ordered to put ourselves in as good order as our circumstances would admit," Martin wrote, "to see (what was the completion of our present wishes) the British army march out and stack their arms."[9]

7

★

FREEDOM'S GUARANTEE

"To disarm the people; that is the best and most effectual way to enslave them . . ."[1]

—George Mason

George Washington presiding over the Philadelphia Convention

What could induce seventy colonial Americans—most of them farmers—to stand against seven hundred highly trained British fighters in the town square in Lexington? For that matter, what induced the wealthy and intellectual classes of the colonies, men and women with so much to lose, to support an all-out war against what was considered the most powerful empire in the world? What drove Joseph Plumb Martin and another approximately 200,000 British subjects in North America to enlist in an insurrection against the Crown over the next seven years?

As with any conflict, there was an array of factors, but one thing was clear: the American colonialists were more religious, puritanical, zealous, and hyper-idealistic about their natural rights than any other people in the world. And the most vital and practical right they knew was the one that would allow them to protect all the others: the right to self-defense.

In the writings and speeches of the American Founders, the threat of disarmament was always a casus belli. Which makes some ironic sense when we consider that of all the natural rights codified in the Constitution, none—not freedom of speech, press, or religion, or the ability to vote or to demand due process—had a longer or deeper history in English common law and tradition than the right to defend oneself. Not even government officials or Loyalists who had hoped to disarm rebellious colonists in order to avert that war would ever offer a broader philosophical argument for depriving the common man of his right to own weapons.

In some sense, these colonists' understanding of the right to bear arms was forged by their violent history, sparse population, inhospitable environment, and geography, but the ideological foundations for the Second Amendment had been well established by the time the first English landed in Massachusetts. And as Alexander Hamilton later noted, "We think in English."[2]

The historian Joyce Lee Malcolm, in her classic study of the origins of the Second Amendment, *To Keep and Bear Arms: The Origins of an Anglo-American Right*, points out that the "colonists were men and women steeped in English laws, English customs, English prejudices, and English habits of mind."[3] One of the reasons the British had been more successful than their European rivals in enticing their countrymen to colonize North America was the promise that their rights and customs continue to be honored and flourish. It was within this framework that British subjects staked their claim to revolt when the king came for their weapons.

The idea of personal arms and collective militias goes back to at least the days of King Alfred I, who called on all subjects to arm themselves for service in the late 800s. In 1181, King Henry II issued the Assize of Arms, calling on all freemen to own weapons in the service of the king—or else. The arms these men were required to provide depended on their wealth and status, but nearly everyone contributed. The citizen army was rooted in English life for centuries. Correspondingly, so was the idea of having a weapon in the home. Henry VIII would decree that all fathers had a responsibility to purchase longbows for any sons between the ages of seven and fourteen years and teach them to shoot. Anyone from the age of fourteen to the age of forty was obligated to practice and be able to show that they were owners of bows and arrows "contynually in hys house."[4] Anyone who failed to own and use a longbow was subject to a fine. To make the longbow even more widespread, the king banned the ownership of crossbows and "handgonnes" and instituted price controls, but the idea was soon abandoned as both weapons gained in popularity.

It is difficult to pinpoint with any certainty the number of arms the average person possessed in England in the 1500s and 1600s, but records illustrate that criminals had easy access to guns during this time, engaging in everything from poaching to illegal hunting to highway robbery. This suggests that guns were plentiful. Even in times of confiscation, usually during civil and religious strife, it is likely that a discreet person could own a firearm or a crossbow without much worry.[5]

In Elizabethan England, the idea of the local militia grew. Many towns were tasked to create and train men to be prepared for invasion and domestic discord. Some of these groups were afforded special training and provided firearms purchased by the Crown, while others were on their own. These traditions, as we've seen, endured in America, culminating in the Minutemen and other Continental militia. During the subsequent upheaval, civil war, and religious violence, those in power might occasionally attempt to disarm the citizenry. The Game Act of 1671, perhaps the most well-known instance of the Crown severely limiting the ownership of weapons by the average citizen, made possession of a firearm by anyone not qualified to hunt illegal and provided for confiscation of the weapon.

It was the English Bill of Rights, a document cataloging the crimes of James II and codifying the "ancient and indubitable" rights of English citizens in 1689, that would in many ways be the blueprint for the American revolutionaries. It was a unique document because it listed the ways that the authority of the Crown was to be limited. One such limitation forbid the disarming of the populace (in part a reaction to James II's Catholic officers disarming Protestants). "These the subjects which are Protestants may have arms for their defence suitable to their conditions and as allowed by law," it read. Whether this clause largely concerned a potential Catholic coup or not, it transformed into something much deeper in American life. By 1765, William Blackstone, whose writings helped define the English common law legal system, affirmed "the natural right of resistance and self-preservation, when the sanctions of society and laws are found insufficient to restrain the violence of oppression."[6] The revolutionaries relied on Blackstone's writing to confirm their own claim to resist tyranny with the musket. "To vindicate these rights, says Mr. Blackstone," wrote Samuel Adams in 1769, "when actually violated or attack'd, the subjects of England are entitled first to the regular administration and *free course of justice* in the courts of law—next to the right of *petitioning the King* and parliament for redress of grievances—and lastly, to the right of *having and using arms for self-preservation and defence.*"[7]

The responsibility of self-defense—for yourself and your community—would be coupled with the right to own property. Republicanism was an American credo, and colonists—not only among political leaders, businessmen, and intellectuals, but men of God as well—took these ideas and shaped them to make sense in their own situation. "Some of the ministers," wrote a Tory in the days leading up to the Revolution, "are continually in their sermons stirring up the people to resistance."[8] It was true. Whether implicitly or explicitly, the colonists would see themselves in both the political and moral right.

One such man, Reverend Jonathan Parsons, a well-regarded Presbyterian minister in Newburyport, Massachusetts, told his flock in 1774 that defending one's liberty—or "repair[ing] our injuries at the point of the sword"—was a moral imperative, "for if one man may defend himself and his rights against an assailant, much more may a whole country defend themselves when their rights are invaded, because the concern is greater."[9] The Reverend Simeon Howard, speaking the same year, argued that Christianity was not incompatible with the notions of self-defense of those who fought in the Revolution: "Defending ourselves by force of arms against injurious attacks, is a quite different thing from rendering evil for evil. The latter implies doing hurt to another, because he has done hurt to us; the former implies doing hurt to another, if he is hurt in the conflict only because there is no other way of avoiding the mischief he endeavours to do us: the one proceeds from malice and revenge; the other merely from self-love, and a just concern for our happiness, and argues no ill will against any man."[10]

Howard would go on to praise militias over standing armies, an idea that soon became one of the sticking points over the ratification of the

Constitution. Many American notions of self-defense had been codified by the anti-military and anti-government sentiments that had been festering among English Protestants during the 1600s. The American apprehension over standing armies would persist for years.

The First Amendment of the Bill of Rights lists the most vital freedoms of man. The second lists the only way to attain them and preserve them. Without the second, there is no first. It was in this context that the newly minted nation enshrined this natural right. The words written by James Madison in 1791, "A well regulated militia, being necessary to the security of a free state, the right of the people to keep and bear arms, shall not be infringed," would not be controversial until the twentieth century when a seemingly ungrammatical comma plunked in the middle of this sentence offered a generation of gun-control advocates a justification to question whether individuals were afforded the right to self-defense.

Modern anti-gun advocates argue that the Founding Fathers never imagined individuals would have a right to bear arms. The Second Amendment, they claim, was intended only to arm the militia. It is an expedient historical fantasy. In late eighteenth-century America, there was no debate over what those words meant. They were so self-evident that the only question was whether they were even necessary.

As Justice Antonin Scalia noted two centuries later when reaffirming the right to bear arms, "The Amendment's prefatory clause announced a purpose, but does not limit or expand the scope of the second part, the operative clause. The operative clause's text and history demonstrate that it connotes an individual right to keep and bear arms." The Second Amendment explicitly mentions "the right of the people," just as the Fourth, Ninth, and Tenth Amendments do, all of which have been found to protect individual rights.

Nearly every intellectual, political, and military leader of the founding generation, stressed the importance of self-defense and the individual right to bear arms. John Adams, in his 1770 defense of Captain Thomas Preston, one of the British soldiers responsible for the Boston Massacre, argued that all men had the inherent right to defend themselves. "Here every private person is authorized to arm himself, and on the strength of this authority," Adams said in his opening statement, "I do not deny the inhabitants had a right to arm themselves at that time, for their defense, not for offence." But, the future president added, even soldiers of the Crown, even if they were unwanted and intrusive, had cause to defend themselves when assaulted by a mob. Self-defense was "*the primary* canon in the law of nature," Adams argued, quoting Blackstone (emphasis mine).

The revolutionary pamphleteer Thomas Paine would note that locals in Boston "found it necessary to arm themselves with heavy Walking Sticks or Weapons of Defence" when they went outside. "Arms like laws discourage and keep the invader and the plunderer in awe . . . ," he wrote. "Horrid mischief would ensue were one half the world deprived of the use of them; for while avarice and ambition have a place in the heart of man, the weak will become a prey to the strong."[11]

When Pennsylvania became the first colony to explicitly guarantee the right to bear arms, it was Benjamin Franklin who presided over the conference. In 1776, the year he wrote the Declaration of Independence, Thomas Jefferson's first draft of the Constitution of the Commonwealth of Virginia stated, "No freeman shall ever be debarred the use of arms." (By the third draft, the sentence read: "No freeman shall be debarred the use of arms [within his own lands or tenements]." Many anti-gun advocates point to this parenthetical as evidence that Jefferson didn't envision guns being carried outside of private property. But it is far more reasonable to suggest that parenthetical was an admonishment of the potential of British-style gaming laws that prohibited common men from hunting on their own lands.)[12]

Jefferson's amendment came too late and, in the end, it wasn't adopted in the Constitution of Virginia. Instead the state used George Mason's Declaration of Rights, which included the right of "the proper, natural, and safe defence of a free state." The same Mason also noted the importance of the militia and right to bear arms by reminding his compatriots of England's efforts "to disarm the people; that it was the best and most effectual way to enslave them . . ."

Many Americans, in fact, would soon see the Second Amendment as superfluous in a world filled with weapons. For one thing, they made little if any distinction between the militia and the individual, as the former does not function without the latter. While it is convenient for contemporary advocates of gun control to claim that evidence for individual gun rights is still inconclusive, what we do know for certain is that not a single soul in the provisional government or at the Second Continental Congress or any delegate at the Constitutional Convention—or, for that matter, any new American—ever argued against the idea of individuals owning a firearm. Not a single militia leader asked his men to hand over their firearms after the town's drills had ended.

The real point of contention between the Federalists and Anti-Federalists over the Second Amendment was never about individual ownership. The Federalists argued that the Bill of Rights was not necessary because states would be empowered to run their own affairs. Anti-Federalists argued that the Bill of Rights would be another safeguard that protected individual liberty from federal control. Though no one debated the right of people to arm themselves, one of the most contentious debates over the Constitution revolved around who would have control of the militias, the states or the federal government.

The skepticism regarding a standing army during peacetime went back to the English, and was regarded as one of the most obvious abuses of the Crown. The Boston Massacre in 1770 had moved many Americans further into the British Whig camp, which viewed peacetime armies as anathema to liberty. William Pitt, friend of the colonists, warned that in America, "these three millions of Whigs—three millions of Whigs, my Lords, with arms in their hands—are a very formidable body."[13] The founding generation was equally fearful of the idea of soldiers suppressing the rights of the people. An army should be temporary, raised and paid to fight foreign adversaries, not internal threats. Americans believed that militias, stocked with unpaid, ordinary civilians (which is to say armed), could repel invasions, deal with insurrections, and rise to the threat of tyranny.

The Federalists' position in this debate, however, is also testament to just how widespread individual ownership of guns was among the populace. They contended that concerns over protections from government were overblown because there were *so many guns in private hands* that it was unimaginable that any tyrannical army could ever be more powerful than the general public. Noah Webster, writing as "A Citizen of America," reasoned that "the supreme power in America cannot enforce unjust laws by the sword; because the whole body of the people are armed, and constitute a force superior to any band of regular troops that can be, on any pretense, raised in the United States."[14]

During the debate over the Bill of Rights, Samuel Adams proposed that the Constitution should "never [be] construed to authorize Congress to infringe the just liberty of the press, or the rights of conscience; or to prevent the people of the United States, who are peaceable citizens, from keeping their own arms; or to raise standing armies . . ."[15] Richard Henry Lee, Sam Adams, and Patrick Henry littered their constitutional arguments with explicit mentions of individuals keeping arms.

In Federalist 46, Madison also defended the Constitution by offering the opinion that a standing army was acceptable because the size of the armed civilian population creates a balance of power that guards against abuses. "Besides the advantage of being armed, *which the Americans possess over the people of almost every other nation*," Madison wrote, "the existence of subordinate governments, to which the people are attached and by which the militia officers are appointed, forms a barrier against the enterprises of ambition, more insurmountable than any which a simple government of any form can admit of. Notwithstanding the military establishments of the several kingdoms of Europe, which are carried as far as the public resources will bear, the governments are afraid to trust the people with arms."

The Constitution was ratified on June 21, 1788, by nine of the original thirteen colonies. However, five states—Virginia, New York, North Carolina, Rhode Island, and New Hampshire—demanded the Bill of Rights be adopted by Congress. Within that text of these demands, every one of them asked that the right to bear arms be afforded special mention. New Hampshire's language was the most compact: "Congress shall never disarm *any Citizen* unless such as are or have been in Actual Rebellion."[16] (Emphasis added.)

Robert Whitehill, a delegate from Pennsylvania, proposed a number of amendments to the Constitution that many historians believe were used by James Madison as a guide for his own text. One of them was a right to bear arms. "That the people have a right to bear arms for the defense of themselves and their own state, or the United States, or for the purpose of killing game; and no law shall be passed for disarming the people or any of them, unless for crimes committed, or real danger of public injury from individuals . . ." After numerous drafts, James Madison simplified the language and distilled it to its essential parts, throwing in a comma, as we'll see, that would be seized upon many years later.

The Bill of Rights was ratified on December 15, 1791.

There are modern Americans who find the very notion of the individual right in the Second Amendment violent, ugly, and antiquated—particularly the idea that it empowers individuals to rise up against domestic tyranny. It is true that the founding generation didn't intend to bestow Americans with a license to rebel. Rather, they believed in the right to rebel against a government that undermines the rights of the people and thus the nation itself. Whether it required repelling hostile Indians, the French, the Dutch, or ultimately the British, for the founding generation self-defense was the principal manifestation of their rights, universal and inalienable. Now guns would take on a different role. The onetime colonists were in charge of their own destinies. They turned their gaze from Europe to the vast lands of the West over the next one hundred years. They waged war against the indigenous populations of those lands and, soon enough, each other. In the meantime, they constructed a system of unimaginable wealth. They did most of it with the help of guns.

PART II

★

DISCOVERY

Daniel Boone Escorting Settlers through the Cumberland Gap

8

★

GO WEST

"A good gun, a good horse and a good wife."

—Daniel Boone

Daniel Boone
by Alonzo
Chappel, 1862

O n May 14, 1804, the Corps of Discovery, the unit of the United States Army that would form the nucleus of the Lewis and Clark Expedition, gathered in Camp Dubois, near the confluence of the Missouri and Mississippi Rivers, to kick off their historic journey. As the final provisions were being loaded onto the keelboat and two pirogues that would sail north up the Mississippi and then into the largely unknown continent, one of the men went from boat to boat testing out the swivel guns that had been mounted on each of the vessels.

One of the guns the men tested that day was likely a small-bore cannon, while the other two were blunderbusses. The blunderbuss was a short smoothbore gun, typically with a flared muzzle that looked something like a bell-bottom. Some historians believe the gun's name originated from the Dutch words meaning thunder and pipe. Whatever the case, the brawny weapon could be loaded with up to seven musket balls, scrap or iron, and stones.[1] Its lock could withstand moisture more effectively than the average musket's, making it popular with the British Navy and other seafaring types. In some ways it was like the shotguns of the future: devastating at close range. To mount such guns on swivels allowed for a wide arc of movement, making it perilous for anyone who might be thinking about ambushing the boats.

These guns would, as far as we know, be loaded only twice in anticipation of violence. More often than not, they were used to impress the locals—or, more specifically, to impress *and* deter locals from any thought of attacking—or for saluting crowds, which was why they were fired at around four p.m. the day the men left on their journey. The guns were shot again to greet the boats in St. Louis two and a half years later, on September 23, 1806. Between those two dates, Captain Meriwether Lewis and Second Lieutenant William Clark traversed more than 8,000 miles of largely unexplored terrain, losing only one of their men due to a ruptured appendix.

Lewis and Clark departed the East Coast right before the dawn of the first industrial age, an era that saw great leaps forward in gun technology. At the time Lewis was first procuring his muskets for the western expedition, most of the soldiers and hunters in North America might be able to fire their guns twice in a minute. By the end of the century, men would be able to shoot hundreds of times in that span without ever having to manually reload. They would be able to do this with smokeless powder, self-contained cartridges, and telescopic sights. In a number of ways, Lewis and Clark's journey portended the technological possibilities of the coming century.

With the Louisiana Purchase in 1803, the United States had attained approximately 828,000 square miles of territory from France, stretching from the Mississippi River in the east to the Rocky Mountains in the west and from the Gulf of Mexico in the south to the Canadian border in the north. At the eminently affordable price of three cents per acre, President Thomas Jefferson had doubled the size of the republic. Fifteen states would, fully or in part, be carved out of the land procured in this one deal. In the same year, Jefferson commissioned the Corps of Discovery to follow the Missouri River west, past the Continental Divide, to the Columbia River, by which the men could journey to the Pacific Ocean.

The entire Lewis and Clark trip cost the United States government approximately $40,000 (around $8 million today). Yet it helped to forever cement the nation as the dominant power of North America, setting the stage for a century of explorers, trappers, traders, hunters, adventurers, prospectors, homesteaders, ranchers, soldiers, entrepreneurs, missionaries, and masses of Americans spurring a rapid settlement of this vast land. The peopling of the West gave birth to a new culture, disrupted the cultures of the American Indian, and ultimately created the most dynamic economy in the world. Guns would be a vital tool in this project, not only as a means of self-defense and war, but for hunting, trading, and exploration.

Even before the purchase, Americans had long been ignoring the Spanish and French claims and pushing westward. One of these men, the backwoodsman Daniel Boone, famously proclaimed that all he needed was a "a good gun, a good horse and a good wife."[2] It seems unlikely that Boone, born in a log cabin near what is now Reading, Pennsylvania, in 1734 to Quaker parents who had emigrated from England, was exaggerating. Boone's only real classroom, like many others of his time and place, had been the wilderness. His skills at traversing and surviving on the frontier became legendary, and his amazing tales were firmly tethered to his long rifle, a weapon he had mastered as a hunter in his early teens. "D Boon cilled a bar" read a carving on a nearby beech tree in Washington County, Tennessee, until at least 1917.[3]

Boone's specialized frontier skills served him in the French and Indian War, when he was a wagoner for Edward Braddock during the general's disastrous expedition to Fort Duquesne, barely escaping with his life. Boone also fought in the American Revolution, defending settlements in the proxy war against Indians who were allied with Britain. Boone would really make his name after the war, crossing the Appalachians via the Cumberland Gap, carving out the two-hundred-mile-long path known as "Wilderness Road"—and others—forever opening up the West. Boone led men on months-long hunts into what is now Kentucky. John Filson's widely read 1784 book, *The Discovery, Settlement and Present State of Kentucke*, features an appendix detailing Boone's exploits called the "The Adventures of Col. Daniel Boon," and it made the first Kentuckian famous around the world.

The Boone story became equal parts Western ethos and mythos, forever defining the prototypical American woodsman. For the next two centuries, the famous frontiersman would be portrayed in illustrations, movies, and TV shows wearing his buckskin leggings and shirts of animal skins. His possessions included a large hunting knife, an Indian hatchet, a coonskin cap (which Boone rarely wore in reality), but most importantly his powder horn, a pouch with lead balls, and his Kentucky rifle. One of the allegedly surviving Boone rifles was used against the Shawnee Indian warriors at the Revolutionary War Battle at Blue Licks on August 19, 1782. As the story goes, Boone was trapped and wounded and pulled off the escape with sixty other American men. A family member, it is said, later found the rifle, which Boone had discarded in his hasty retreat. Although the gun has gone through a number of modifications since its recovery, this .45-caliber Kentucky rifle with "Daniel Boone—1775" carved in the barrel and fifteen notches carved into the stock is still the type of firearm a backwoodsman would have used in the late eighteenth century.

The frontier that Boone traversed was one of violence and turmoil. During the French and Indian War, Native American raiding parties allied with French interests had begun marauding English settlements. More than 2,000 Americans from New Jersey to Carolina were killed by Indians during the war. Pontiac's Rebellion of 1763 saw more tribes from the Great Lakes joining together and attacking British interests and killing hundreds more colonists. By this time the gun had also proliferated among the Indian tribes and become a necessity for their own survival. As we've seen, this increased the deadliness of conflicts—among themselves and with the white man—as well as competition over hunting grounds.

The frontier was a rough place that attracted unsavory characters, adventurers, and those fleeing population centers. Most of them were armed. One traveler named Elias Fordham noted in the 1760s that "there are a number of dissipated and desperate characters, from all parts of the world, assembled in these Western States; and these, of course, are overbearing and insolent. It is nearly impossible for a man to be so circumspect, as to avoid giving offence to these irritable spirits . . ."[4] As we will soon see, those on the frontier could only intermittently rely on the law, so guns and knives became increasingly indispensable. And guns would soon be more accurate, reliable, formidable, and cheaper.

More vital even than protection from Indians, the new guns were used to procure food. The significance of hunting is prevalent throughout the diaries of Lewis and Clark. A simple search for the word "meat" in the expedition diaries brings back 783 results—and this doesn't take into account all the specific instances of animals. As Lewis pointed out, "we eat an emensity of meat; it requires 4 deer, an Elk and a deer, or one buffaloe, to supply us plentifully 24 hours. [M]eat now forms our food prinsipally . . ." He wasn't kidding. The men likely ate around nine pounds of meat daily when it was available. This sounds like an astronomical quantity to our modern ears, but meat was often what the explorers ate exclusively.

Though the Lewis and Clark Expedition hunted deer, rabbit, squirrel, wild turkey, elk, beaver, and other animals they were acquainted with on the East Coast, soon they were running across animals they'd never seen before. The expedition tried and failed to kill something called a "Prairie Wolf." It was the first time Americans had noted seeing a coyote. They tried to catch "praire dogs"—in the process naming the animal forever. In the summer of 1804, the expedition ran across a herd in the Great Plains that became a staple of nutrition from then on. None of the participants in the American expedition had hunted buffalo before, but they quickly became fans, eating everything from the rump to the tongue. In due time the buffalo became so abundant that the explorers ate the tongues and left the rest to the wolves.

The explorers also hunted (and on occasion defended themselves from) grizzly bears. The bear, which was used to feed the men but also for their expeditionary needs, proved exceptionally difficult to bring down with the weapons the men had in hand. The musket's stopping power from fifty yards was not enough to kill the beast. Considering the musket's low accuracy at long range, they had to get close and shoot the grizzly in the head. This was a dangerous proposition.

Of the two famous explorers, Lewis was more proficient in the use of guns. Decked out in moccasins and a fringed deerskin jacket, Lewis would have been recognizable to Boone or any of the first western explorers. Everywhere Lewis went, he carried a notebook, meat jerky, a large knife, his flintlock pistol, a half-pike (what was called an "espontoon"), and his rifle. A fine marksman, Lewis used the pike as a walking sick but also as a rest for his rifle to allow him a steady shot. Lewis had been a member of the Virginia state militia and then the imposing force of 13,000 militiamen who marched with George Washington to suppress the Whiskey Rebellion of 1791 to 1794, later joining the army proper and achieving the rank of captain. By 1801 he had become President Thomas Jefferson's private secretary, leading to his role as leader of the expedition.

In preparation for this trip, Lewis had traveled to Lancaster, Pennsylvania, home of the Kentucky rifle, in 1803 to oversee "the fabrication of the arms with which he chose that his men should be provided." Over the years, the prestige of the Lancaster gunmakers had not abated. There were around sixty of them working in and around the city by the early 1800s.[5] Lewis purchased flintlock rifles in Pennsylvania, but that was not the end of the shopping spree. That month he wrote Jefferson that "my Rifles, Tomahawks & Knives are preparing at Harper's Ferry, and are already in a state of forwardness that leaves me little doubt of their being in readiness in due time."

The Harpers Ferry armory, along with another one in Springfield, Massachusetts, would become the leading centers of gun technology for the next century. They played an integral part in spurring America's first industrial revolution and experiments in interchangeable parts and precision machinery, soon to be imitated in other trades and by other nations.

One of the prevailing concerns of Americans between the Revolutionary War and War of 1812 was being pulled into another conflict with the British or the French. In 1798, after France began menacing American ships on the East Coast, Congress voted to create a 15,000-man standing army and gave the president authority to double that number in an emergency. Less famously, the legislation also authorized the creation and production of 30,000 muskets to stock the new American armory.[6]

During the Revolution the fledging nation had created a dispersed system of small armories to maintain and store munitions. As the internal threat began to subside at the end of the war, a centralized armory was deemed necessary by Washington. The general approved a site in

Springfield, Massachusetts, due to its geographical proximity to the roads and waterways that allowed them to both import resources and export the final product more efficiently. By 1793, Springfield was home to an array of weapons left over from the war. Within a few decades, however, it was developed into the production center for new American arms, a role it would fulfill until well into the Vietnam War.[7]

The southern states, unsurprisingly, wanted an armory as well. So a year later Congress passed a bill calling on the executive branch to build another center for "erecting and repairing of Arsenals and Magazines" in Harpers Ferry, Virginia. In the long run, the second armory would be less successful than Springfield due to deficiency in waterpower, location, and mismanagement. It saw a major renovation before the Civil War, and became infamous when the abolitionist John Brown raided the armory before attempting to initiate an armed slave revolt in 1859.

The Model 1803 rifle, a short-barreled gun with a .54-caliber flint-lock, had been adopted by Jefferson's secretary of war, Henry Dearborn, to become the Army's official rifle. It was the first gun manufactured in an American armory, the Harpers Ferry Armory producing more than 4,000 of these rifles between 1803 and 1807.[8] The Lewis and Clark Expedition

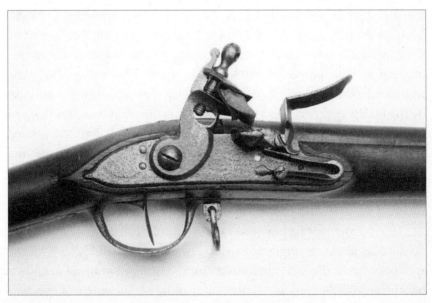

Springfield 1795 flintlock musket

may have carried a prototype of the gun, but we don't know for sure. None of the weapons the Corps of Discovery carried is known to exist today. All of the weapons, as well as musket balls, powder horns, axes, and other arms, were sold at a public auction in St. Louis shortly after the expedition's end in September 1806 for a grand total of $408.62.

In truth, the duo's cache would soon be antiquated anyway—except for one gun, that is, which was a portent of the precision, speed, firepower, and innovation that would come to dominate gunmaking over the next fifty years. The expedition might have brought only one, but it proved to have an outsized importance, not only impressing locals but discouraging them from resorting to violence against the expedition. On the first page of the first entry of Lewis's journals, in fact, the explorer introduces us to the "air gun."⁹

Lewis and Clark mention the air rifle thirty-nine times in the journals of the trip.¹⁰ In nearly every instance that the expedition encountered a new Native American encampment, the duo decked themselves in their most impressive, colorful, and polished military uniforms. They then marched into the native camp with flags, attached bayonets, and donned swords as if they were meeting a dignitary in a European court. The Indians were given an array of beads, medallions, and colorful clothing as gifts. Then Lewis showed off the air gun, a weapon that even tribes that had experienced guns before had never encountered. According to Lewis, many of the tribes considered it "something from the gods."

A private on the expedition named Joseph Whitehouse described one meeting in the summer of 1803, at a Yankton Sioux village along the Missouri River: "Captain Lewis took his Air Gun and shot her off, and by the Interpreter, told them that there was medicine in her, and that she could do very great execution." Indeed it could. The Indians stood amazed as Lewis kept firing the gun without reloading. When he was done "the Indians ran hastily to see the holes that the Balls had made which was discharged from it. [A]t finding the Balls had entered the Tree, they shouted a loud at the sight and the Execution that suprized them exceedingly."

Lewis wrote that he purchased the air gun in 1804, although he gave no specifics about its origin or model. The explorer would keep both the specifics of how the lock functioned and the number in his possession a secret from nearly everyone. The idea of using air pressure to fire a lead ball goes back to the 1500s. The earliest surviving example of an air rifle, dating to around 1580, can still be seen in Stockholm's Livrustkammaren (Royal Armory) museum. But it was in 1780 that an Italian inventor in the Austrian province of Tyrol named Bartolomeo Girandoni developed an air-powered rifle that could fire .46-caliber lead balls. He sold the idea to the Austrian army, which used the weapon from 1780 to around 1815. An Austrian government report in 1801 found that Girandoni air guns had been lost in battle, so it's plausible that many were circulating in Europe and one had made its way into the hands of an American gun merchant.[11]

Whatever the case, the gun featured a higher rate of firing capacity than any other weapon in existence at the time. It was a smokeless repeating gun that could hold up to 800 pounds of compressed air. Its tubular magazine held up to twenty-two .46-caliber round balls. It could fire up to forty times before it began losing muzzle velocity.[12] It was one of the first truly successful attempts at a repeating gun. The problem was that it would take around 1,500 strokes of a hand pump to create the pressure needed to fire the weapon. Its specialty parts were nearly impossible to fix.

Most of the guns Lewis and Clark brought with them retained the downsides, glitches, and vagaries that had plagued the machine for over two centuries. But—conceptually speaking, at least—the air gun was a weapon of the late nineteenth century. It gave men a glimpse into the kind of potency that would soon dominate gun technology through the revolver, the repeating rifle, and the automated gun.

For now, with the immediate gains made in workflow, division of labor, and interchangeable parts, American arsenals produced around 10,000 muskets per year in the early 1800s.[13] Many people contributed to make this impressive feat possible. One was the noted inventor Eli Whitney. Born in 1765, the Yale-educated engineer from Massachusetts became most famous for inventing the cotton gin, a device that streamlined the process of extracting fiber from cotton seeds (although some historians dispute Whitney's claim to it). Whitney portrayed himself as a pioneer in the new musket-making process, a man who wrestled with how to produce all the components in the most efficient way. "A good musket is a complicated engine and difficult to make," he wrote, "difficult of execution because the conformation of most of its parts correspond with no regular geometrical figure."[14] For years he would be credited for pioneering the machine-made interchangeable parts. The truth is more complicated. Whitney had obtained his huge government contract to produce weapons before he ever wrote or suggested interchangeability. While the historical consensus acknowledges him as a competent producer of guns, he also likely exaggerated his own role in the early production of firearms.

Whereas Whitney took more credit than he deserved, others would not get enough. If one person can lay claim to have systemized and standardized the manufacture of weapons, it was John H. Hall. Born on January 4, 1781, in Portland, Maine, the day before Richmond, Virginia, was burned by British naval forces led by Benedict Arnold, Hall grew up with a fascination with gadgets. A volunteer in the Portland Light Infantry, Hall worked as a cooper, carpenter, and shipbuilder, attaining a hard-boiled determination that at various times aided and hampered his career.

Hall filed his first patent for a breech-loading gun (a technology that, as we'll see, soon dominated rifle making in the mid-1800s) at the age of thirty, only to find out from William Thornton, the superintendent of the patent office, that the gun had already been conceived of by someone else. Incredibly, that someone else was none other than William Thornton. Skeptical of this astonishing coincidence, Hall traveled to Washington to confront Thornton and take a look at the evidence for himself. Thornton, unsurprisingly, was unable to provide any substantial proof of having designed such a gun. After spending months lodging complaints with government officials, Hall decided to avoid years of bureaucratic entanglements and instead hand Thornton half of all royalties moving forward. Hall's gun became not only the first breech-loading rifle patented in the United States but the first new gun patented, period.[15]

At the time, most military long arms were smoothbore .69-caliber muzzle-loading flintlock muskets. Hall's rifle "could be loaded and fired . . . more than twice as quick as muskets . . . ," wrote the inventor in his patent application. "[I]n addition to this, they may be loaded with great ease, in almost every situation." Hall began advertising his gun in 1812, but sales were slow. It was unfamiliar, difficult to maintain, and carried a hefty price of $35 per gun.[16]

Military leaders were also initially dubious about the functionality of this new technology. Testing was delayed for years due to the War of 1812 and postwar funding issues. Hall continued to push for civilian sales and a military contract, making the case that speedy reloading was the future. "The time necessarily required in the loading of Rifles, has long formed a serious obstacle to their general use. It is even conceived by some," Hall later wrote, "that circumstances outweigh all the advantages to be derived from superior accuracy."

Finally, in 1817, Hall produced one hundred handmade muskets for evaluation by the U.S. Army Ordnance Board. Impressed, the government offered Hall an abandoned sawmill that was perched on the Shenandoah River at the Harpers Ferry armory. Due to the complexity of this new firearm, as well as the requirement that the parts be interchangeable, Hall spent nearly five years developing the tools and machinery necessary for the production of his rifles. Once done, it outperformed every other model in contention, proving exemplary in testing, one firing over 7,000 times without a single malfunction.

In 1819 the Hall-patented rifle was adopted by the U.S. Army, although the gun was not widely used for years. The Hall carbine, produced in varying calibers, would become the principal long arm of the United States cavalry for the next two decades.[17] It would be used in the Black Hawk War in Illinois and Michigan Territory and the Seminole War on the Florida frontier. A unit of this type required a carbine as its primary arm, as it was easier to use when fighting on horseback, and Simeon North took on the task of developing a breech-loading carbine based on Hall's rifle design. The result was a .58-caliber smoothbore percussion arm that featured a sliding rod bayonet.

During his two decades at Harpers Ferry, Hall developed a number of innovative tools, including drop hammers, stock-making machines, balanced pulleys, drilling machines, and special machines for straight cutting—a forerunner of today's milling machine, a critical tool used in the fabrication of precision metal firearm components.[18] His precision-manufactured machine-made rifle parts were completely interchangeable, thus eliminating the need for skilled craftsmen to repair broken arms. As with other important techniques, many innovators took part in creating the "American system of manufacture," but Hall was certainly one of the method's pioneers and played an important role in its realization.

By most accounts, Hall was not an easy man to do business with: he had constant run-ins with his superiors. At one point there were congressional calls for more study of the utility and costs of Hall's rifles, the aim of which was to show that they were a waste of funding. In the end, the episode only enhanced Hall's reputation when the resulting report found that the guns "have never been made so exactly similar to each other by any other process. [The] machines we have examined effect this with a certainty and precision we should not have believed, till we witnessed their operation."[19] After this, Hall's ideas spread rapidly to the Springfield Armory and other private armories. He devised gauging systems to maintain accuracy, and when Simeon North began building Hall rifles in Connecticut, these gauging systems ensured that parts were interchangeable between rifles from the two armories. Others in the private sector would soon take those ideas and, without bureaucratic meddling, perfect them and change the way the guns operated.

9

★

PEACEMAKER

"God created men, Sam Colt made them equal."

—Unknown

Steel engraving of
Samuel Colt with
a Colt 1851 Navy
Revolver

Like the Kentucky rifle before it, the revolver was a distinctly American invention. Unlike the Kentucky rifle, however, the revolver's development, production, and popularity can be largely attributed to one man, Samuel Colt. The Connecticut native was not merely a mechanical virtuoso but a promotional and manufacturing mastermind who would become a template of the nineteenth-century American industrialist, epitomizing the exuberance and possibilities of the populist era of mid-1800s American life. A self-made man, Colt was prodigious, a tireless self-promoter, innovator, autodidact, and mythmaker. His nose for opportunity made him one of the wealthiest men of his day. With this success came a leap forward in firearm technology. Colt invented the first hands-on, workable, mass-produced revolving firearm. And with his gun, he became one of the first industrialists to take advantage of mass marketing, celebrity endorsements, and corporate mythology to sell his product—a success that laid the groundwork for twentieth-century businessmen, including Henry Ford. In practical terms, his gun was more deadly, more accessible, more dynamic, and more useful than any that had ever been designed. It would play a part in carving out the West, revolutionizing war, and transforming the role of the gun in modern American life.

The Colts had been in Connecticut since the 1630s. Samuel's maternal grandfather, John Cakhvell, had established the bank in Hartford, while his grandfather, Peter, a Yale graduate, played a role in the Revolutionary War, working on the Committee of Inspection in New Haven. Peter's experience during the war, obtaining provisions not only for American troops but for the French army, helped secure contracts and trade deals in major power centers of the budding nation. Peter's post-revolutionary life was the epitome of what the historian Barbara Tucker referred to as the "ethos of the new capitalism" of the early nineteenth century. It was a time that saw the egalitarian ideas about commerce that had dominated the previous century start to dissipate. Men like Peter, John, and Sam engaged in speculation, making and losing fortunes, often living restless and nomadic lives. Ambition became a Colt family trait.

Sam Colt was born in the Lord's Hill neighborhood in Hartford—named not after the Almighty but rather one of the city's original settlers, Captain Richard Lord—on July 19, 1814, only a few days before the Americans and British would fight one of the bloodiest battles of the War of 1812 at Niagara Falls. For all its success, the Colt family was also seized by tumultuous affairs, mental instability, and tragedy. Sam's mother passed away when the future gunmaker was just six years of age. One of Sam's sisters passed away in childhood. Another, Margaret, died from tuberculosis at the age of nineteen. His older brother John tried his hand at various vocations, struggling at all of them, before he was convicted of the infamous murder of a printer named Samuel Adams. The pair had argued over a bill of less than $20 before John murdered Adams with a hatchet and then allegedly stuffed the body into a packing case, which he put on a packet bound for New Orleans. John committed suicide before his execution. Colt's sister Sarah Ann also committed suicide.[1] His other brother, Christopher, who had married into a family of slave traders, lived a wayward life that included intermittently demanding money from his far more successful brother. He struggled with depression and resentment until his death.

Sam was different. Growing up, Colt worked first in his father's dye and bleaching factory in Ware, Massachusetts, before apprenticing on a farm. From all accounts, the young Colt's upbringing was almost entirely free of parental supervision. In this environment, the curious boy could focus on his interests, one of them being guns. In a fawning and sometimes unreliable account, his first biographer tells the story of a search party finding the missing young boy "sitting under a tree in the field, with a pistol taken entirely to pieces, the different parts carefully arranged around him, and which he was beginning to reconstruct. He soon, to his great delight, accomplished the feat."[2] Whether this tale serves as a self-serving myth or not, it's clear that Colt had a propensity for mechanical things and great resourcefulness. He was already experimenting with new technology in the field in his mid-teens. After a home-brewed pyrotechnic display during a Fourth of July celebration at his local high school, Colt, anticipating expulsion, took leave of formal education forever.

Prompted by his father, Sam began toying with the idea of becoming a sailor—traveling as far as England and India on a merchant ship. Although the physical hardship of seafaring life quickly cured him of any ideas of taking to the sea as a way to make a living, it's during this time that he first carved a crude model for a wooden revolver.[3] Returning to the United States, Colt borrowed money from family and took his mock-up to Anson Chase, a Hartford gunsmith, asking him to transform this skeletal idea into a gun. He did. But when the young inventor tested out his new machine in the back firing range, it blew up in his hand at the first squeeze of the trigger.

Colt offered various accounts of how and why he had hatched the idea for a chambered rotating weapon. He maintained, for example, that as a sailor he had been transfixed by the motions of the rotating mechanism of the ship's capstan. Other times, Colt claimed that the idea had been birthed after reading harrowing tales of Native American attacks on settlers heading to the West. Why was the settler able to shoot only once, he wondered, before being seized upon by Indians who could unleash a torrent of arrows at the same time? In 1851, Colt told the Institution of Civil Engineers in England that after years of reflection and repeated trials, "without having seen, or being aware, at that period (1829), of any arm more effective than a double-barrelled gun having ever having been constructed, and it was only during a visit to Europe, in the year 1835, that he discovered he was not the first person who had conceived the idea of repeating fire-arms with a rotating chambered-breech."[4]

Although he certainly reimagined and perfected the idea, it seems unlikely that Colt was unaware that multi chambered guns already existed. Pepperbox pistols, for instance, were widely owned and used by the time Colt was carving out his wooden model. Named after the pepper grinders they resembled, these handguns had to be manually rotated, and were notoriously unreliable and difficult to aim because of the front-loaded weight of the multiple barrels. The year Colt was born, the Boston inventor Elisha Collier (along with a colleague, Artemus Wheeler) had taken out a patent on a five-shot flintlock model pistol. Collier's development was to invent a gun that was "self-priming": in other words, when the hammer of the weapon was cocked, a compartment automatically released a measured amount of gunpowder into the pan for another charge. Had the United States Army showed more interest in the idea, perhaps Collier would have come to worldwide renown. As it was, the British ordered 10,000 pieces, using them in colonial India. Many problems plagued Collier's early models, however, namely the cost of creating revolving mechanisms and the excruciatingly long time it took to load the gun. This impediment made the most attractive aspect of the gun, the potential to fire it quickly in succession, almost moot. Colt and other inventors would soon fix this problem.

But before Colt undertook his most prosperous projects, he cultivated a knack for showmanship—a crucial aspect of his future success—by joining the popular Lyceum circuit. During the mid-1800s, there was an explosion of traveling shows that entertained teeming crowds on fairgrounds across the United States and Canada. Founded in 1826 by Massachusetts native Josiah Holbrook, the events featured self-styled experts, performers, salesmen, puppeteers, hucksters, polemicists, noted authors, and dozens of other varied speakers and showmen, who sold their wares, exhibited their exotic animals, performed tricks, and gave lectures on issues of the day. In towns across North America, the curious local communities, starved for access to technology, gadgetry, and entertainment, also treated these events as a form of social and intellectual enrichment. In a time before television, radio, or phonographs, this touring event was, for many people, the only way to hear, see, or learn about new ideas.

Colt, we imagine, viewed the endeavor more as a capitalistic opportunity than a societal good. Growing a beard to hide his young age, Colt toured the country as "the celebrated Dr. Coult of New York, London and Calcutta," posing as a medicine man with a portable chemical laboratory. Sam amused crowds by administering nitrous oxide, or laughing gas. Such an act might seem cheap to our modern sensibilities, but it was not only rather harmless but exciting for men and women living in the new and sometimes isolated communities in America.

Colt's forays into the heart of America also helped him comprehend not only the size and scope of the new land but, as he later noted, the overwhelming need of those Americans to feel safe. The excursion was also useful in that Colt learned the art of public speaking, made numerous contacts around the country, and earned enough money to provide seed capital for his planned firearm business. Colt's instincts as a salesman rarely failed him. And throughout his time artificially inducing laughter, he continued to ponder the serious problem of a revolving gun, as letters and blueprints of prototypes from this era show.

Finally, at the age of twenty-one, Colt decided to patent the idea he'd been toying with for years: the repeating revolver. He did so, first in England and France, where it was cheaper and simpler, and then in the United States in October 1835. It made a singular technical advance—what may seem obvious to us now: rather than relying on five barrels, Colt's invention had a rotating cylinder that came into alignment with a single barrel. When cocked for firing, the next chamber revolved automatically to bring the next shot into line with the barrel. The gun included a locking pawl to keep the cylinder in line with the barrel, and a percussion cap (more on this later) that made it more reliable than any other gun available. His design was a more practical adaption of Collier's earlier ideas and created a far more balanced and lighter weapon with a sleeker design. In a short time this modernization would become the dominant mechanism of American weapons. The patent protected Colt's fundamental ideas until 1857, by which time he was enormously wealthy and world-famous.[5]

First the young inventor had to figure out how to mass-produce his idea. Although Colt relied on members of his family for funding, he lived in an era when high debt and speculative investment were no longer frowned upon—and Colt wasn't shy about participating. In 1836 he began wooing wealthy investors, demonstrating his inventions in an upscale showroom in Manhattan, raising around $300,000—a huge amount at the time—to launch his project, the Patent Arms Manufacturing Company. Based in Paterson, New Jersey, then one of the fastest-growing industrial hubs in the nation, Colt paid himself $1,000 a year, half of the profits semiannually, and another $6,000 for the patent. His ambitious plan was reflected in the ostentatious design of his new factory, a four-story armory featuring an ornate exterior. "On the spire which surmounted the bell tower was a vane very elaborately made in the design of a finished gun and in front of the mill was a fence, each picket being a wooden gun," one contemporary commenter would note.[6]

The first gun manufactured in the new Paterson factory was not a pistol but a Model Ring Lever rifle. However, it was followed shortly by the first Colt Paterson, a five-shot revolver that came in a .28-caliber, although soon Colt also began producing a .36-caliber model. The original gun featured no loading lever, so a shooter had to partially disassemble the revolver every time he wanted to reload it. But by 1839 a reloading lever and a capping window were incorporated, allowing the shooter to reload without disassembly, making it the most user-friendly gun ever invented.

Colt understood that on some level he would be reliant on military contracts for his success. More than merely a fiscal benefit, such deals were a way to spread the word. "Government patronage . . . is an advertisement if nothing else," he later noted. So when, in 1837, the Senate passed a resolution calling for testing of new weapons at West Point, Colt submitted a number of his guns for review. They would not be favorably evaluated. The most common complaint about the Colt guns was the prohibitive cost, but there were bad reviews about the quality as well. Certainly the first Patersons were unreliable when compared to later models. Among other problems, the Army noted that they were difficult to figure out because the new percussion arms were not yet being widely used. The Ordnance Department observed that the Colt was "entirely unsuited to the general purpose of the service."[7]

Not for the last time in his career, Colt would feel that he had been treated unfairly by the government. He wrote a five-page letter meticulously contesting every single criticism offered by the board. Colt rapped the board for reaching the "wrong conclusion," not only offering his own pushback but offering testimonials from military men, including one sergeant who wrote Colt that "in passing through Indian country, I have always felt safer with one of your rifles."[8]

Colt's fortunes would change soon enough. In the winter of 1838, the United States was plowing tens of millions of dollars into the Seminole Indian War, which left more than a thousand Americans and an unknown number of Indians dead. It was an ugly affair that saw the sides lobbing brutal attacks back and forth, the Indians effectively deploying guerrilla warfare and Americans ratcheting up the violence in retaliation. At the height of the conflict, Samuel traveled to Florida to demonstrate his guns to the troops. With an array of his rifles and new revolvers, the inventor made his way to Fort Jupiter and put on a demonstration that went far better than his previous endeavors. Major General Thomas Jesup had only praise for the revolving weapons, writing a superior that "I am still confident that they are the only things that will finish the infernal war." Now there was a new technology to deal with a new kind of war. The guns were put to immediate and effective use—so much so that Colt complained in 1851, in rather blunt terms, that by the effectiveness of his gun in "exterminating the Indians, and bringing the war rapidly to an end, the market for the arms was destroyed."[9]

Although never shy about lobbying government officials in Washington, Colt spent the rest of his life directly approaching military men, building relationships that helped him not only sell his gun but build its legend. Sam had a particular knack for sensing the flows of history, and during his relatively short life he befriended many of the great names of the era, including General Zachary Taylor, Franklin Pierce, and Colonel Jefferson Davis (a man who would become secretary of war before being elected president of the Confederacy), among many others. Colt kept a book in which he saved all the letters of prominent men who used his gun, including revolutionary nationalists like the Italian Giuseppe Garibaldi and the Hungarian Lajos Kossuth, King Victor Emmanuel II of Italy, and the king of Siam, among many others.

By the time the Civil War was brewing, in fact, Colt could count on enough military supporters to print a twenty-page brochure extolling the virtues and tangible upside of using the Colt. He attached a long list of "distinguished officers" who could provide testimonials. It included military heroes, future presidents, and senators known to most Americans.[10]

In Florida, however, fate seemed to be undermining Colt's big breakthrough. On his voyage home, Sam's ship capsized in St. Augustine Bay and he lost the Army check for $6,000. The Army refused to send another one, and his investors were dubious about his tale, leaving him in trouble.

At this point his first foray into production was unsuccessful not only because the demand for the new gun was slow but because of Colt's habit of profligate spending. Shareholders in the Patent Arms Manufacturing Company had begun to push him out. By 1842 his company had shuttered and auctioned off its most valuable machinery to many rivals and one of his largest stockholders. It was during these years that Colt began to invest his time and energy in other innovations.

One of his most notable creations was a galvanic cell and underwater explosive—a "submarine" mine—meant to protect American ports from renewed threats of British naval assaults. The British had already made well-known advances in mining harbors, and Americans were concerned that they would again threaten the Eastern Seaboard over a dispute regarding the waters off New England.[11] While researching his project at New York University, Colt collaborated with other inventors and scientists, including a teacher named Samuel Morse, who later invented a single-wire telegraph system. The two worked together on a partially implemented scheme to install a telegraph line from lower Manhattan to New Jersey. Morse used the battery from one of Colt's mines to transmit a telegraph message from Manhattan to Governors Island when his own battery was too weak to send the signal. (The line was never completed.)

Colt sought to privately fund his experiment, informing the Navy that he would conduct a demonstration of his underwater mine "without any expense to the government or exposure of any secrets connected with my plans of defense." On July 4, 1842, in front of a large crowd of politicians and military officials, Colt blew up a sixty-ton schooner in spectacular fashion on the Potomac River using underwater cables and his mine. Many of the onlookers found the show to be horrifying and unnecessary. Some in the Washington establishment thought Colt a swindler. John Quincy Adams, then a congressman, who had sponsored a popular resolution undermining the Colt project, called it an "un-Christian contraption." Colt, always the showman, proposed blowing up another ship, this time in New York Harbor. His request was denied (although he did blow up three other ships on his own dime).

The project went nowhere. Colt, perhaps due to his Paterson experience, was disinclined to share his engineering secrets with the government. Government engineers, conversely, were apprehensive about Colt's invention for a number of reasons. "As experiments, these, as many others have been, were very beautiful and striking, but in the practical application of this apparatus to proposed war, we have no confidence," an assessment in the *Army and Navy Chronicle, and Scientific Repository* noted.[12] Although, of course, Colt never stopped soliciting its business, he nursed a lifelong enmity toward government officials in Washington—"the great city of humbug," he called it. It wasn't until the Civil War that the United States began to seriously explore underwater mines.

It would, however, be American providence that rescued Colt from obscurity. Jacksonian democracy had manifested in expansion, which didn't merely render territorial growth but a spectacular opening of individual economic opportunity. Colt's revolver would play a big part in the settlement of the West, the annexation of Texas, the fighting in the Mexican-American War, the conflict with Native Americans, and the Gold Rush; all these events made him extraordinarily rich. This expansion of American life was inconvenienced by the presence of Native Americans, who weren't especially inclined to hand over vast tracts of their ancestral lands to the newcomers. This is not a place for a moral debate on the methods of populating the West but rather a place to note that the revolver would, as Colt had imagined, afford the settler an undisputed upper hand.

"They are the only weapon which enabled the experienced frontiersman to defeat the *mounted* Indian in his own peculiar mode of warfare," Daniel Boorstin writes. "[Y]our six-shooter is the arm which has rendered

the name of Texas Ranger a check and terror to the bands of our frontier Indians."[13] In 1844, two dozen Rangers led by Captain Jack Hays
fought off a far larger force of Comanche, a battle that was to be firmly
entrenched in Western lore and Colt's sales pitch. "They were two hundred in number, and fought well and bravely, but our revolvers, fatal as
they were astounding, put them speedily to flight," wrote Ranger Nelson
Lee, who pointed out that a man with a Colt Paterson had five times the
firepower of a man with a single-shot gun.[14] This and other smaller victories in Texas helped bolster Colt's reputation in military circles.

When James Polk became president in 1845, he would facilitate Texas
joining the Union as the twenty-eighth state and conclude negotiations
with Great Britain for the annexation of the Oregon Territory south of the
49th parallel. The Mexican government, however, was less pliable about
the disputed lands between the Nueces River and the Rio Grande. So Polk
sent General Zachary Taylor to secure Texas. With war on the horizon,
Captain Samuel Walker of the Texas Rangers, a Western celebrity who had
become familiar with Colt and his gun doing battle with Indians, came
east looking for recruits and weaponry. Walker convinced the U.S. government to place an order of 1,000 guns, launching Colt's revolver for good.

Walker would, however, ask the gunmaker to make a number of upgrades to the existing Paterson model. Could Colt, for example, create a
gun that could hold six bullets instead of five? Could he create one that
was even easier to reload than the Paterson? Could he build a gun that was
effective enough to kill the enemy with one shot? He could. The 1847
"Walker," christened after its sponsor, was a weighty four pounds and shot
a .44-caliber black powder cap and ball through a barrel that was nine
inches long. It was the most powerful handgun produced anywhere in the
world until the .357 Magnum came along in 1935.

With a $25,000 government order in hand, Sam persuaded Eli
Whitney Jr., the Connecticut contractor for Army muskets, to help him
produce the revolvers. They were ready six months later. (A pair of guns
for Walker, who had hounded Colt for delivery, arrived in Mexico only
four days before he was killed in action.) With money coming from the
Mexican-American War, Colt could build his own factory and finally put
his entire production assembly-line production into motion at Colt's Patent Fire-Arms Manufacturing Company.

After what must have felt like a lifetime of false starts, the determined Colt was finally poised to become one of America's preeminent industrialists. After more than a decade of refining his ideas, Colt was making an elegant weapon that distinguished him from his competitors. Certainly there would no longer be a shortage of wars or interest in his revolver. Nor, where his business was concerned, would he ever have to answer to others. "I am working on my own hook and have sole control and management of my business and intend to keep it as long as I live without being subject to the whims of a pack of dam fools and knaves styling themselves a board of directors . . . ," he wrote after securing loans for his new factory.

For his factory, the Patent Fire Arms Manufacturing Company, Colt picked his hometown of Hartford. The armory, according to his first biographer, Henry Barnard, was located "within a short walk of the State House, railroads, and the business centre of Hartford. It has at hand all the water required for its manifold necessities; it is close to a navigable stream, so that coal, iron, and all the stock, can be landed at its doors, and its products, whenever it may be desirable, can be shopped by the Connecticut [River]."[15] Although he would find a dedicated workforce, most of the technical work was to be done by machines, while hand-fitting was needed to finish the product.

A number of great engineers of the age, like Elisha K. Root, Christopher Spencer, George Fairfield, and Charles Billings, would work for Colt during the early years. By pushing manufacturing efficiency, Colt could ensure that his gun's price was consistently competitive—from $50 for the first Paterson to $20 for his later models. As the chairman of the Committee of Patents noted, Colt was intent to "perfect his armory by the increase and subdivision of machinery, so that he will be able to furnish . . . a perfect arm at a price which will defy . . . spurious imitators."[16] And there would be many.

Hartford, already one of America's leading industrial hubs in the 1850s, was transformed by the Patent Fire-Arms Manufacturing Company. It became not only the city's leading employer but a place that featured a utopian village that served as the social, religious, political, and labor center of his workers. Colt was intent on building a modern industrial community to surround what was to become the largest gun armory in the world.

By 1856, Colt's company could produce 150 weapons per day using interchangeable parts, efficient production lines, and specially designed precision machinery decades before Henry Ford. Visiting the plant in the late 1860s, Mark Twain, then living in Hartford, described it as "a dense wilderness of strange iron machines . . . a tangled forest of rods, bars, pulleys, wheels and all the imaginable and unimaginable forms of mechanism . . . It must have required more brains to invent all these things than would serve to stock fifty Senates like ours."[17]

A Russian-style bright blue onion-shaped dome emblazoned with golden stars topped by a statue of a horse could be seen on the grounds. The factory was augmented by a self-contained town, something comparable in many ways to a modern "campus" built by a Silicon Valley company. H.S. Pomeroy and Elihu Root designed a complex for about 145 families that sprawled out around the brickwork of the factory. Ignoring more nativist trends of the time, Colt hired from all ethnicities and backgrounds and nations, but especially from Germany. The gunmaker even sent one of his top assistants, Fredrick Kunkle, to Prussia to find artisans, building Swiss chalets and a beer hall to lure them. The neighborhood was referred to as "little Potsdam."

Colt had somewhat of a schizophrenic relationship with his workers. He appreciated that manufacturing was monotonous, grinding work, and took pains to ensure his workforce was taken care of. He made certain there was proper lighting—big windows and skylights—and good ventilation. He installed a modern heating system and a state-of-the-art fire prevention system. He paid his workers (including the unskilled sector) well-above-average wages. Colt introduced a ten-hour day and mandated one-hour lunch breaks.

More than that, those who lived in Coltsville had all the conveniences that a modern American middle-class nineteenth-century family could desire. There was a church and a concert and dance hall that could seat up to 1,000 people. The Colt Brass Band became celebrated throughout the region, playing at many of the huge parties organized for the community by Colt, especially the fireworks extravaganzas on the Fourth of July. Colt encouraged workers to engage in social leisure activities. A Colt employee could go to the newspaper reading room and peruse periodicals from around the country, or sign up for one of the many social clubs or educational programs (which created a number of future notable gun engineers). Or he could go on a picnic with his family near orchards, greenhouses, sculpted lawns, man-made lakes, and botanical gardens in the huge Coltsville park—all of it stocked with an array of exotic animals and flowers.

It is here, in June 1856, that Colt married Elizabeth Hart Jarvis, the daughter of a prominent Hartford Episcopal clergyman. A steamboat and a fleet of liveried carriages chauffeured the entire wedding party to the nearby town of Middletown for the ceremony. The couple honeymooned in Europe, attending the coronation of Czar Alexander II. When they came back to the complex they moved into the Armsmear, an opulent Italian villa replete with towers and domes and surrounded by large reflecting pools decorated with fountains. It stood high on the hill overlooking the grounds running down to the factory. "Beyond all this luxury," wrote Martha J. Lamb in *The Homes of America* in 1879, were the "towers of the great armory . . . also the outline of the pretty Swiss village, which grew out of the planting of willows by the dike . . ."[18] The jewel of the estate is still there, a pink-hued mansion.

It must be remembered that the beautiful environs and societal advantages of Coltsville had been thought up, shaped, and constructed to serve only one purpose: Colt's guns. In the heart of the complex was the H-shaped brickwork armory. Colt was a demanding boss who laid out tough quotas and gave no quarter to those who failed to meet his demands. A sign hung prominently on the factory floor stated: EVERY MAN EMPLOYED IN OR ABOUT MY ARMOURY WHETHER BY PIECEWIRK OR BY DAYS WIRK IS EXPECTED TO WIRK TEN HOURS DURING THE RUNNING OF THE ENGINE, & NO ONE WHO DOSE NOT CHEARFULLY CONCENT TO DU THIS NEED EXPECT TO BE EMPLOYED BY ME. This was no idle threat.[19]

Colt was not above social engineering and did not shy away from politics. He was no free market fan, using lawyers and government contacts to undermine competition. He could, by today's standard, rightly be accused of embracing crony capitalism and rent seeking. A Democrat, Colt pushed his workforce to vote accordingly, going so far as firing apostate Republicans. The elite of Hartford were Republican, and one paper accused Colt of "a most oppressive and tyrannical exertion of the money-power, against which it is the duty of every freeman solemnly and earnestly to protest."[20] When the Civil War broke out in 1861, Colt began making weapons exclusively for the Union. During the first year of the war he was producing 27,000 guns. By 1863, the company's output dramatically increased to 137,000 and to nearly 300,000 the following year, making it the largest private armory in the United States.[21] By the time the war ended, more than 1,000 people worked at the company's factory.

It was the Single Action Army—more famously known as the "Peacemaker"—that would embody Colt's legacy. An elegant gun with a practical and streamlined design, it took on near-mythological status not merely because of its easy use but because of the legendary men who claimed to use it. The first model gun had a solid frame that weighed around three pounds, a .45-caliber with a 7.5-inch barrel, blued steel, and an oil-stained walnut grip. It was soon one of the most popular guns ever made. Mechanically, it still incorporated much of the technology that Colt propagated during his lifetime. In 1872, the Army's Ordnance Board would adopt the new gun for service and ordered 40,000 between 1873 and 1891, when it was the standard military service revolver.

It was likely Colt himself who came up with the moniker "Peacemaker" for his gun. It was not merely a stab at irony or an adman's clever copy. Colt often, and vigorously, argued that this gun could empower the average American. The weapon could be brandished for self-protection, of course, but it was a firearm so formidable that war was to become too

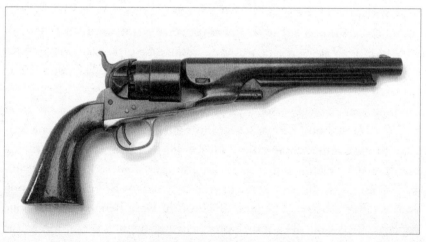

Colt Model 1860 Army Percussion Revolver

destructive to be worth engaging in. The gun was, to him, an imperative tool in fulfilling the American dream on both a personal and providential scale. "Living in a country of most extensive frontier, still inhabited by hordes of aborigines, and knowing of the insulated position of the enterprising pioneer, and his dependence, sometimes alone, on his personal liability to protect himself and his family, [I] had often meditated upon the inefficiency of the ordinary double-barreled gun and pistol," he said in an 1851 speech to British engineers.[22] A Colt made one man six. "Place a revolver in the hands of a dwarf . . . and he is equal to a giant," noted the industrialist.[23]

Even more significantly, the average man could order one through the mail for the somewhat affordable price of $17 and have a light but powerful weapon within weeks.[24] And selling his guns to civilians—every civilian, if possible—would be Colt's principal goal. In a nation coming to terms with growing wealth, power, and size, Colt capitalized on Americans' romanticized view of the rugged frontier to sell pistols. With all the complex mechanical modernizations of the gun, Colt's success was also wrapped up in aesthetics and storytelling. Embedded in his guns were the adventurous attitudes of the era, the Western impulse and individualistic notions, patriotic fervor, and American life. These were weapons, elegant and utilitarian, but they told stories. Literally.

Colt built a relationship with the artist George Catlin, who had made numerous forays into the West during the 1830s to paint scenes of Indian life. Catlin not only produced many of the first artistic renditions of the Wild West, but he was a meticulous collector of artifacts and stories. In 1838 he began delivering a series of popular lectures about his time on the Plains, publishing two volumes of engravings detailing his adventures. His sense of drama caught the eye of Colt, who commissioned the artist to produce a series of oil paintings portraying his adventures in the West—with one stipulation. All ten, known as the Firearm Series, depicted Colt revolvers and rifles either being used in hunting or impressing the local Native Americans. Colt used these images as a promotion to bolster the legend of Colt as the premier weapon of the frontier.

Colt had also heard about Waterman Ormsby, a man who later created intricate and beautiful etchings used by the United States on its banknotes to repel counterfeiters. His invention, the "grammagraph," could roll-die

Colt Second Model Dragoon Revolver

artistic engravings onto steel, allowing Colt to create numerous cylinder scenes that made his guns more visually attractive and further evoked visions of the West. These beautiful images—created by the noted engraver Gustave Young, who worked for the Colt company from the 1850s to the 1870s and would be poached by Smith & Wesson from the 1870s to the 1890s—depicted scenes of legendary battles and individual bravery. They were featured on the Dragoon Revolver, the Model 1849 Pocket Revolver, the Navy 1851 Revolver, and other models.

Colt did what he could to personalize guns in several other ways, often playing on his own celebrity by sending his gun "compliments of the inventor" and running ads signed by Colt in which he spoke directly to his consumers. He would, if possible, whet the consumer's appetite by offering slightly modified models with customizable elements at additional cost. Colt included quirky add-ons that created a more unique experience, like a gun case that looked like a reference book with a serious-sounding title like *Colt on the Constitution: Higher Law & Irrepressible Conflict*. One was inscribed *Law for Self Defense*.

Colt embraced a modern notion that is recognizable to anyone who owns an iPhone, constantly churning out "new and improved" models—an expression he may have coined—to keep people clamoring for the latest iteration of his products.

The gunmaker also created a national network of sales reps, running ads in newspapers that featured professional artwork. Colt had been aware of the emergence of the "penny newspapers" since his days on the Lyceum circuit. These papers were mass-produced in the United States from the 1830s by means of steam-powered printing. Colt would be one of the first to use them as marketing tools, publishing ads that explained his guns, defended them from critics, offered specifics on technical changes to the design, and, perhaps for the first time, running celebrity endorsements to vouch for his product. In 1857, Colt paid the popular *United States Magazine* to publish a fawning twenty-nine-page illustrated feature in its March issue titled "Repeating Fire-Arms: A Day at the Armory of Colt's Patent Fire-Arms Manufacturing Company." Colt pursued and compensated publications for this sort of coverage his entire career.

Colt may also have been the first internationally renowned American businessman. His European patents put him in the position to sell new weapons to perpetually warring continental powers, making him a global player in the arms market. Back in 1851, Colt had operated an exhibit at the United States section of the Great Exhibition of the Works of Industry of All Nations, an international demonstration of the newest and most brilliant innovations from around the world that took place in Hyde Park, London. It was the first of many world's fairs that would become popular in the nineteenth and twentieth centuries. Colt's exhibit was a big draw and was enthusiastically received by the British. At his stand he displayed more than four hundred of his revolvers, including the prototypes of the Colt Navy and also his older Walker and Dragoon models. All were hung on the wall in the shape of a giant shield. The guns were also open to public handling. One contemporary writer noted that "the gentlemen, who handle the revolvers, are principally officers, but we noticed one individual pressing to be instructed in the use and mystery of the instrument, who evidently intended to carry out the theory into practice at the very earliest opportunity."[25] Colt used this time to glad-hand officials, sending ornate revolvers to a number of British royalty and military commanders.

Colt also became the first American manufacturer to open a plant in England, a building that would take its place in the smoke-spewing pillars that dotted the landscape of the industrial age. In 1853 an impressed Charles Dickens toured the state-of-the-art factory, with "the complete manufacture of a pistol, from dirty pieces of timber and rough bars of steel, till it is fit for the gunsmith's case."[26] The great writer's escort gave him one of the finished revolvers for testing, and "after a little practice," Dickens wrote, "I find that a mere novice may, with one hand, discharge the six rounds as rapidly as the eye can wink."[27]

In the end, however, the British factory would be the only one built outside the United States. And it did not last long. According to early twentieth-century historian Charles Winthrop Sawyer, American workers, unaccustomed to British society and soggy English weather, were constantly abandoning the factory and heading home. The Englishmen who replaced them, both the engineers and workers, did not carry out Colt's wishes and, at least according to the boss, did not share the American work ethic.

At home Colt experienced no such difficulties. Legendary names of the Old West and American life were to become users of "Judge Colt and His Jury of Six," from self-declared lawman Judge Roy Bean, who once fined a dead man $40 for carrying a concealed weapon, to Bat Masterson and Wyatt Earp. (Not long ago, a Colt revolver that may—or may not—have been used by the lawman and gambler at the OK Corral sold for $225,000.) As did Teddy Roosevelt and George Patton, who special-ordered an ivory-stocked, custom-engraved single-action in 1916 that he would carry through World War II. The Colt .45 Peacemaker became so popular, it would have second- and third-generation models.

Alas, for all of his success, Colt's life was marred by personal tragedy. Of his four children, three died in childbirth or soon thereafter. (His son Caldwell drowned on a sailing trip off the coast of Florida in 1894.) Colt died on January 10, 1862, at the age of forty-seven. "The funeral of Samuel Colt, America's first great munitions maker, was spectacular—certainly the most spectacular ever seen in Hartford, Connecticut," the historian Ellsworth Grant wrote.[28] All of Colt's 1,500 workmen filed in pairs past the metallic casket in the parlor of Armsmear. He had died one of the richest men in America, leaving his estate to his wife and Elisha Root, who would run the company. In 1901 the Colt family sold the company to a group of investors.

By the end of his life, Colt had likely personally overseen the production of some 400,000 guns, changing both the technology of firearm production and the role of the gun designer. Before him, gunmaking was largely a regional affair. Colt was known worldwide. Most importantly, he had modernized and industrialized the gun. Sam Colt's success had ignited an era of modernization. From now on things moved quickly.

10

★

BULLET

"A fanatic is one who sticks to his guns whether they're loaded or not."
—Franklin P. Jones

Claude Étienne Minié

Just as Colt's patent on the revolver was ending in 1857, two Massachusetts gunmakers, Horace Smith and Daniel B. Wesson, were busy prepping the release of their own new gun, one that would complement many of Colt's advances but add one revolutionary change. The Model 1, as it would become known, was the first revolver to use self-contained metallic cartridges—or what people typically (but, as we'll see, incorrectly) refer to as "bullets" today. The cartridge, one advance that had first escaped Colt's grasp, was a technology that helped alleviate many of the complications that had plagued gun owners since the inception of firearms. It allowed the shooter not only to repeatedly fire, but to reload rapidly. Its creation hybridized an array of innovations from some of the most renowned names in gunmaking history.

For hundreds of years, shooters had been loading round lead balls of various sizes into their muskets and rifles. The round shape made loading marginally quicker, and the lead, which was both common and had a low melting point for malleability, made weight standardization of ammunition possible. Yet, as we've seen, guns were often problematic to load, with shooters having to jam a ball of equal diameter into the barrel of the rifle by force. Sometimes this task was so challenging that shooters had to use mallets to pound the ammunition down the barrel. And because the spiral grooves of the new rifles would quickly foul from powder residue, it was necessary for the shooter to constantly clean out his firearm; otherwise it might be rendered useless.

There is evidence that paper cylinders containing ball and black powder were already being used in the mid-1500s.[1] By 1777 the British had patented paper cartridges. At first these containers merely held the components together, allowing the soldier to rip open the paper package with his teeth and pour the contents down the barrel before ramming it all in the bore. Later those paper cartridges were coated in wax or tallow to protect the powder and ball from the elements and pushed down the barrel whole—and, as an added bonus, the wax melted from the heat and helped soldiers clean out the resulting fouling.

Before a proper cartridge could be conceived, there had to be something more advanced than the flintlock ignition system to propel the ball. As we've noted, shooting a gun was contingent on the sparks generated by the flint igniting a pan of priming powder, so any kind of wet weather or dampening could mean misfiring, which happened quite often. Inventors had experimented with alternative explosives as a way to overcome the moisture problem, but most of the combustible materials turned out to be even more unstable than black powder, though only slightly easier to keep dry. That is, until Joshua Shaw, an English painter who would later migrate to the United States, claimed to have fortuitously run across an idea in 1814 when accidentally detonating powder in a sealed steel can.

Shaw's concept resulted in the construction of a small metal cylinder that held inside highly sensitive explosives, like mercury fulminate. This explosive concoction, known to chemists for some time, was made of ethanol and mercury in nitric acid. What made it useful for the gunmaker was its shock sensitivity. By the 1820s these "percussion caps" would be placed over a hollow metal "nipple" at the back of the barrel of a revolver or other gun. When the trigger was pulled the hammer hit the cap and ignited the primer inside, and the flame from the powder traveled through the hollow nipple and ignited the main charge. Percussion caps could be made in an array of sizes for an array of guns. Early caps could sometimes be hazardous, because they exploded and sent copper shards at the shooter. When properly designed, the cap expanded so that it fell off the nipple when the hammer was re-cocked, allowing faster reloading. Soon, most rifle and revolver makers adopted the system and old flintlock guns were rapidly being converted.

At around the same time percussion systems were being implemented, inventors were figuring out ways to enhance the trajectory of the bullet that was being propelled. A British captain named John Norton had invented the first known cylindrical bullet in 1832. The design was based on the blowpipe darts he had witnessed locals using when he was stationed in South India. The conical shape, far more aerodynamic as it pierced the air, had a hollow base. William Greener, the renowned London gunmaker, took Norton's idea even further, designing a cylindrical bullet with a wooden plug in that hollow base to increase muzzle velocity. But it was a French ordnance officer named Claude-Étienne Minié who would be credited with making one of the bullet's most deadly advances in 1849, when he created a cylindrical lead bullet that featured a conical point and a hollow base with an iron plug.

What made the Minié bullet so advantageous was that it was smaller than the diameter of a rifle barrel, so even if the barrel had been fouled—which it often was—one could load the bullet into the muzzle around seven times faster than a typical musket ball. One of the keys to firing a rifle properly was figuring out how to tightly seal the bullet within the barrel so that gases wouldn't escape. Typically this was performed by placing the lead ball in a greased cloth. The Minié bullet alleviated all of this inconvenience. Rather than escaping, gases from the combustion of the gunpowder expanded the lead as it filled the hollow base of the Minié bullet, triggering the soft metal to flare and grip the barrel's grooves, spinning it to fly farther and more accurately. In effect, the bullet went in one size and came out another.

In early trials, the Minié bullet performed exceptionally well. Testers hit more than 50 percent of their targets from 400 yards using the new bullet—as opposed to 4.5 percent when using a traditional ball.[2] Suddenly an average soldier with only rudimentary training could fire a gun with passable accuracy from many hundreds of yards away. This feat would have sounded fantastical only a few decades earlier. James H. Burton, a disciple of John H. Hall's who worked at the armory at Harpers Ferry, soon eliminated the need for the iron plug, making it even easier and cheaper to manufacture the bullet. Jefferson Davis, United States secretary of war, adopted the Minié ball—an ounce in weight and half an inch across—for the United States Army in 1855. The Union would end up making nearly 3,000 of them every hour at the height of the Civil War, producing tens of millions of Minié balls by the end of the conflict.[3]

It is believed that the Minié bullet accounted for more than 90 percent of the casualties during the Civil War.[4] The new bullet was devastating to the soldiers who encountered it. Rather than pass through the body, as a round ball might, the Minié flattened on impact, shattering and splintering bones, bouncing around inside the body, and doing massive damage. When the bullet did drive through the body, the soft lead left the victim with an exit wound that was far larger than the entrance wound. As we'll see, Civil War surgeons were initially unable to deal with these horrific wounds and shattered bones.

Exploding caps and conical bullets were not enough. While it was certainly true that a revolver could transform one man into five or six, once the handgun was emptied of bullets, there would still be the cumbersome process of loading each separate chamber with powder and ball *and* percussion cap on the nipple of each chamber. There had to be a better way. And that better way was to integrate the cap, powder, and projectile into a single metal package.

In 1848 an inventor named Walter Hunt, best remembered for his tendency to sell off his ideas and not his prolifically creative mind—he invented the safety pin, lockstitch sewing machines, and the ice plow, among many other useful and enduring items[5]—created the "Rocket Ball." Similar to the Minié ball, the Rocket Ball could be shot even farther by packing the cavity of the bullet with powder. For ignition, Hunt soon added a cap with a small hole and then combined lead, powder, and ignition into one container. There was no casing, as the entire cartridge was fired out the muzzle. It was an invention that allowed the lever-action rifle and other quick-firing guns to exist.

The next year Hunt patented a rifle that could shoot this new cartridge, called the "Volitional Repeater" rifle. This rifle featured a tubular magazine with a lever mechanism located in front of the trigger, which, when pulled, would push one Rocket Ball from the cylinder to the next position and cock the hidden hammer. Although the design was mechanically unreliable, the contours of the lever-action rifle, soon to dominate the market, were set.[6] But Hunt, as was his wont, sold the design, this time to shirtmaker George Arrowsmith, for a mere $400. And by 1854 his ideas had slowly worked their way to the desks of two engineers named Smith and Wesson at the Robbins & Lawrence plant in Vermont.

B y the age of sixteen, Horace Smith, born to a Massachusetts carpenter and his wife in 1808, was working in the Springfield Armory as an apprentice. He spent the next twenty years there. Like Sam Colt and many other great American gunmakers, Smith had little formal education. Smith worked his way through a number of gun firms, focusing on creating more efficient techniques to make weapons and quicker loading times for the weapons he did produce.

Daniel Wesson was seventeen years younger than his business partner, and the age difference would be mirrored in a relationship that was more like a father and his son than equals, as the older Smith was the dominant force in their business partnership. Wesson was used to this arrangement, as he had made his bones apprenticing with his brother, a well-known Massachusetts rifle maker. Those years gave Wesson an education not only in gunmaking but in the ins and outs of patent law, increasingly important in the nineteenth century.

In 1850, the year California would become a state, the two came together in Windsor, Vermont, at the Robbins & Lawrence factory, a groundbreaking center of the precision tool industry started by Richard Smith Lawrence and Samuel E. Robbins. The firm, which played a vital role in the first American industrial revolution, was home to an array of machines and procedures that were aimed at increasing productivity. By the time Smith and Wesson showed up, the factory was pumping out 10,000 military muskets every year at the amazingly low cost of $12 per item. The system developed by the American armories in Springfield and Harpers Ferry—and private factories like Robbins & Lawrence—was the most advanced in the world. Although the "American system" of manufacturing was not solely about weaponry, it wasn't until gunmakers like Sam Colt and others appeared at London's Crystal Palace exhibition to show off their wares that British engineers, and soon the other Europeans, began to embrace it. The British Army, in fact, was impressed enough not only to place a large order for rifles but to purchase Robbins & Lawrence–designed metalworking machines. The Crown's armory at Enfield would rely on them for years.[7]

Despite going on to create many manufacturing innovations and producing tens of thousands of rifles for the Union during the Civil War, the names Robbins and Lawrence would be largely forgotten by history. The lesson, of course, is that if you want your name to endure through the annals of time, make sure to put it on the gun. On this front, Smith and Wesson, who had a small but important role in gun design history, would not be outdone. In 1855 they took their first crack at independence with the Smith & Wesson Company. The venture limped along until investors took a controlling interest and renamed the firm Volcanic Repeating Arms Company. One of these stockholders, a man whose name was soon to be stamped on millions of guns in the coming century and a half, was Oliver Winchester.

Unlike many of the enduring names in the industry, Winchester was neither a mechanical innovator nor an engineer nor particularly interested in guns at all. Rather, he was an astute businessman with an aptitude for spotting pioneering ideas, profitable patents, and talented men. Born in 1810 into a family that had inhabited the city of Boston for five generations, Winchester's hardscrabble upbringing sparked an unrelenting drive for success.[8] The man was born at the right time for men of his disposition. By the mid-1830s, Winchester had helmed a string of successful business ventures, including running a highly profitable men's furnishing store in Baltimore. Winchester soon decided to move to New Haven, where he partnered with a New York industrialist named John M. Davies to become one of the leading shirt manufacturers in America—and, according to him at least, the entire world. In Connecticut, Winchester found himself amid a vibrant wave of early industry. Factories dotted the town, producing everything from clothes to clocks to horse-drawn carriages and, of course, guns. With a nose for profit, Winchester soon expanded his manufacturing efforts.

Much like Colt, Oliver imbued his workforce with the idealism of the industrial age, entwining capitalism with strains of religiosity and patriotism. "Let us, therefore, be united in our efforts and purpose," he once lectured his workers, "to devote to our several departments, all the energies we possess, nor be satisfied while a stitch is misplaced, a stain unremoved, or a wrinkle unsmoothed; remembering that a shirt, however coarse, is an emblem of purity, and as the work of our hands, which are directed by our minds, it is the index to our character, to which the close observer of human natures requires no more certain key."[9]

Well, perhaps one. Money was to be made, and lots of it. Considering the time and place, it's unsurprising that the enterprising Winchester would have been drawn to gun manufacturing. And at the age of forty-five, Winchester, although he knew practically nothing about the business or mechanics of firearms, pulled together a group of investors and took a controlling interest in the newly minted Volcanic Repeating Arms Company from Smith and Wesson. The technology was not there yet, however, and although Winchester plowed his own money into the flailing enterprise, the attempt went belly-up in 1857.

Smith and Wesson would give it another shot, founding the Smith & Wesson Revolver Company in Springfield less than a year later. It was

Smith & Wesson Model 1

here that they brought together many of the ideas they had worked on in the past decade to create the Model 1, the first revolver to use rimfire cartridges instead of powder, ball, and percussion cap. The cartridges would make the gun easier to reload than any ever made. The Model 1 held seven .22-caliber bullets that were mounted in copper casings that held the black powder. At the bottom was a hollow rim with priming compound. When the firing pin on the hammer hit the rim of the cartridge, the priming powder was ignited, leaving a spent copper casing in the chamber but propelling a cylindrical bullet. The gun fired a small .22-caliber, so it did not interest the Army. But the revolver soon became a favorite of many gun slingers and went through various iterations: the Model 2 featured a .32-caliber, and then the Model 3, a .44-caliber.

The duo also began experimenting with innovations like an unsnapping latch that allowed both barrel and cylinder to drop down and forward, or a spring-loaded ejection that would clear the used casings from the cylinder. All of which made reloading faster. While the Colt company outdid them with a gate-opening mechanism that pushed out all the spent casing when opened, soon every new revolver was utilizing the cartridge technology, and guns would never be the same.

In 1862, Winchester wrote stockholders to say that, since "the commencement of our organization, till the past three months, five years and a half, there has not been a month in which our expenditures have not exceeded our receipts."[10] Winchester's company teetered on the edge of insolvency for years. That is, until a Winchester employee named Benjamin Tyler Henry, an engineer who had worked with Smith and Wesson, cobbled together a number of existing patents and invented his namesake, the Henry repeating rifle. The obsessive Henry would have a complicated relationship with Winchester, who was impatient with the slow development of his firearm. Henry was, in modern parlance, a workaholic. Perhaps even this is an understatement. Henry lived virtually full-time in the factory and worked inhumane hours for years trying to perfect his ideas.

In 1860, Henry finally fixed all the problems with his gun and gave Winchester what he wanted: a lever-action (behind the trigger) breech-loading rifle with a sixteen-shot tubular magazine that could repeatedly fire. During one Navy test, the Henry fired 187 shots in 340 seconds. In time, the Ordnance Board placed an order of nearly 1,700 of his rifles for use, mostly by the cavalry.

Although it proved less sturdy in wartime conditions than some of the repeaters that would come, many soldiers purchased the gun on their own dime. Rather than rely solely on federal purchases, Winchester took a page from Colt's book and made inroads with local editors, politicians, and military men, showering them with praise and gifts—and always selling the new technology. Winchester's company, the New Haven Arms Company, reorganized after the Civil War and was renamed the Winchester Repeating Arms Company, with Oliver taking the helm as president, treasurer, chairman of the board, and about everything other than janitor. Winchester became a tireless advocate for his weapon.

The year after the Civil War ended, Winchester introduced the Model 1866, nicknamed the Yellow Boy due to the bronze-brass alloy receiver.[11] (Western Indians often referred to it as "many shots" and "spirit gun.") The rifle found a big market on the western frontier. Initially, the brass-framed rifles and carbines used .44 rimfire caliber. The "rimfire" cartridge is shot when the firing pin strikes the rim cartridge base, igniting the primer. Most of the future models featured "center-fire" ammunition, which is still today's predominant style of cartridge, in which the pin strikes the center of the cartridge base.

As the revolver made the flintlock pistol obsolete, the repeating rifle—and the cartridge that fueled it—would add a new, dangerous dimension to firearm technology.

11

★

THOSE NEWFANGLED GIMCRACKERS

"That damn Yankee rifle you load on Sunday and shoot all week."
—Confederate soldier

Frank Leslie's scenes and portraits of the Civil War, 1894

On August 17, 1863, the inventor Christopher Spencer arrived at the White House to meet President Abraham Lincoln. The president would later refer to the inventor as "a quiet little Yankee who sold himself in relentless slavery to his idea for six weary years before it was perfect."[1] Lincoln, who typically had great curiosity about the functioning of firearms, was, unsurprisingly, distracted that day. The Battle of Gettysburg, the bloodiest of the Civil War, may have thwarted Robert E. Lee's hopes of invading the North only a month earlier, but the end of the war was nowhere in sight. Draft riots had recently broken out in New York

City and elsewhere in protest of the newly passed conscription law. Busy, the president asked the inventor to return the next day so he could shoot the carbine himself.

It was the next morning that the two men, surrounded by cabinet members and a smattering of other government officials, strolled to a spot not too far from where the Lincoln Monument now stands to have a shooting contest. "The target was a board about six inches wide and three feet high, with a black spot on each end, about forty yards away," Spencer recalled. "The rifle contained seven cartridges. Mr. Lincoln's first shot was about five inches low, but the next shot hit the bull's-eye and the other five were close around it."

" 'Now,' said Mr. Lincoln," according to Spencer, " 'we will see the inventor try it.' The board was reversed and I fired at the other bull's-eye, beating the president a little. 'Well,' said he, 'you are younger than I am and have a better eye and a steadier nerve.' "[2]

The Spencer rifle that Lincoln shot that day would take less nerve to use than any of the muzzle-loaded rifles being fired by the soldiers battling in the Civil War. To comprehend its importance of functionality, consider that of the more than 27,000 rifles recovered from the field of Gettysburg, the *Annual of Scientific Discovery* reported that a staggering 24,000 were still loaded. Of the guns found loaded, 12,000 had been loaded more than once without firing, and half of them had been loaded between three and ten times without shooting—one of them twenty-three times.[3] There are numerous theories to explain these statistics, but the most convincing is that men felt safer with loaded weapons. The *Annual*, for instance, points out that muskets "in the hands of cowardly or incompetent men are actually useless." (One wonders if the author of that judgment had ever seen action himself.) It is almost certainly true that there were many soldiers who had tried to create the impression of fighting, while looking for avenues of retreat. Some, with fouled rifles, had been unable to shoot. Other men, no doubt, preferred holding on to a loaded gun to protect themselves to being caught by a bullet in the midst of reloading.

Repeating rifles helped eliminate many of these fears. Even in the best of conditions, the bravest and most competent soldier could fire a single-shot, muzzle-loaded gun—the dominant gun of the Civil War—perhaps three times in a minute. The Spencer rifle offered the soldier a spring-loaded, seven-shot tubular magazine in the butt of the gun. Its lever action ejected a spent cartridge and chambered a fresh one. A man could empty his entire magazine well within a minute and already be reloaded. The "Blakeslee cartridge box," invented by Union infantryman Erastus Blakeslee, was a leather-covered box that could fit up to ten tubular Spencer magazines with seven cartridges each. It made reloading even faster.[4]

When a captain named Alexander Dyer tested the Spencer rifle for the Union Army, he fired it more than eighty times without a single misfire. He then let the gun sit outside in the rain and sun. No problem. It still fired perfectly. Dyer buried the weapon in the sand, yet there was still no clogging of the mechanisms—even without cleaning. When he put the breech mechanism in salt water for twenty-four hours, it still worked. "I regard it," he would write, "as one of the very best breech-loading arms I have seen."[5] Most people who used it agreed. General Ulysses S. Grant called Spencer's rifles "the best breech-loading arms available."[6]

Like many of the other major gunmakers of the eighteenth century, the Connecticut-born Spencer was entirely self-taught. At eleven, Spencer moved in with his grandfather, Josiah Hollister, a veteran of the Revolutionary War, who taught him basic woodworking and blacksmithing skills. At thirteen, Spencer recalled, he picked up a hacksaw and cut his grandfather's Revolutionary War musket to carbine size to see if he could make it fire faster for hunting purposes. By the time the boy was fifteen, he was said to have fabricated a homemade steam engine.[7] With these skills Spencer found himself serving an apprenticeship as a mechanic. He was soon working for numerous plants in America's first industrial age, including, for a short time, the revolver-fabricating machinery of the Colt factory in Hartford. By the time Spencer met with the president, he had created a horseless steam-powered buggy, allegedly driving it back and forth from his Manchester home to Hartford until local officials asked him to stop, since the noise was disconcerting to locals.

It was Spencer's association with one of New England's wealthiest families, the Cheneys, that became one of the most beneficial relationships in his professional life. It was in their factory that he invented a revolutionary automatic silk-winding machine and there that he became obsessed with inventing a breech-loading gun.[8] Although such a mechanism might seem obvious to us, making breech-loading work was one of the big innovations in gunmaking in this era. The idea had been fermenting for hundreds of years. For example, in London Tower sits a sixteenth-century breech-loading carbine that belonged to King Henry VIII. The gun used by the oft-married English monarch was probably for hunting and showing off. Others, in France and elsewhere, had experimented with guns with a chamber that could be exposed so as to load loose powder and a ball. Because gas leaked, and black powder created residue, intricate parts necessary for such a gun corroded easily. Only the advent of the cartridge made it possible.

By 1859, Spencer had completed his design for a lever-action breech-loading rifle. The Cheneys helped back the production of proto-types of the weapon.[9] When the Civil War broke out, they underwrote Spencer's operations, securing meetings with Lincoln administration officials. According to lore, the president was so impressed by the functionality of the Spencer rifle the day they went shooting that he was moved to personally intervene and override the wishes of the close-minded ordnance general James Wolfe Ripley, ensuring that the gun would become a mainstay of the Union Army and change the complexion of the conflict. The truth is a bit more complicated.

Before the Civil War, Ripley had been the commanding officer of the national armory at Springfield, Massachusetts, which had for the most part been governed by civilians powerless to make demands of the government employees. "Every day at eleven in the morning and four in the afternoon, the men would drop work, go down to the spring back of the shops and regale themselves with rum, cider brandy and impromptu wrestling matches," Civil War historian Robert V. Bruce noted.[10] Ripley would bring much-needed order to Springfield, and with it improved morale and production. In 1854, Ripley hosted a delegation of British engineers and military men curious to adopt production methods with interchangeable parts for the Royal Small Arms Factory in Enfield, north of London, as a means of improving production of the 1853 pattern Enfield rifle-musket for the Crimean War. Within ten years the British would be sending the Confederacy 400,000 Enfield rifles.

As a brigadier general in the Union Army during the Civil War, the rigid Ripley instituted a number of successful upgrades, including modernizing supply chains and artillery ordnance. Yet it was Ripley's dislike of breech-loading repeating rifles—he called one a "newfangled gimcracker"[11]—for which he is best remembered. Ripley had been witness to numerous allegedly game-changing inventions that failed during his time in Springfield, which made him skeptical of new loading techniques. Specifically, he believed breech-loading guns promoted waste and undermined discipline in battle. Anticipating a short war, Ripley was also concerned about funding and training troops to use brand-new weapons. He did not believe in complicating supply lines and was a proponent of reconfiguring guns already in the armories.

None of these concerns were particularly outlandish. Yet many historians blame Ripley for prolonging the Civil War and costing lives with his archaic views on weaponry. Robert V. Bruce argued in his book *Lincoln and the Tools of War* that if the Union had adopted the repeating rifle earlier, "Gettysburg would certainly have ended the war. More likely, Chancellorsville or even Fredericksburg would have done it, and history would record no Gettysburg Address, no President Grant, perhaps no carpetbag reconstruction or Solid South."[12]

Counterhistories are interesting to debate but ultimately unsatisfying. For one thing, even if the North had been able to ramp up production to arm enough troops to make a difference, it is unlikely the military would have been able to instill the principles and training necessary to make it the dominant gun of the war. Moreover, Ripley was not very different from military leaders throughout history who have valued tradition, doctrine, and logistical concerns over new technology. The truth is that in this age of invention there were plenty of false starts and terrible creations that wasted the military's time.

So whether Ripley had stayed or not, the move to breech-loading and repeating rifles, though slow, had already begun. Lincoln, after all, had already directed Ripley to order Spencer repeating rifles: more than 10,000 of them would be delivered to the Army and Navy by 1862,[13] and another 37,000 had already been ordered.[14] The gun, in fact, had already seen action by the time the two men were shooting at their targets. Union troops commanded by Colonel John T. Wilder's "Lightning Brigade" had defeated the notably larger Confederate forces at the Battle of Chickamauga using some of the new repeating guns.[15] One dazed Southern prisoner asked a Union officer, "What kind of *Hell-fire* guns have your men got?"[16] The gun fared well at the Battle of Hoover's Gap as well: the Union drove the Confederates from central Tennessee, which was two months before Lincoln challenged Spencer to a contest of aim. Within a week, regiments of the Michigan Cavalry carried Spencer repeating rifles at the Battle of Gettysburg, as did General George Armstrong Custer's brigade.

In fact, President Lincoln had shot a repeating rifle more than two years before he met Spencer outside the White House. While reviewing Hiram Berdan's green-coated marksmen of the 1st United States Sharp-shooters, a company put together to harass Confederate lines. Lincoln asked to shoot one of the men's rifles. Berdan, a nondescript mechanical engineer from the urban environs of New York City, happened to also be one of the best marksmen in America at the start of the Civil War. As soon as the conflict began, he hatched plans to pull together the North's best shots to aid in the war effort. When the War Department finally took him up on his idea in 1861, Berdan circulated an announcement in papers across the North. "No man would be enlisted who could not put ten bullets in succession within five inches from the center at a dis-tance of six hundred feet from a rest or three hundred feet off hand" read the call for marksmen published in local newspapers.[17] When the would-be sharpshooters showed up in Weehawken and various other loca-tions in the Northeast, they were asked to shoot ten times from 200 yards, as fast as possible, and hit a ten-inch bull's-eye. If a participant missed the shot by more than five inches on average, he was disqualified. There were so many good shooters that the Union ended up creating two regiments, one commanded by Berdan (ten companies) and one by a colonel named Henry A. V. Post (eight companies).

For a number of reasons, including the comfort they felt with their personal weapons, Berdan's marksmen were initially allowed to bring their own rifles. The government promised to reimburse the men $60 for each of these usable weapons (and later reneged). However, the self-arming idea immediately became problematic. Without standardized weapons, the Army had difficultly providing the array of ammunition and parts necessary to keep the regiments stocked and ready to fight. So Berdan decided that what he needed was breechloaders with new hair triggers and sights. Instead the men were equipped with Springfield muzzleloaders.

Berdan's continued aggressive push to arm his men with repeating rifles made him detest the military and the armament office. One gen-eral referred to Berdan as "most unscrupulous" and "totally unfit for a command." The head of the Springfield Armory at the time also thought him "unscrupulous," adding that everything Berdan said should be taken with "a grain of salt."[18] Still, Berdan had Lincoln and popular opinion on his side. As with the Revolutionary War–era Kentuckians, civilians were soon coming out to see the marksmen do their thing. When the regiment toured Washington, crowds came to watch them. It was then, in September 1861, that Lincoln, accompanied by a contingent of cabinet members and family, took a look at the sharpshooters himself. Berdan walked with the president as he reviewed the troops and then invited the party to the rifle pits where men were training. Lincoln reportedly fired three shots "like a veteran marksman," to the cheers of the big crowd.

One of the onlookers, then–assistant secretary of war Thomas Scott, a skeptic of breechloaders, asked Berdan, who until recently had been a civilian, what he knew of war and shooting, challenging him in order to prove the worthiness of the repeating gun. Berdan, no doubt happy to show off his marksmanship, took up the challenge and a target labeled "Jeff Davis" was set up six hundred yards away.

Berdan initially expressed some concern about targeting the head of the Confederacy, but Lincoln reportedly told him, "Oh, Colonel, if you make a good shot it will serve him right."

"Now," Scott instructed him, "you must fire standing, for officers should not dirty their uniforms by getting into rifle pits."

"You are right, Colonel Scott," Berdan allegedly answered. "I always fire from the shoulder."

"What point are you going to fire at?" Scott asked.

"The head," Berdan said as he took aim.

"Fire at the right eye!" Scott shouted desperately.[19]

Apparently, Berdan did. When the target was brought to him, with a bullet hole in Davis's head, Lincoln laughed. And as he climbed into his carriage, he said, "Colonel, come down tomorrow, and I will give you the order for the breechloaders." This story, retold by nineteenth-century historians, paints an exceptionally neat picture of the emergence of the breechloader. At first the regiments were firing Colt five-shot revolving rifles, better than muzzleloaders, on the front. "It was a proud morning for us," one of Berdan's men wrote, "as we marched past camp after camp, and battery after battery, waiting for us to get ahead and for their places in the column." They performed admirably, disrupting enemy lines, taking their shots at officers and artillerymen. Soon many more Union troops were equipped with superior single-shot breech-loading rifles. The simplicity and precision made these guns popular not only with Civil War snipers but, as we'll see, civilians, hunters, and soldiers in the West.

The South recruited their own sharpshooters to push back against the Union snipers. They would often be hampered by inferior guns, although they made great efforts to get their hands on Union arms. "Soon after we reached Yorktown, we discovered the rebels had Sharp Shooters also," wrote one officer, "and I will give them the credit of having as good shots as I ever saw, and some better than I want to see again." The two sides became ensnared in sniper dueling that foreshadowed future wars. But the Spencer—and other guns like it—was a mechanically complex arm whose manufacture was beyond the capability of Southern industry.

Even if they had been able to produce the technological advances of the North, the South simply did not have the capacity to manufacture metallic cartridges used by the repeaters or make the guns themselves. The North wasn't inhibited by a lack of industrialization—although perhaps they lacked some imagination. By the time Ripley was replaced by Lincoln in 1863, Spencer had already set up shop in a Boston piano factory and began delivering weapons. But the rise of the repeating rifle would still be slow going. To put it in perspective, the Union would purchase fewer than 100,000 repeating rifles and make 1.5 million muzzle-loading rifles during the war.[20]

Even when soldiers did get their hands on the new repeaters, the armies that deployed them had not yet developed proper doctrines for their use.[21] The guns' benefits—range and speed—were often negated when commanders utilized troops equipped with the gun as if they were muzzle-loading percussion cap rifles, the prevailing weapons of the Civil War to the very end. Many battles were still being decided using tactics of mass formation and armies lining up at 100 yards, throwing lead volleys at each other.

However, Ripley's contention that rapid-firing rifles were wasteful did not come true. "There is no doubt that the Spencer carbine is the best fire-arm yet put into the hands of the soldier, both for economy of ammunition and maximum effect, physical and moral," Major General James H. Wilson noted.[22] "Our best officers estimate one man armed with it [is] equivalent to three with any other arm. I have never seen anything else like the confidence inspired by it in the regiments or brigades which have it."[23] Or, in somewhat starker terms, a Confederate soldier is said to have remarked that the guns could be "loaded on Sunday and fired all week."[24]

Spencers were used by American cavalry and civilians on the frontier after the Civil War, but wartime production created a surplus that undermined the company's future. By the end of 1868 the Spencer Repeating Rifle Company was no more and Spencer himself signed a deal with the Winchester company, selling them all his future repeating rifle designs and improvements. The War Department eventually fully came around to the new breech-loading rifles. The problem was cost. The war-weary nation had taken on considerable debt and was in no mood for ratcheting up military spending.

With this problem in mind, Erskine Allin, a self-taught gun engineer who had risen through the ranks of the Army to become master armorer at the U.S. Armory at Springfield, hatched an idea. Why not take the thousands of existing muzzleloaders—with their perfectly sound barrels and butts—and convert them to breechloaders? Allin came up with the idea of a "trapdoor" to the receiver. Basically, this entailed cutting off the back end of a Civil War musket and fitting it with a trapdoor that could fit a cartridge. The armory would convert more than 25,000 Springfield Model 1863 rifles with these trapdoor breech systems. The Model 1873, adopted by the United States War Department, became the fifth iteration of Allin's design. These Springfields were no longer shipped to the South to quell a rebellion but rather to the West to conquer a continent.

12

★

FASTEST GUN IN THE WEST

"When the war closed, I buried the hatchet, and I won't fight now unless I'm put upon."

—Wild Bill Hickok

Wild Bill Hickok

At around six p.m. on July 21, 1865, "Wild" Bill Hickok, sometime gunman, lawman, gambler, and former Union spy, spotted Davis Tutt, a former Confederate soldier, emerging from the Springfield, Missouri, courthouse on the north end of the town square. "Dave, don't cross that square with my watch," he instructed Tutt.[1]

What happened next was the violent culmination of a dispute that had spilled over from the day before at the Lyon House Hotel gambling hall. There, Hickok had reportedly refused to play cards with Tutt due to a long-standing dispute over a gambling debt—although others claimed the two were quarreling over a woman. Whatever the cause, and there would be countless versions of the story, Tutt was holding one of Hickok's favorite possessions, his gold pocket watch.

The tension was immediately palpable as both parties understood what would happen next. Hickok and Tutt squared up in the sensible sideways stance of the gunfighter, not in the open stance so often depicted in old Hollywood Westerns, which would have been suicidal. For a few apprehensive seconds the two stared at each other. Then Tutt, considered a good shot by most who knew him, made the catastrophic decision of reaching for his six-shot revolver. According to witnesses, two shots were fired, although they sounded as one. In a flash, Tutt clutched his chest, stumbled toward the courthouse, spun around a column, and uttered the words "Boys, I am killed" before falling to the ground.

Hickok was arrested, charged, and speedily acquitted, in what can only be termed a blatant case of jury nullification. Not that this sort of frontier justice was rare. The men who sat on juries in the Old West regularly ignored the letter of the law and leaned on conceptions of fairness that comported with the realities of their environment and place. Tutt had embarrassed Hickok, after all. And it had been a fair fight.

Because of the duel, Hickok's fortunes soon turned forever and a new mythology was born. In September of that year, a writer for *Harper's New Monthly Magazine*, George Ward Nichols, interviewed the gunfighter and, with great specificity, detailed his exploits for a story that appeared in the February 1867 issue, turning the then-unknown gunfighter into one of the great legends of the Old West. In the piece, Nichols described Hickok as "6'2", long flowing hair, chest like a barrel, thin waist adorned by twin Colts, graceful, dignified bearing . . ." From then on, gunfighters, criminals, gamblers, and lawmen—sometimes the very same person over a long and wayward career—would be immortalized in magazine articles and dime-store Westerns that were sold across the United States. The folklores created by these writers would in due time be picked up by novelists, painters, musicians, and Hollywood studios, and persist to this day. Many men portrayed in these books did indeed lead hardscrabble existences tinged with genuine violence and danger. But these grizzled showmen learned to dramatize their stories for money, adorning them with exciting and romantic flourishes. Few were as good at it as Wild Bill.

James Butler Hickok's family had ventured from Massachusetts—one great-grandfather had grabbed a musket and met the British on their march to Concord—to Vermont before ending up in Illinois. "Bill," who would take his grandfather's name, was born in 1837. By the time he hit his late teens, Hickok was on his way to Kansas, where a civil war was playing out over the question of slavery. Bleeding Kansas saw violent political confrontations and terrorism between anti-slavery Free-Staters and pro-slavery "Border Ruffians." Hickok joined the former, becoming a skilled gunman, soldier, and spy. After the war, the young man used those skills to work—at least according to his own telling of his life—as a wagoner, a scout, a lawman, a gambler, and what can rightly be described as a performance artist.

It was Hickok's gunfight with Tutt that dominated cultural depictions of the Western duel. Americans had taken to dueling rather quickly over the years. Unlike Europe, where these deadly contests were based on aristocratic honor codes and restricted to men of certain classes, in egalitarian America men of all backgrounds could and did participate. "In France, one hardly ever fights a duel except in order to be able to say that one has done so," Alexis de Tocqueville wrote in 1831, noting the more violent tinge of dueling. "In America one only fights to kill; one fights because one sees no hope of getting one's adversary condemned to death."[2] The "Code Duello," written by an Irishman in 1777, contained more than two dozen rules for aspiring duelists (for example, the number of shots or wounds that would satisfy honor) that were often followed by Americans. In 1838, South Carolina governor and dueling enthusiast John Lyde Wilson wrote an American version of the dueling etiquette called *The Code of Honor; or Rules for the Government of Principals and Seconds in Duelling*. The book offers not only a fascinating look into the honor codes of the pre–Civil War South but also the rationalizations for it. "If a man be smote on one cheek in public, and he turns the other which is also smitten, and he offers no resistance, but blesses him that so despitefully used him," explained the theatrical Wilson, "I am aware that he is in the exercise of great christian forbearance, highly recommended and enjoined by many very good men, but utterly repugnant to those feelings which nature and education have implanted in the human character."[3]

These wouldn't be the only American figures to engage in the practice. The populist president Andrew Jackson allegedly participated in six duels over his lifetime. These sometimes deadly run-ins were typically prompted by some untoward talk about Jackson's wife, Rachel, who, it was said, had married the future president without properly divorcing her previous husband. Jackson, shot in the chest in one of these confrontations, staunched his wound and proceeded to gun down his antagonist. Jackson, in fact, was wounded three times total while dueling. Most often, however, men would do a lot of talking about dueling but little shooting. No less an American hero than the young Abraham Lincoln was nearly involved in a duel before honor was restored. In the Wild West, there was less time for seconds to work out the differences between men.

With the flood of men seeking adventure and riches came brutality, and new guns were easier to use in rapidity and thus far more deadly. It's one thing for an aggrieved man to shoot a flintlock pistol in the general direction of his rival, and quite another thing to engage in spontaneous acts of violence with six-shot revolvers and repeating rifles. Many authors and editors made a good living romanticizing the Old West for audiences back home, bringing them the graceful heroics of gunslingers and adventurers. Yet in truth many of the men they wrote about were cruel and immoral, with little real gallantry or heroism to speak of. Many of the most famous Western duels were really nothing more than cold-blooded murder.

In the West, duels rarely featured protracted negotiations to recover honor. In male-dominated frontier towns that sprung up at the intersections of cattle trails and railroad stops, where ranchers, prospectors, gamblers, and merchants would carouse, drink, and compete, violence was often the only way to preserve one's dignity—and vengeance was often taken spontaneously. Few of these encounters ended in a Hollywood-like showdown. Most often combatants opened fire during drunken brawls or engaged in small-scale warfare that pitted feuding clans and interests against each other. "Where this is the common custom, brawls or personal difficulties are seldom if ever settled by blows," wrote Bill Hickok's friend General George Armstrong Custer. "The quarrel is not from a word to a blow, but from a word to the revolver, and he who can draw and fire first is the best man. No civil law reaches him; none is applied for. In fact there is no law recognized beyond the frontier but that of 'might makes right.'"[4]

Many of these men were legendary for being "the fastest gun in the West." Yet, while speed was important—men like Wild Bill Longley, another probable psychopath, was reputed to be able to outdraw anyone, and often did—most gunmen didn't rely on the quick draw to survive. For one thing, though some holstered their guns, many did not. Western gunmen, as we can plainly see in the majority of surviving pictures from that era, preferred carrying their pistols in their pockets or in their belts. "Whenever you get into a row be sure and not shoot too quick," Hickok explained. "Take time. I've known many a feller to slip up for shootin' in a hurry."[5]

In the fantastic and also largely fictitious 1880 book, *The Life and Marvelous Adventures of Wild Bill, the Scout, Being a True and Exact History of All the Sanguinary Combats and Hair-breadth Escapes of the Most Famous Scout and Spy America Ever Produced*, James W. Buel claimed that one of Bill's favorite activities was charging onlookers a dollar to see him shoot a silver dime from fifty paces. "He would place the dime in a position that the sun's rays would concentrate on it, thus affording him a good sight" before sending a bullet through the dime "nine times out of ten," writes the author. In another trick, Hickok drove a cork through the neck of a bottle from thirty paces, knocking the bottom out without breaking the neck. He could shoot a chicken's head off "at thirty or forty paces nineteen times out of twenty." Some of these were plausible, as many Western heroes entertained crowds with their incredible proficiency with guns. This was an American tradition, after all.

And shoot they did. "The fear of the law is not half so great as the fear of the bullet with characters we have to deal with," a ranch foreman in Texas would say in 1879.[6] Tutt, for example, had not been the first person Hickok gunned down. In 1861, a man named Dave McCanles mocked Wild Bill, insulting his courage and manhood. So naturally, as a measure of revenge, the twenty-four-year-old began an affair with his tormentor's mistress. When McCanles learned of the relationship, he tracked Hickok down inside a train station and threatened to whip him. "There will be one less son-of-a-bitch when you try that," Hickok claimed to have replied. When McCanles ignored this threat, Hickok shot him in the chest.

He wasn't alone. Clay Allison's tombstone may read "Gentleman, Gun Fighter," but in truth the man was probably a homicidal maniac, the kind of person who allegedly cut off another gunman's head and carried it thirty miles in a sack before placing it on a bar and having a drink. The infamous gunfighter John King Fisher gunned down unarmed men as a matter of habit, including members of his own gang. James "Killer" Miller, a teetotaling Methodist, also moonlighted as a paid assassin who began a decades-long killing spree by offing his own brother-in-law. To call him a "gunfighter" might be a generous concession, considering most often he would use his double-barreled shotgun to finish off the unsuspecting victims. After evading conviction for years, Miller was finally lynched by a Texas mob in 1909, reportedly yelling "Let 'er rip" before stepping off the crate he was on to finish the hanging himself.[7]

As with many other figures of the West who concocted stories about their own lives, it's difficult to know how many were assassinated by the infamous gunman John Wesley Hardin, who maintained he shot down forty-two men, although he was indicted on a still-impressive twenty-seven bodies. At fourteen Hardin stuck a knife into another boy who insulted him. At fifteen he emptied his revolver into another boy to whom he had lost a wrestling match. When a group of Union soldiers caught up with him, Hardin claimed: "I waylaid them, as I had no mercy on men whom I knew only wanted to get my body to torture and kill."[8]

Henry "Billy the Kid" McCarty, perhaps the most famous of the gunfighters, was a marauding thief and murderer who purportedly pulled his gun, a .44-caliber Colt Peacemaker, at the slightest provocation. There were others, of course: Sam Bass, "Curly Bill" Brocius, Doc Holliday, Jesse James, Butch Cassidy and Henry Longabaugh (the "Sundance Kid"), and noted lawmen like Dallas Stoudenmire (most famous for the "Four Dead in Five Seconds Gunfight"), Wyatt Earp, and many others. Many of these men had careers as lawmen and criminals. Some of them were honorable. Some of them were frauds. Few of them cared much about the ancient code of gentlemen. Most died violently at the wrong end of a gun.

Virtually every man on the frontier owned a gun. Many had been brought back from the battlefields of the Civil War, but the eastern manufacturers were making serviceable weapons at affordable prices. The new revolvers, owing to the ease with which they could be used and carried, were both widespread and dangerous. Once Smith & Wesson's patent ran out, the all-in-one cartridge came to dominate the guns of the West made by nearly every manufacturer.[9] "In the streets one constantly meets hardy, sun-tanned men with long hair and beards who carry unconcealed in their belts the hunting knife and revolver, inseparable companions of the plainsman," wrote the French émigré Philippe Régis de Trobriand on a visit to Omaha.[10] The Colt was the most popular of these revolvers. "Wild Bill always carried two handsome ivory-handled revolvers of the large size; he was never seen without them," wrote Hickok's friend George Custer. Hickok's waist, George Ward Nichols noted, was "girthed by a belt which held two Colt's Navy revolvers." Hickok had pulled his favorite .36-caliber, six-shot, 1851-built revolver on Davis Tutt.

All the Colt percussion revolvers made at this time were single-action, which is to say they could be fired only by cocking the hammer and then squeezing the trigger one shot at a time. Other manufacturers, like Remington, likely the second-most-popular gunmaker of the western era, offered both single- and double-action revolvers. The latter allowed the owner to fire single-action or simply squeeze the trigger to fire, thus the "double action." The British gunmaker Robert Adams had been the first to patent the double-action system, in which the external hammer could not be cocked by thumbing it back. Once the patent expired in the mid-1870s, other companies featured the system in their own revolvers.

The Smith & Wesson Model .44-caliber "American" was a popular single-action big-bore six-shooter. Remington sold the New Model 1875, which was, for the most part, a knockoff of the Colt Peacemaker. When the outlaw Frank James, brother of Jesse, surrendered to Missouri governor T. T. Crittenden in 1882, a reporter asked him why he preferred the .44-40 caliber 1875 Remington (which was, apparently, the sort of thing journalists asked outlaws in those days). "Because," the former Confederate soldier reportedly replied, "the Remington is the hardest and the surest shooting pistol made, and because it carries exactly the same cartridge that a Winchester rifle does . . . [W]hen a man gets into a close, hot fight, with a dozen men shooting at him all at once, he must have his ammunition all of the same kind."[11] Staving off a dozen men of a posse might not have been a top concern for most western arrivals, but practicality almost surely was.

For those inclined to conceal their weapons there was the derringer, a small single-shot large-bore gun that was another widely popular weapon of the West. The gun was a misspelling of the name of its inventor, Henry Deringer, son of a colonial gunsmith who had produced Kentucky rifles in the late 1700s, then began to perfect and mass-produce the small pocket pistols out of Philadelphia. Its popularity soon induced other major gunmakers to copy its design, often adding their own flourishes. The most

Remington New Model Army Percussion Revolver

advantageous aspect of the derringer was that it could be concealed—either as an extra gun or in saloons that had limited gun-carry restrictions—yet it was deadly accurate at short range. John Wilkes Booth used one of his derringer pocket pistols to assassinate President Abraham Lincoln in April 1865. It was during the reporting of this event that an extra *r* was added to the inventor's name by reporters. The gun remained popular into the twentieth century, and not only among assassins.

While the revolver and the derringer (and certainly the rifle) were the dominant weapons of the West, the double-barreled shotgun was also in widespread use by this time because of its affordability and practicality. The shotgun—often known as the "scatter gun," because it strewed pellets—provided versatility as a weapon for hunting, war, and defense. Developed from the smoothbore hunting guns, there were both muzzle-loading and breech-loading cartridge types. Many thousands of shotguns from a variety of makers and countries were the mainstay of settlers, lawmen, and express coach mail companies. The popular saying "riding shotgun" referred to guards sitting next to stagecoach drivers to protect their cargo and passengers from outlaws and Native Americans. Western dime books were littered with stories of shotguns saving the day. When two deputized men armed with six-shooters, rifles, and derringers attempted to apprehend John Wesley Hardin, he wrote, "I covered them with a double-barreled shotgun and told them their lives depended on their actions, and unless they obeyed my orders to the letter, I would shoot first one and then the other."

Nevertheless, despite the prevalence of these new, lethal guns and the sometimes lack of reliable law—and the many men who took advantage of the situations they found themselves in—the Old West did not see the kind of mass violence portrayed in popular depictions. For the many thousands of men and women who would never be written about in dime novels or portrayed in Western films, the gun protected their home and property from criminality. For most of them, firearms were the means of hunting for sustenance and a way to ward off danger. The majority of men and women who trekked westward in the second half of the nineteenth century did so to find prosperity and peace. Most never fired, or even had to point their gun, at another human being.

There has been a long-running debate among scholars regarding the proper way to calculate the homicide rates of the frontier West. Whatever the precise number is, it's clear that the average agricultural, ranching, or mining community was far from the violence-ridden place depicted in movies. No, the West wasn't a tranquil Eden, as we've noted. There was danger, criminality, and "range wars" that broke out between competing clans—although usually the number of casualties in these conflicts hardly justified the moniker of "wars."

In 1883, for example, the Associated Press breathlessly reported that the "Dodge City War" had broken out, making the frontier town sound like a combat zone to eastern readers. This "war," it must be noted, yielded exactly zero casualties. Dodge City was often treated as the epitome of alleged western unruliness. It had its share of violence. But as historian Robert R. Dykstra has pointed out in his book *The Cattle Towns*, the problem these communities faced "was not to rid themselves of visitors prone to violence, but to suppress the violence while retaining the visitors."[12] Dodge City, Dykstra observes, witnessed an average of only 1.5 homicides per year over the ten years it was the leading cattle-trading center of the West.

The reputation of debauchery and gunfighting was often exaggerated by locals, who found not only a warped sense of pride in portraying their towns as centers of brutality and depravity but also a pretty good marketing campaign. In 1879 a Dodge City editor wrote that "to live in the 'wickedest city in the west' is a source of pride" because locals measured the "accomplishments and glorious ends" of those who were buried in the town's cemetery, Boot Hill.[13] We all know the slogan "What happens in Vegas stays in Vegas." Well, the 1870s version of tourist promotion was not much different. "Everything goes in Wichita" read the welcome sign on the outskirts of town. "Hell is still in session in Ellsworth"[14] was the sign that hung in the Kansas cowtown, claimed one reporter. The truth was less spectacular. Ellsworth probably saw only one shooting of note in 1872, and no murders.[15] Another town, Ogallala, Nebraska, considered the "cowboy capital" of the West and sometimes the "Gomorrah of the trail," saw six killings from 1875 to 1884.[16]

Many contemporary gun control advocates argue that the lack of violence can be attributed to the fact that there was more gun control in the West than there is in modern America. These days, there are numerous articles, columns, and "fact-checkers" making these absurd claims.[17] One of the most popular pieces of evidence bolstering this assertion is to point to a picture of a Dodge City ordinance that read: "Any person or persons found carrying concealed weapons in the city of Dodge or violating the laws of the state shall be dealt with according to the law."

It's true that, by 1879, Dodge City had nearly twenty businesses licensed to sell liquor and many whorehouses teeming with intoxicated young men. It seems reasonable not to want these men to be armed with revolvers as they packed into a red-light district. However, the men *voluntarily* handed over their weapons in exchange for the chance to find entertainment and drink. Not in the wildest recesses of the westerner's imagination would he think a person had to ask for permission—or get a license—from the government to own a firearm. Nor do we know how rigidly the law was enforced or for how long. Moreover, the Dodge City ordinance—and some other towns, featured similar ones—typically applied only to the area north of the "deadline," which was the railroad tracks and a kind of red-light district. In the rest of the city, guns were allowed.

There is, in fact, a much stronger case to be argued that guns made crime like robbery and assault less prevalent. In reality, a man walking into town with gun blazing would almost surely see the retribution of a gun-wielding citizenry—many of whom had learned to use their weapons during the Civil War—that was far more interested in building a peaceful community. To put this in some context: during the frontier period, which historians typically define as 1859 to 1900, a survey of primary and secondary sources from all the states of the "West" could find fewer than a dozen confirmed bank robberies—in total—over those forty years.[18] There were more than 1,000 in those same states in 2015 alone.[19] Yet there were probably tens of thousands of such crimes depicted in movies over the past century. Despite the perceptions we've created, guns were far more likely to keep the peace than be used in wanton acts of violence.

13

★

THE SHOWMAN

"The West of the old times, with its strong characters, its stern battles and its tremendous stretches of loneliness, can never be blotted from my mind."

—Buffalo Bill

Buffalo Bill Wild West Show

I t was only a matter of time before an industrious American began to package and monetize the mythology of the West for widespread consumption. William F. Cody—or "Buffalo Bill," as he would be known to millions—was born in Scott County, Iowa, in 1846, the year the territory would become a state. Sam Colt might have romanticized the guns of the frontier to his consumer base, but Buffalo Bill brought the frontier and the personalities and distinctive lifestyles and their weapons to the world. The man who modeled his looks on Hickok (who would end up working for Cody) was portrayed as everything from a gunslinger to a chivalrous warrior to a madman to a preening effete to a sniveling coward in movies and books in the coming century. Maybe he was a little bit of all those things.

Cody, nearly a decade younger than Hickok, lost his father when the future showman was still in his adolescence. The youngster grew up quickly as his family found itself swept up in the Kansas-Missouri wars over slavery. In his early teens, Bill took a job riding horseback in a wagon train and delivering messages between the drivers and workmen. Cody witnessed an economic boom in Kansas sparked by a new wave of emigrants moving westward after the completion of the First Transcontinental Railroad in 1869. An industrious young man like him, fearless and good with a gun, could profit from "railroading and trading and hunting. I went out to make money and I was just looking for anything that could come along."[1]

Cody claimed to have ridden for the Pony Express, which famously employed around eighty men and used hundreds of horses to travel the nearly 1,800 dangerous miles between St. Joseph, Missouri, and Sacramento, California. We don't know if this is true. But we do know that Cody won a medal of honor in 1872 as a scout in the U.S. Army during the Indian Wars, famously engaging in a rifle duel in which he killed and supposedly scalped the Cheyenne warrior Yellow Hair. It's a story he would retell often.

It was at some point in 1867 when the young veteran began hunting buffalo herds to feed the crew working on the Kansas Pacific Railroad. Although there were probably dozens of "Buffalo Bills" wandering the West at the time, it was during an eight-hour shooting match with a hunter named William Comstock that Cody won the moniker. He used a .50- to .70-caliber Springfield trapdoor rifle that he named after the Italian femme fatale Lucretia Borgia.[2]

The buffalo were intricately entwined in the vibrancy and health of American Indian life and the sustenance of the expanding white presence after the Civil War. The eradication of these massive herds not only changed the complexion of the North America, it hastened the end of Indian dominance of the land. While doing it, however, buffalo hunters became nearly as legendary as the gunslingers.

In 1840 the United States estimated that there were around 17 million American bison west of the Missouri River. Today it is estimated that 30 million of these animals roamed the West in giant, nearly inconceivably massive herds. One frontiersman claimed that he had come upon a herd that was seventy miles long and thirty miles wide. Others confirmed herds of comparable sizes. Not only would new guns drive the hunting, they created a growing market for the animal. Buffalo tongues, for example, became a delicacy in the East. By the 1870s a new process for tanning the hides—using a strong lime solution to soak the skins—was perfected. Because of such technological developments, the only limits set on buffalo hunters were their own. By the mid-1800s, hundreds of thousands of buffalo were being killed annually.

For thousands of unskilled and uneducated men like Cody who were searching for riches and adventure, buffalo hunting was an easy way to make good money quickly. Buffalo hunting wasn't merely profitable; it was easy *and* profitable. The U.S. government and the railroad companies endorsed the hunting as a way to populate the West. The railroads didn't just rely on bison hunting grounds for food; they marketed them as vacation areas for sports hunters. One *Harper's* story from 1867 describes these hunting excursions:

> Nearly every railroad train which leaves or arrives at Fort Hays on the Kansas Pacific Railroad has its race with these herds of buffalo; and a most interesting and exciting scene is the result. The train is "slowed" to a rate of speed about equal to that of the herd; the passengers get out fire-arms which are provided for the defense of the train against the Indians, and open from the windows and platforms of the cars a fire that resembles a brisk skirmish. Frequently a young bull will turn at bay for a moment. His exhibition of courage is generally his death-warrant, for the whole fire of the train is turned upon him, either killing him or some member of the herd in his immediate vicinity.[3]

The new guns made all of it possible. And perhaps the most effective of these guns was the Sharps rifle, which would overtake the Springfield Army rifle as the hunter's weapon of choice. Some called the Sharps rifle the "Big Fifty," others the "Poison Slinger" or "Beecher's Bible," after the anti-slavery minister Henry Ward Beecher told the *New York Tribune* in

1856 that he believed shipping a Sharps rifle to the fighters in Kansas's anti-slavery effort "was a truly moral agency, and that there was more moral power in one of those instruments, so far as the slaveholders of Kansas were concerned, than in a hundred Bibles."[4] Around 1,000 of these had been sent to anti-slavery "Free Soil" settlers who were fighting against pro-slavery forces in "Bleeding Kansas" during the 1850s. One of the most famous Free Soilers was John Brown, who later used Sharps Model 1853 carbines in his ill-fated attempt to capture the U.S. Armory at Harpers Ferry, Virginia, in 1859.

Christian Sharps had built on John Hall's idea of interchangeable parts. The New Jersey–born inventor worked under Hall at Harpers Ferry and patented his own rifle in 1848. By 1850 he had set out on his own and set up shop in Mill Creek, Pennsylvania, producing two models of his ever-improving rifle. A year later he moved to Hartford to be among the many leading gunmakers. Lacking production facilities, he contracted Robbins & Lawrence to manufacture his new breechloader.

While the earlier models of Sharps could not bring down the buffalo with one shot, the later models had no such difficulty. The Sharps rifle used three-inch-long cartridges and weighed over nine pounds when loaded. One noted western hunter wrote in 1883 that "I saw probably a hundred of these in my travels, and only three of four of any other kind. I questioned a great many of these men who use them, as to their effectiveness and adaption to frontier use, and all pronounce them the best arm in use, all things considered, for that purpose."[5] The weapon also featured a unique "two-trigger" setup in which pulling a rear trigger set the front trigger ready for discharge at the slightest pull, allowing the gun to be steadied for a long-distance shot.

"A large majority of the frontiersmen I met with—in fact, nearly all of them—used Sharp's [sic] rifle," another traveler wrote.[6] Although it was most lethal to the bison—one 1887 government survey estimated that the Sharps rifle had killed more buffalo between the years 1867 and 1882 than any other—it was widely used in warfare. The Indians sometimes referred to it as the "shoot today, kill tomorrow" gun.[7] In June 1874, its reputation would grow when around two dozen buffalo hunters repelled a force of hundreds of Comanche Indians at the small town of Adobe Walls in the Texas Panhandle. A hunter name Billy Dixon purportedly

Sharps rifle

shot an Indian from 1,500 yards, convincing the war party to give up on their three-day siege.

Bill Cody made his name hunting these buffalo, once claiming to have downed over 4,000 of them during an eighteen-month span. In his career as a buffalo hunter, he had amassed a total kill of 20,000 bison between 1870 and 1879. Others would make him look like a lightweight. There was Orlando A. Brown, who in a two-month span shot nearly 6,000 buffalo.[8] He shot so often with his loud Sharps gun that he would go deaf in one ear. Tom Nixon, one of the most notorious of the bison hunters of the day, slaughtered 3,200 of them in a thirty-five-day hunt—120 of them in one forty-five-minute span. What's more, buffalo rarely ran from their killers. A man like Cody could saunter to within one hundred yards or less of his prey, and even after the loud bang of the rifle—even after a beast had collapsed in a heap on the prairie ground—the other buffalo typically continued grazing as if nothing had happened. When the herd did take off, hunters learned that shooting the lead buffalo would stop the entire herd. In essence, a hunter like Buffalo Bill could kill as many as he could skin and carry. A western hunter with even a middling work ethic could probably make around $35 a day in the late 1870s killing buffalo.

Cody would, at various times in his life, fight, champion, befriend, and exploit Indians, whose history has also been distorted by culture. As we've seen, guns began to play a major role in Indian life from the time they were introduced by the newcomers in the seventeenth century. Many Native American tribes of the West would become exceptionally skilled at using both horses and guns as a means of hunting and warfare. For a number of decades, Indians relied predominantly on smoothbore muskets, for which they could sometimes fabricate their own ammunition. However, since they were unable to fix or produce new guns, obtaining and maintaining them was often a major concern of tribal leadership. Trading guns and ammunition with Indian tribes was legal but often restricted. In 1837, for instance, the United States Office of Indian Affairs limited trade to "a pound of lead" for ammunition to "not make less than forty-five, nor more than one hundred [shots], and must be of a length and weight corresponding properly with the size of the ball." Most westerners ignored these restrictions, as the tribes traded for all types of weaponry.

In 1846, a twenty-three-year-old Harvard Law School graduate named Francis Parkman traveled west to live with the Plains Indian tribes, roaming with various parties between the Mississippi and the Rockies. In his widely read books and articles, Parkman offered eastern readers remarkably beautiful and meticulous accounts of the tribes and their relationship with the buffalo herds that blanketed North America. Over the next decades, Americans began to romanticize the Indians' treatment of the bison and, in turn, take responsibility for their own role in decimating it. Things were, perhaps, not that simple.

What Parkman found was a bucolic lifestyle that featured plenty of guns. Before the 1840s, some historians estimate that 60,000 Plains Indians were killing about half a million bison a year for sustenance.[9] The fact is that tribes killed as many as they could, but significant changes in climate and the introduction of disease were also big factors in finishing off the enormous bison herds. Indian tribes, galvanized by the introduction of the rifle, were just as inclined to overhunt and just as ready to compete for the buffalo hides as the newcomers.[10]

What's more, the white men would not always have the upper hand. When tribes in the Montana Territory missed their federal deadline to move to the reservations in June 1876, Lieutenant Colonel George Armstrong Custer and the 7th Cavalry were sent to compel the Indians to obey. When they showed up, a coalition of Lakota Sioux and Cheyenne warriors confronted them in the Battle of the Little Bighorn in the Montana Territory. The Americans were famously decimated. The five companies of the 7th Cavalry had been armed with their Army-issue Colt Single Action Army revolvers and their Model 1873 Springfield carbines. While these guns are said to have won the West, it was not to be on this day.

For more than a century after the battle, theories, including conspiratorial ones, swirled around the incident. The prevailing cultural depiction of Custer's last stand includes overwhelmed American troops being slaughtered under hails of arrows. One theory had it that most of the American guns jammed, leaving the troops helpless. Later testing would confirm that the copper casings of the rounds that were lugged around by the troops in leather pouches formed a green film that sometimes fouled and jammed the guns when fired. This jamming of the rifles prevented extraction of the fired cartridge cases. The U.S. Army replaced the copper with brass moving forward.

Yet it is far more likely that Custer's troops were simply and literally outgunned. While archaeologists who began excavating the sites of the battle in the 1980s found that the Lakota and Cheyenne used ancient weapons like lances, clubs, and arrows, they were also equipped with some of the most sophisticated firearms of the day. Forty-six models of guns were used by the warriors led by Sitting Bull and Crazy Horse, and at least 415 separate guns were used by the Indians. The investigators found more than 2,000 spent cartridges. The Native Americans had an arsenal of the best American-made weaponry of the day: Colts, Henrys, Remingtons, Smith & Wessons, Sharpses, Spencers, and Winchesters, among many others.[11]

The first idealized version of Custer as a heroic figure falling in a hail of arrows came to Americans through one of Cody's Wild West extravaganzas. In fact, by the time he was twenty-three, "Buffalo Bill" was already famous. Philip Sheridan, the assertive Civil War general and veteran of the Indian Wars, persuaded Cody to accompany him on a hunting trip with Russia's Grand Duke Alexis. The event was widely reported on and Cody became nationally known. And in 1869, on a trip to New York, the hunter and soldier met Ned Buntline (whose real name was Edward Zane Carroll Judson Sr.), one of the early sensationalists of the western experience. Buntline falsely took credit for the Colt's "Buntline Special"—a 16-inch-barreled version of the Colt Single Action Army revolver—although there is no evidence of his involvement in its creation or production. A prodigious womanizer, Buntline, who was also married at least seven times, was forced to move around the country to avoid the messy repercussions of his love life.

First Buntline wrote a completely fantastical biography of Buffalo Bill's exploits, titled *Buffalo Bill, the King of the Border Men*, the first episode of which appeared in the popular *New York Weekly* newspaper. Later he convinced Cody to tell him his tales, which were immediately dramatized for the bestselling book *The Scout of the Plains*. Nearly 2,000 Buffalo Bill Westerns would be written, mostly concocted accounts written by one of his employees, Prentiss Ingraham. It was not until Owen Wister's bestselling 1902 novel *The Virginian*, which depicts the rugged life of a cattle rancher in Wyoming, that Americans got their first true literary Western. By that time, the violent life of the cowboy and the gunfighter had been well established. Such images were further reinforced with the emergence of the rodeo and shooting contests adding to popular conceptions of the American West. Cody personified them in his books and shows.

By 1872, Buntline convinced Cody to come to Chicago with western personalities to put on a stage production of *The Scout of the Plains*. The group sat down and wrote their first play in only four hours.[12] Despite reviews that pointed out the atrocious acting and implausible storylines—perhaps Cody was ill prepared to enact situations that he had never actually experienced—the play was a giant hit. Cody, who had a good sense of humor and a knack for showmanship, performed the play for the next eleven years. In 1883 he took the show on the road, forming Buffalo Bill's Wild West, which brought together all the facets of western lore and life, including buffalo hunts, duels, reenactments of famous battles against Indians (including Custer's last stand), and early rodeos. Often the shows featured Native Americans, real gunfighters, and buffalo. For the next thirty years, Bill performed in the show, which became a massive hit not only across North America but in Europe as well. Buffalo Bill's Wild West shows were, as he coined it, "the Drama of Civilization."

The most consistent and popular aspects of these shows focused on western battles, quick-draw dueling, and sharpshooting. Bill Hickok, now the "Prince of Pistoleers," became one of Buffalo Bill's most famous draws. In 1884, Cody met the four-foot-eleven-inch Phoebe Ann Mosey, the fifth child of a twice-widowed mother, performing trick shots at a circus in New Orleans. Mosey, soon to be known to the world as Annie Oakley, had shown amazing prowess with guns as a child in rural Ohio. As an adolescent, she trapped and hunted for food to help sustain her mother and half-dozen siblings. As a teenager, she began showing off her prodigious talents with a rifle for money. It was during this time that she challenged a trick-shot artist named Frank Butler to a contest and beat him. Butler became immediately enchanted, married her, became her manager, and stayed with her until their deaths only a week apart in 1926.[13]

Word spread as the couple toured the country, soon coming to the attention of Cody, who negotiated for a three-day trial run with Buffalo Bill's Wild West. They stayed on for sixteen years. In an era when deception was accepted as part of the entertainment, Oakley—no one is sure why she took the name—was the real deal. "Miss Annie Oakley," "Little Sure Shot," or "Little Miss Sure Shot" had an astounding capacity for shooting that combined with an understated assuredness and flash that could rarely be matched.

There would be other sharpshooters—women as well—yet none could match Annie Oakley's showmanship and skill. She could shoot holes in playing cards that were thrown in the air by her husband from thirty paces. At ninety paces she could hit a dime, snuff out a candle flame, and shoot the ash off a cigarette. In 1885 she participated in a nine-hour contest, hitting 4,772 glass balls out of 5,000. She once took a $5,000 bet that she could hit forty out of fifty pigeons at thirty yards. She hit forty-nine. She performed in front of Queen Victoria and King Umberto I of Italy, and supposedly shot the ashes off a cigarette held by German kaiser Wilhelm II. She became a huge draw for Wild Bill and soon an international star.

We can never know how many women in the West and rural areas mastered their rifles and revolvers. But Oakley was a champion of the sport and spoke about guns with the kind of conviction that would be familiar to any Second Amendment advocate these days. She gave women lessons on shooting and advocated that they take up guns. "I want to see women rise superior to that old-fashioned terror of firearms," she said. "I would like to see every woman know how to handle them as naturally as they know how to handle babies."[14] Oakley encouraged women not only to own guns but to use them in self-defense. "I have had an ideal for my sex," she once wrote. "I have wanted them to be able to protect their homes."[15] Oakley liked to tuck a revolver into an umbrella when taking walks alone in case she was attacked, even demonstrating her system of self-protection in the *Cincinnati Times-Star*. "If I were accosted, I could easily fire," she told the paper. "A woman cannot always rely on getting help just by calling for it." When the New York State legislature passed a bill barring women from having guns in the home, she spoke publicly against it.

In 1894, Oakley and Butler performed in a Thomas Edison Kinetoscope production and appeared in *"Little Sure Shot" of the "Wild West,"* an exhibition of rifle shooting at glass balls, one of the first films ever made. In April 1898, long after she was world-famous, Oakley wrote President William McKinley, offering the government the services of a company of fifty "lady sharpshooters" who would provide their own arms and ammunition should war break out with Spain.[16]

One imagines the Spanish were lucky that she was rebuffed.

Oakley's rise signified the nadir of the Old West. In October 1901, a freight train would crash into another train carrying many of the performers of Buffalo Bill's show. More than a hundred horses perished in the accident. Oakley was severely injured, although she recovered. But by then America was already moving on. Cody's friend Wild Bill, who almost always sat facing the doorway of whatever room he was in, had made the lethal mistake of taking a chair facing away from the door of the Nuttal & Mann's Saloon in Deadwood, Dakota Territory, in 1872. He was shot in the back of the head with a Colt Model 1873 Single Action Army at point-blank range by a man named Jack McCall. Cody, on the other hand, died peacefully in 1917, surrounded by friends a day after being baptized in the Catholic Church at the age of seventy. Annie Oakley lived until 1926, when she passed away from old age, followed by her husband eighteen days later. By this time, however, the guns that had made Western heroes famous were nothing but romantic relics of a time long past. The next evolution of firearms would be the most consequential. Its genesis went back to the mid-nineteenth century and the American Civil War, but its capabilities would truly be felt initially in Europe during the first mechanized war.

In Annie Oakley's forty years of shooting, Americans went from firing one bullet at a time to firing hundreds per minute. They went from stuffing a lead ball down the muzzles of rifles to feeding perpetual firing machines with cartridges in high-capacity magazines. The era of rapid fire was here.

PART III

★

MODERNITY

Recruits, 18th Penn. N.G., Pittsburgh

14

★

HELLFIRE

"The discharge can be made with all desirable accuracy as rapidly as one hundred and fifty times per minute, and may be continued for hours without danger."[1]

—*Scientific American* magazine

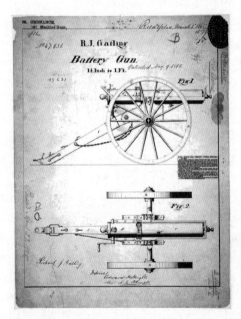

Battery Gun by Richard Jordan Gatling

They showed us the new battery gun on wheels—the Gatling gun, or rather, it is a cluster of six to ten savage tubes that carry great conical pellets of lead, with unerring accuracy, a distance of two and a half miles," Mark Twain remarked in one of his 1868 columns. "It feeds itself with cartridges, and you work it with a crank like a hand organ; you can fire it faster than four men can count. When fired rapidly, the reports blend together like the clattering of a watchman's rattle. It can be discharged four hundred times a minute! I liked it very much."[2]

Dr. Richard Jordan Gatling's hand-driven machine gun was far more reliable and faster than any other gun before it, introducing to the battlefield the prospect of continuous firing of weaponry. Twain may have found the creation to his liking, but for millions of soldiers in the upcoming century the idea of unremitting fire added a specter of violence that altered conflicts in the bloodiest way imaginable—for both the soldiers and their commanders. When a Union army of the Civil War sparingly used a hand-cranked Gatling gun for covering fire during skirmishes around Petersburg, Virginia, in 1862, it held little consequence. By the time World War I ended, the British estimated that machine guns had been responsible for somewhere around 80 percent of all casualties.[3]

None of this was the intention of Gatling. Born on a southern plantation to a slave-owning father in North Carolina in 1818, the inventor, who would have friends on both sides of the Civil War, lived a restless life, moving often and dabbling in an array of professions, including spending time as a county clerk, merchant, planter, and dry goods store clerk. Gatling moved to St. Louis in 1844 and became a doctor, or what passed as a doctor in those days, although he never practiced, before ending up in Indianapolis on the eve of the Civil War, where he worked in speculative real estate.

In 1861, the year war broke out, Gatling attended a lecture in Ohio where he heard a speaker expounding on the lifesaving benefits of breech-loading weapons and quicker reloading times. The speech sparked an idea that began to percolate in his mind. Spurred by the horrors of war, his notions about speedy firing began to gain traction. "It occurred to me," he wrote a friend in 1877, recalling the daily comings and goings of the wounded, sick, and dead in the early days of the war, "that if I could invent a machine—a gun—which could by its rapidity of fire, enable one man to do as much battle duty as a hundred, that it would, to a great extent, supersede the necessity of large armies, and consequently, exposure to battle and disease be greatly diminished. I thought over the subject and finally this idea took practical form in the invention of the Gatling Gun."

Gatling had already witnessed wounded Union infantrymen returning to Indianapolis. Although the men he saw slogging back from the bloody battlefields of the Civil War were lucky to have escaped with their lives, many had done so with catastrophic injuries. With the great technological advances of weaponry in the mid-1800s came a wave of shattered bones and lead amputations. The sheer numbers of casualties were shocking. For many years Civil War casualties were thought to be around 620,000, but now some historians put the estimates much higher. "The number of men dying in the Civil War is more than in all other American wars from the American Revolution through the Korean War combined," J. David Hacker, a demographic historian from Binghamton University in New York, has written. "And consider that the American population in 1860 was about 31 million people, about one-tenth the size it is today. If the war were fought today, the number of deaths would total 6.2 million." Using digitized census records from the 1800s, Hacker has recalculated the number of casualties to be closer to 750,000, and many scholars are increasingly coming around to this view.

Whatever the actual number was, it was unprecedented. It is true that most Americans who died during the war did so from disease and factors that did not include being shot at by the enemy. Still, at least 100,000 from each side perished in battle. The Civil War featured soldiers with increasingly advanced weapons and ammunition, and yet most of the military leaders didn't grasp the consequences, using antiquated methods to deploy their troops and weapons.

It is unsurprising, then, that doctors were initially unprepared to deal with the overwhelming number of wounds and injuries. In the mid-nineteenth century, medical school was often no more than two years—if that. Many Army doctors at the outset of the Civil War were nothing more than political appointments or, worse, quacks. There was not only a dearth of doctors, but of the doctors who did deal with bullet wounds, only a fraction had ever performed surgery before the war. Of the 11,000 Union doctors, only 500 had any surgical experience before the war. In the Confederacy, only 27 of the 3,000 doctors had prewar surgical experience.[4]

Yet the truth about how Americans wrestled with the repercussions of new gun technology is complicated. The common perception is that physicians during the Civil War knew precious little about sterilization or infections, and permitted unsanitary conditions that cost many lives. As the war progressed and family members saw the results of these amputations and wounds for the first time, the reputation of the doctors diminished and a distorted view of their work began to first coalesce.

It is true that surgeons did not even wash their hands before sticking and prodding wounds to determine if they should amputate. They often used blood-splattered sponges and dipped them into dirty water to clean the wounds. Most of this was due not to negligence but rather a lack of knowledge. In many ways, the Civil War saw great advancements in medicine. Doctors were not the hapless butchers often depicted in movies and novels. One of the grisly benefits of the war, in fact, was the ability of doctors to study outcomes. As war pushed man toward innovative new ways of killing, it also pushed others toward advances in lifesaving techniques.

Compiled by the government, *The Medical and Surgical History of the War of the Rebellion* was a massive six-volume work detailing medical care during the war. It found that of the 174,000 wounds inflicted during the conflict, around 4,600 were treated with surgical extraction and nearly 30,000 ended up as amputations. The mortality rate among the latter was 26 percent. To put this number in context, during the Franco-Prussian War fought in 1870, the mortality rate for amputations was 76 percent.[5] Moreover, by 1846, anesthesia using ether had been developed. The next year saw the use of chloroform. Anesthesia was used by war doctors in approximately 80,000 cases for the Union and 54,000 for the Confederates, saving thousands of soldiers horrifying pain, most often brought on by amputation. Civil War doctors soon discovered that amputation performed within twenty-four to forty-eight hours after being wounded—"primary amputation"—saved lives. These procedures were performed quickly by sawing off limbs in a circular motion. The amputations were most often left to heal by granulation, in which thick tissue was allowed to naturally form around the wound. If not, surgeons used the "fish-mouth" method, cutting flaps of skin that were sewn into a rounded stump. These amputations were many, and they would be a constant reminder of the war.

This is what Gatling saw in 1871, and this is what he wanted to stop with a high-powered rapid-fire gun. Often depicted as a tragic figure, Gatling attempted to belittle the importance of his invention, framing it as a means of diminishing mass death rather than creating it. "The best way to ameliorate war is to shorten it," he would say.[6] That it would not do—although it would make him rich and famous. Whether his dovish intentions were merely a retroactive justification after remorse struck the man is certainly up for debate. We can't bore into Gatling's soul to find out. Of course, as we'll see, if Gatling hadn't invented the rapid-fire gun, someone else would have.

What we do know is that Gatling, a completely self-taught mechanical engineer, *almost* solved the long-standing problem of automatic fire. Throughout history, engineers had attempted to rig guns that could fire multiple rounds without reloading. From the first days of gunpowder, soldiers rammed as many pellets and shards as they could into pot guns. Leonardo da Vinci drew up plans for a thirty-three-barreled organ gun with three rows of eleven guns each, all connected to a single revolving platform. Attached to the sides of the platform were large wheels. Ribauldequins—guns that often featured ten or more iron barrels in a row—were first said to be used by King Edward III of England in 1339 against France, and would be used, in various forms, by numerous armies over the next centuries.

In the mid-1500s, Sir Francis Walsingham, then secretary of state, turned up at court with a mysterious German who, "among other excellent qualities," had promised to produce a harquebus "that shall contain balls or pellets of lead, all of which shall go off one after another, having once given fire, so that with one harquebus one may kill ten thieves or other enemies without recharging it."[7] There is no record of what became of the experiment. In the early 1700s an Englishman named James Puckle patented a flintlock cylinder crank-propelled gun that could hold eleven shots. It probably never went past the prototype stage.

Even as Gatling was attempting to build his gun, a number of other inventors were already toying with the idea. In 1861, the Billinghurst company would test its Billinghurst-Requa battery gun in front of the New York Stock Exchange, hoping to lure investors.[8] Invented by a dentist named Josephus Requa—who was apprentice to once-prominent upstate New York gunmaker William Billinghurst, thus the name—the gun fired off 175 shots per minute, reaching 225 shots in a minute and fifteen seconds in later trials. The gun featured twenty-five horizontal barrels mounted on a light artillery carriage that were loaded at the breeches with "piano hinge" magazines with .52-caliber cartridges. The gun used percussion caps on one nipple that detonated one round that passed in domino fashion from one cartridge to the next until it was exhausted. Although the gun had its champions, including members of the New York Light Artillery, it was barely used by the Union, as it often failed in damp weather and was difficult to reload and aim.

Around the same time Requa was impressing investors on Wall Street, an edition of *Scientific American* reported that an offer had come from an English firm to sell the Union Army an armament called the "Perkins steam gun" that could discharge ten twelve-pound balls per minute. Although the inventor, Jacob Perkins, had died more than a decade earlier, he was already well-known to many Americans. The Massachusetts-born Perkins, who had moved to England after his banknote engraving methods (soon to be widely adopted), had a difficult time finding traction with United States investors. Perkins was behind numerous well-received creations, including the first patented vapor-compression refrigeration cycle.[9] The steam-powered gun generated some excitement among political leaders on both sides of the Atlantic, including Lincoln.

Military leaders, on the other hand, were less impressed. Steam, as it turned out, was a lot less robust as a propellant than gunpowder, making a "steam gun" a step backward. Or, as the Duke of Wellington is said to have quipped after seeing an exhibition of the weapon, "if steam guns had been invented first, what a capital improvement gunpowder would have been."[10]

Inventors kept getting closer. The year Gatling witnessed the wounded hobbling back to Indianapolis, a man named Wilson Ager was already testing a hand-cranked machine gun in America. President Lincoln, after an exhibition of Alger's so-called Coffee Mill Gun, wrote, "I saw this gun myself, and witnessed some experiments with it and I really think it worth the attention of the Government."[11] The idea was sound, the execution less so. Military leaders complained that the Coffee Mill Gun overheated and failed to feed ammunition and allowed gas to escape from the breech during firing, lowering the weapon's velocity. By March 1863, *Scientific American* reported that Coffee Mill Guns had "proved of no practical value" and the remaining guns were put in storage in Washington. The Union had ordered a number of these unreliable contraptions, in turn souring Lincoln on Gatling's similar invention, even though the president was typically a fan of firearm innovations.

"I assure you my invention is no 'Coffee Mill Gun,'" Gatling wrote in an 1864 letter. "The object of this invention," he went on, "is to obtain a simple, compact, durable, and efficient firearm for war purposes, to be used either in attack or defense, one that is light when compared to ordinary field artillery, that is easily transported, that may be rapidly fired, and that can be operated by few men."[12] But it was like a Coffee Mill Gun. While Gatling's brainchild would evolve over the years, at this point the fundamental mechanism was similar. It was equipped with anywhere from four to ten barrels—most of the time six—organized around a central axis featuring a magazine that loaded each barrel separately. A person could theoretically fire the barrel as fast or as slow as the hand-crank allowed. In reality, since the metal barrel experienced a tremendous heat, each barrel had an opportunity to cool as it revolved.

When it worked, it was terrifying. In an era that was not fully removed from the use of flintlock muskets, this constituted a nearly incomprehensible speed of fire. Early models of the gun could shoot 200 rounds per minute. Later models fired up to 1,000 rounds per minute. In 1870 it was reported that Gatling personally fired 1,925 rounds in 2 minutes and 30 seconds.[13] While the rapidity was certainly impressive, what also enticed those who tested the gun was its simplicity. "The mechanical construction is very simple, the workmanship is well executed, and we are of the opinion that it is not liable to get out of working order," a Union officer reported after trials of the gun at Washington Navy Yard in 1863.[14] Gatling, normally a reserved man, participated in a number of public demonstrations to impress crowds and grow more comfortable with salesmanship. "The newly invented gun of Richard J Gatling, of this city, was put through an experimental trial yesterday, with blank cartridges, at the State House square, in the presence of the Governor and a large crowd of citizens," one Indiana newspaper reported.[15] "It operates very successfully and will prove to be a weapon of war both novel and deadly."

Some Army officers bypassed the Army ordnance bureaucracy and purchased Gatling guns for their troops. The flamboyant Union general Benjamin Butler, for instance, bought twelve of them in 1864. Gatling claimed that Butler "fired them himself upon the rebels. They created great consternation."[16] A lieutenant from the 4th New Jersey Battery wrote a friend that "Gen. Butler brought one his favorite Gatling guns, which throws 200 balls per minute, in this Battery on Friday, and pointing it through one of the embrasures, began to 'turn the crank.' This drew the fire of the Rebs on us, and one captain and a private were severely wounded." In the same year, a Gatling demonstration so impressed future Democratic Party nominee for president Winfield Scott Hancock, he ordered a dozen for his corps. It was only at the end of the war that the Army officially adopted sixty Gatling guns for general use.[17]

Yet, overall, the Gatling gun saw scant action during the war—and when it did, it was near the end of the conflict. Despite all the potential and plaudits, it would take years for the gun to be ready to be adopted by the U.S. Army as a standard armament. The early models were heavy and cumbersome, mounted on old cannon carriages that were difficult to move during battle. The early models did not provide lateral fire, which often made them nearly useless. After the war, the Army created a specialized wood carriage to lighten the burden and gave it a 12-degree sweep at 1,200 yards, but the life span of the gun would be short.

Gatling was more successful selling his guns abroad to the Russians, Austrians, and Turks. Other Europeans had already taken up similar lines of thinking during the mid-1800s. The Mitrailleuse gun—*mitraille* means grapeshot—was a multibarreled rifle gun that could fire up to 444 times per minute. Invented by Captain Fafschamps and Joseph Montigny in 1851, it went through numerous iterations. By 1867, Emperor Napoleon III of France was so impressed by a display of the weapon that he made a large purchase for his army. However, its performance in battle would be lacking, as it suffered from many of the tactical problems of the Gatling gun. It was heavy and difficult to move and offered little lateral fire. It was dropped within two years. Some historians argue that the Mitrailleuse's poor showing in the Franco-Prussian War resulted in lagging interest in machine guns for many European armies. It cost them.

Many other inventors took their shot. There was the Nordenfelt gun, invented by a Swedish engineer named Helge Palmcrantz (it was financed by a banker named Thorsten Nordenfelt, thus the name), which was an updated version of the Mitrailleuse. Patented in 1873, it was also a multiple-barreled gun that was mounted laterally, and a wooden strip would feed the gun at a rate of 350 shots per minute by a hand-cranked mechanism that fed cartridges in through an overhead hopper. There was the Gardner gun, invented in 1874 by William Gardner of Toledo, Ohio, a former captain in the Union Army. The British Army took an interest after seeing the five-barreled gun fire 16,754 rounds before a failure occurred, with only 24 stoppages. When operator-induced errors were taken into account, there were only four malfunctions in 10,000 rounds fired. The Army adopted the weapon, although its introduction was delayed because of opposition from the Royal Artillery seeing some action. There were others: the Lowell Machine Gun and the Wilder Machine Gun, to name just two.

Each of them brought some specialized aspect to the table. In the end, none of them were successful, because a new gun—one that could sustain self-perpetuating fire—was about to change everything.

15

★

AN AMERICAN IN LONDON

"Whatever happens, we have got the Maxim gun, and they have not."

—Hilaire Belloc

Sir Hiram Maxim

Many years after he was already wealthy and famous, Hiram Maxim, who suffered from bronchitis his whole life, invented the first steam inhaler to mitigate his suffering. One of his critics soon accused him of wasting his time and "prostituting" his talents on "quack" devices for the sick. "From the foregoing it will be seen that it is a very creditable thing to invent a killing machine," Maxim sarcastically retorted, "and nothing less than a disgrace to invent an apparatus to prevent human suffering."[1]

The fact was that the American would one day be knighted by Queen Victoria, and it wasn't because he had helped people breathe easier. Maxim invented guns that did more than simply introduce automatic rapid fire to the battlefields of Europe. They decimated long-standing notions about courage and ingenuity and changed the contours of warfare forever. Men, no matter how brave or resourceful or talented with a gun, could now be mowed down by a contraption that took little skill or bravery to use.

In 1871, the *New York Times* published an editorial informing its readers of a new creation, one that it referred to as a "terrible automatic engine of war." Rather than lament the power of Maxim's new automatic weapons, the newspaper remarked that such an easy-to-use, perpetually killing machine would almost certainly impel world leaders to end their disputes through diplomacy rather than violent conflict.[2] "Machine guns and automatic weapons are the highest types of firearms that have been invented," the unnamed author of the editorial notes, "and indeed it seems impossible to imagine anything more likely than they to bring about a general state of peace among all nations."

It would not. Although there is no way to properly quantify just how many people Maxim's inventions would leave dead or mutilated on the muddy battlefields of Europe over the next fifty years, Edward C. Ezell, curator of armed forces history at the Smithsonian Institution, once speculated that the "numbers must be astronomical."[3] And whereas Gatling, like other gunmakers of the nineteenth century, claimed his invention was conceived for humanitarian reasons, Hiram Maxim offered no such moral justifications. In fact, years later he recalled that the reason he'd gotten into the gun trade in the first place was because an American expat had told him figuring out ways to allow European nations to kill each other was the fastest way to get rich. He was right.

Born in 1840 in Sangerville, Maine, Maxim described himself as a "chronic inventor."[4] He probably deserves to be considered one of the greatest this country has ever produced. By the age of fourteen he was apprenticing to a carriage maker, and by the age of twenty-six he obtained the first of his 271 patents in the United States. Maxim's inventions were as imaginative as they were wide-ranging. His earliest biographer describes his impressive list of patents as "multifarious devices" that would lie on a spectrum of interests, including a modern mousetrap, an automatic sprinkling system, an automatic steam-powered water pump, gas

motors, smokeless powders, flying machines, hair curling irons, gas gener-
ators, steam traps, meters, storage batteries, apparatuses for demagnetizing
watches, regulators, electric lamp fixtures, magnetoelectric machines, a
process for recovering solvents, a riveting machine, and magnetic sepa-
rators.[5] Maxim would later be fixated on flight, eventually concocting a
7,000-pound biplane in 1893 that was equipped with light steam engines
and that successfully rose from the ground, though only a few feet.

Maxim should be properly considered one of the first electrical engineers in the United States. He was hired as chief engineer of the United
States Electric Lighting Company, the main competitor of Edison, in
1878. The self-taught Maxim claimed to have beaten the famous inventor
to the lightbulb, and he produced a lamp with a high-resistance filament.
Edison's fame would constantly intrude on Maxim's own accomplishments and never stop annoying him. As Maxim once explained to his
business partner, the next time any person confused his invention with
Edison's, he "would kill him on the spot."

In 1881 his electric pressure regulator was exhibited at the Paris Exposition, where he was awarded the Légion d'Honneur. And after a falling-
out with a British lighting company, the supremely confident Maxim,
who claimed never to have smoked, imbibed, or drunk caffeine (but had
purportedly left children and marriages—sometimes more than one at the
same time—strewn wherever he went), set up shop in London in 1881
to begin work on his machine gun. "Don't do it," a London competitor
told Maxim after hearing about the inventor's plans to make an automatic
machine gun. "Thousands of men for many years have been working on
guns; there are many hundreds of failures every year; many engineers and
clever men imagine that they can make a gun, but they have never suc-
ceeded; they are all failures, so, you had better drop it and not spend a single penny on it. You don't stand a ghost of a chance in competition with
regular gunmakers. You are not a gun man. Stick to electricity."[6]

Few engineers were more "clever" than Maxim, and he knew it. The
self-perpetuated gun was certainly one that had been wrestled with for a
long time. In 1663 a British inventor known only as "Palmer" presented
a paper to the Royal Society that theorized that recoil and the gases produced by the exploding charge of a gun could reload automatically.[7] The
technology was not there—and it would not be there for another two
hundred years.

It was Maxim's Maine upbringing that ensured his creative mind was exposed to guns. Maxim points out in his autobiography that it was only around the time of his late childhood that fellow Mainers had stopped carrying their muskets to church every Sunday. By the mid-1800s, industrialization had made gun ownership far more affordable and widespread, so they simply tucked their revolvers into their belts.

It was the rifle that captured the young man's imagination. Maxim described being surprised by the "violence and the force" of the first Springfield rifles he fired in the 1870s. "Cannot this great force, at present merely an inconvenience, be harnessed to a useful purpose?" he asked himself. At that moment Maxim claims to have started exploring the idea of rigging a gun to reload using its own recoil energy. Maxim, in fact, claimed to have created rudimentary designs for such a gun as early as 1873, although it was ten years before it was built.[8] In another instance Maxim would take credit for having conceived of the idea of a hand-cranked gun in 1854 when still a young teen. Whatever the case, until 1883, he noted, "no one had ever, to my knowledge, spent a single penny or made a single experiment in the attempt to evolve an automatic gun."

Maxim's first attempt to develop an automatic weapon was one that could be fired from the shoulder. By 1884 his experiments had progressed to a point where he could build his first working model.

The Gatling gun could fire continuously, but it was heavy, became overheated, and required cranking. The Maxim gun, patented in 1883 and introduced in 1886, was a portable machine gun that needed only one barrel to fire all of its bullets automatically—theoretically, for as long as the user had ammunition. It would not be the equivalent of ten soldiers; it would be the equivalent of an army.

This kind of firearm technology was a near-inconceivable improvement. How did it work? Maxim had designed a groundbreaking toggle mechanism that, when fired, remained locked until the bullet left the gun, but when recoiling it unlocked the bolt to let the next bullet fire. Another lever, called the accelerator, ejected the used cartridge case and grabbed a new one from the fabric belt that fed it. The energy made the bolt cock the firing pin, load a new cartridge, and fire. The speed in which the gun could do this through one barrel created much heat. But Maxim solved this problem with a water jacket, a metal tube that surrounded the barrel and was filled with cool water.[9]

The trials for the new gun were widely attended by European military leaders—and extensively celebrated. "It is really wonderful," one of Britain's leading military men, Sir Garnet Wolseley, told Maxim. "You Yankees beat all creation. There seems to be no limit to what you are able to do."[10] When seeing the gun shoot 333 rounds in one minute, Kaiser Wilhelm II exclaimed in 1887, "This is the gun, there is no other." Not only was the Maxim gun consistently lighter than military leaders assumed, but it was faster, more accurate, and exceptionally durable. In one test by Italian officers, the Maxim was submerged in the sea for three days. When the gun was recovered, it was not cleaned, and yet it performed as well as it had before. One of the downsides, a few military leaders observed, was how well it worked. They saw the efficiency as a waste of cartridges, a needless expense.

It should be noted that there was another ongoing technical advance—conveniently, a Maxim patent—that would make the machine gun even more threatening. Because no matter how quickly or accurately a soldier fired his gun, no matter where he hid, his position was almost always given away by the resulting plume of smoke generated by black powder.

There had been many stabs at fixing the problem. A few years earlier a Swiss chemist named Christian Friedrich Schönbein had conceived of "guncotton"—a form of smokeless powder that was made by soaking cotton in sulfuric and nitric acids—to mitigate the problem, but although it was more potent than black powder, with little resulting smoke when fired, it was also unstable in heat, unreliable, and dangerous. In 1865 a Prussian artilleryman created a more propellant smokeless powder by mixing nitrocellulose with barium nitrate.[11] In 1885 a French chemist named Paul Vicille experimented with gelatinized nitroglycerine, which not only eliminated the black plume of smoke but left little or no residue. Then there was Alfred Nobel, the noted inventor of dynamite, who, experimenting with a safer, commercially viable form of nitroglycerin, developed a smokeless powder in 1887. As an outgrowth of those experiments, guncotton was replaced with nitroglycerin. (Maxim, as he did with most of his competitors, quarreled with Nobel, who also claimed to be the first to patent the smokeless powder.)

It was Hudson Maxim, Hiram's younger brother and employee, who would work on numerous innovations, including a delayed-action detonating fuse and the aptly named "Maximite," an explosive more robust than dynamite. A chemist by trade, Hudson refined smokeless powder and, depending on whom you listen to, concocted a far more stable recipe called, appropriately enough, "stabillite." With an inventor named R. C. Schupphaus, they developed a smokeless powder that was first adopted by the U.S. government.[12]

Despite all these advances, Maxim initially struggled at the gun trade. For one thing, there was the Nordenfelt company, one of the leading arms dealers in Europe, which dependably stole his ideas and undermined his business efforts. Perhaps tired of losing these commercial battles, Maxim joined with Nordenfelt in 1888 to form the Maxim-Nordenfelt Guns and Ammunition Company. From then on Maxim's machine would be made famous by the maneuverings of the enigmatic Sir Basil Zaharoff, a Turkish-born Greek who claimed to be a Frenchman. Zaharoff was a master salesman whose wily and often unethical tactics made Maxim wealthy.

Working with Nordenfelt, selling armaments and also things like unusable submarines to small nations, Zaharoff successfully sabotaged many of Maxim's prospects over the ensuing years.[13] (Despite Zaharoff's role in selling the machine gun worldwide, Maxim doesn't mention him once in his autobiography.) Sometimes referred to as the "merchant of death," Zaharoff armed many of the great conflicts of his day—often both sides of them. By 1896 the Maxim-Nordenfelt Guns and Ammunition Company was bought out by Vickers Ltd., and Maxim became a Vickers director. Soon the Vickers machine gun, based on Maxim's design, was standard issue in the British Army.

It was in the First Matabele War in 1893–94, which pitted the Ndebele Kingdom (in what is now Zimbabwe) against British police, that Europeans would first use the Maxim gun on an opposing army. It immediately proved exceptionally deadly. In one engagement, fifty soldiers with four Maxim guns fought off 5,000 Ndebele warriors, losing only four men. At the Battle of Omdurman in 1898, British general Herbert Kitchener annihilated the massive forces of the revolutionary Abdullah al-Taashi—also known as "the Khalifa"—within mere hours. The machine gun gave Europeans an immense technological advantage over their colonial holdings. Once these armies met others with similar technology, the outcomes were predictably horrifying.

Soon other European powers wanted their own machine guns, and Maxim would sell them to anyone who could afford them. He wryly noted that "the Russians have purchased vast numbers of Maxim guns, and it has been asserted by those who ought to know that more than half of the Japanese killed in the late war [the Russo-Japanese War of 1904–1905] were killed with the little Maxim gun."[14] The Russians adapted the gun, helpfully naming it the Pulemyot Maxima Obraztsa 1910—literally, "Maxim's Machine Gun Model of 1910." The Germans, England's future archenemies, licensed the system from Maxim in 1908 and created the Maschinengewehr 08. Thousands were produced in the nation's armor works in Spandau, and the model became the machine gun of the German army during the First World War. At the start of the war Germany had two hundred of Maxim's Maschinengewehre. By the end of the war they were producing over 14,000 every month.[15]

Lord Salisbury pointed out that Maxim was one of the "greatest benefactors the world has ever known." How so? the inventor asked. "I should say that you have prevented more men from dying of old age than any other man that ever lived," Salisbury answered.[16]

Maxim, the man from Maine who had changed the world, died of old age in November 1916, only days after the Battle of the Somme, where, bogged down in trench warfare imbued with machine guns, the French and British armies attempted to break through German lines on the Western Front. The ensuing battle, which lasted more than four and a half months, resulted in 1.5 million men perishing—many of them mowed down by the machine he invented. But it would only get bloodier. At the time of Maxim's death, the United States was debating whether to enter into the Great War, and one American was already working on the ideas that would not only render Maxim guns antiquated but define firearms to this day.

16

★

AMERICAN GENIUS

"The greatest firearms inventor the world has ever known."

—Plaque in front of the Fabrique Nationale
d'Armes de Guerre Herstal, near Liège, Belgium

John M. Browning's son Lt. Val Browning with the M1918 Browning
Automatic Rifle, 1918

On June 28, 1914, Gavrilo Princip, a Bosnian Serb, pulled a Browning pistol from his coat and shot twice, killing Archduke Franz Ferdinand of Austria and his wife, Sophie, the Duchess of Hohenberg. Before the nineteen-year-old was able to turn the gun on himself, a group of bystanders standing nearby on the Sarajevo street tackled him and grabbed the gun. The scene was mayhem. Franz Ferdinand's bloody undershirt and Princip's gun would end up in the hands of a Jesuit priest named Anton Puntigam, a close friend, who had performed the blood-soaked last rites on the archduke and his wife. Puntigam later gave the gun that "killed 8.5 million people" to the Jesuits for preservation. It is now on permanent display at the Museum of Military History in Vienna.

The repercussions of this event, well-known and massive, would embroil millions and change the world forever. Yet we would be remiss not to point out that even a bumbling assassin with a half-baked plan needed only two shots from an FN Browning Model 1910 to plunge the world into conflict. The Browning pistol, after all, was one of the most reliable and sturdy handguns ever produced. What makes the gun even more amazing is that it was one of about a dozen game-changing inventions concocted by its inventor, John Browning.

In one way or another, Browning's ideas played a part in nearly every conflict in the twentieth century as he invented and conceptualized the modern gun. The rest would merely be tinkering and streamlining his foundational ideas. Browning brought his creations to a host of gun manufacturers around the world, and those gunmakers who didn't work with him would copy him. By the end of his career, the man from Utah had a say in virtually every category of firearms in existence: rifles, pistols, shotguns, machine guns, and cannons.

Unlike many other great American gunmakers, Browning was himself the son of a gunsmith. His father, Jonathan, was born in the frontier town of Brushy Fork in Bledsoe Creek, Tennessee, the year Thomas Jefferson was sworn in for a second term as president. His family traced its roots to Captain John Browning, a soldier and explorer who had ventured to North America in 1622 and become head of one of the first families established in Virginia. Growing up in a deeply rural area, the elder Browning did not benefit from any formal schooling and, like his successful contemporary Sam Colt, experienced a childhood without much parental interference. He became fascinated by firearms at an early age and was a self-taught gunsmith by nineteen.

Like many young men of his time and place, Jonathan Browning moved with the currents of American destiny—which is to say westward. His first stop was Quincy, Mississippi, where he began taking advantage of some of the technological innovations filtering down from the Northeast's gunmakers. For example, he tested new percussion caps and attempted to invent his own multi-shot rifle. His version relied on a rectangular bar—something like a harmonica—that held five or six chambered balls with a design that featured a hammer underneath the lock, swinging upward. Although fairly popular among locals, like many of Jonathan Browning's early stabs at repeating guns, it remained cumbersome to load and was never patented.

During this period, Mormon missionaries entered Browning's shop and began converting him to the faith founded by Joseph Smith in upstate New York in the 1820s. It wasn't long before Jonathan, swayed by the group's sense of community, packed up his wife, two kids, and belongings and moved to the Mormon community in nearby Nauvoo, Illinois. There he immersed himself in the church and made himself a valuable member of the community by repairing and making guns. When Browning asked Brigham Young if he could join his coreligionists headed to fight in the brewing Mexican-American conflict, the leader of the Latter-Day Saints told him, "I need you here." Soon enough, Browning would trek to the newly minted Mormon community of Ogden, Utah Territory, in 1852.

Jonathan took the then-Mormon tradition of polygamy seriously, marrying twice more. He was no less negligent in his duty to be fruitful and multiply, siring twenty-two children. Among them was John Moses Browning, born on January 23, 1855. John often stood out as a precocious and friendly boy. In his teens, John and three of his brothers worked as "jobbers," repairing all types of items for the family business. An industrious child, John took on various jobs, including working as a tanner. By the time he had finished school at fifteen, not an uncommon age at the time, Browning had already begun constructing makeshift guns assembled from discarded parts left by the colorful pioneer characters who passed through his father's blacksmith shop.

"A man might come in with an old gun, hoping to raise a little money on it," said one of his younger brothers years later. "Pappy would take one look and shake his head. There was nothing more discouraging than Pappy looking solemn and shaking his head. 'That's a dead mule' was one of his favorite expressions. The man may have hoped to get a couple of dollars for that gun but *dead mule* would jolt him down a dollar at least. Finally, Pappy would say, 'Well, maybe I can use the hammer sometime.' If you want four bits for it, pitch it on the junk pile yonder."[1]

John created many of his early firearms from these "dead mules," as it became obvious early on that the boy had a gift. He made particularly impressive use of his father's lathe (the family would claim theirs was the largest west of the Mississippi), a tool that rotated on its axis to perform various fabrications like cutting, sanding, knurling, and drilling. It was from this tool that many of Browning's inventions sprung, including his first rifle.

At some point in his early twenties, John got his hands on a breech-loading rifle and immediately went about trying to improve the design. In 1879, the year he turned twenty-four, John married, his father passed away, and he won the first of his 130 lifetime patents. This one, a design for a single-shot breech-loading rifle, still sits in the Smithsonian Institution in Washington. It's the gun that launched his career.

"You can't get anywhere without coming to Ogden," claimed the city's chamber of commerce in the late 1800s. For those headed west, this was often true. In Ogden the transcontinental railroad tracks from the east would join tracks being laid from the west. By 1869, the first locomotive steamed into Ogden, and the citizens of the city welcomed the train with a ceremony that evening with banners that read "Hail to the Highway of the Nations! Utah Bids You Welcome." Many thousands of newcomers moved through the frontier hub. Many needed guns. Browning and his brothers met that demand as skillful and popular assemblers of rifles in the center of the railroad town. Using heavy, reliable Remington barrels, they ended up producing around five hundred firearms from 1880 to 1883, constructing them to comport with government-issue .45–70 rounds and Sharps .32–40 rounds. A number of their customers took their guns into the heart of West, where the Browning reputation grew.

By 1883, western arms dealers from major eastern manufacturers were already crisscrossing the frontier, selling their guns and replacement parts to gunsmiths and general stores. As the legend goes, one of these men, a Winchester agent named Andrew McAusland, would, during his travels, come across a rifle stamped "BROWNING BROS. OGDEN, UTAH U.S.A." with the serial number 463.[2]

Two things about the robust rifle immediately caught the man's attention. First was the serial number, which, though not too large, was large enough to indicate there was budding competition in the Utah railroad town. Second, and more concerning to McAusland, was the impressive durability of the rifle, which had obviously seen heavy use but still functioned flawlessly.[3] So concerned was McAusland, in fact, that he sent the rifle back to his bosses at Winchester. Within weeks the company's vice president, T. G. Bennett, got on a train in New Haven and made his way to Ogden, which he would describe as a "vast plain of wind and rocks completely indescribable in its unattractiveness," to purchase the rights to the gun.

A mechanical engineer himself, Bennett was initially skeptical that these brothers, most of whom were barely shaving, could have designed and produced such a potent weapon. Conversely, it did not escape John Browning's attention that an executive from one of the largest gun manufacturers in the country was beckoning. So the budding capitalist asked for $10,000 for his gun, but accepted the tidy sum of $8,000 for the right to manufacture his design.

While Winchester had been one of the dominant producers of repeating rifles, at the time they had no single-shot rifles to offer. This one would certainly do. What really excited Bennett, however, were the other ideas that came pouring out of John. When Bennett asked the inventor if he could design a lever-action repeating shotgun, Browning, never one to lack self-confidence, explained that he could and would, but that he had even better things in mind. "Yes, I've thought a good deal about a lever shotgun," Browning answered. "I think it would sell. But a slide-action gun would be easier to operate and better looking. I think I have one worked out now that's pretty good."

Browning patented his first pump model shotgun in 1887.

This would be the start of a twenty-year collaboration between the gun designer and Winchester. "When back in New Haven I had a gun of each model made up in the finest finish and sent them to the brothers. For many years and many new models, amounting to thousands of dollars, the mutual word or a handshake was sufficient to seal a bargain between the brothers and Winchester," Bennett would later recall. Browning's association with Winchester continued until 1902 and included single-shot rifles, lever-action and pump-action shotguns, and lever-action rifles.

Winchester engineers often made minor improvements to Browning's first design, calling it the Winchester Model 1885 Single Shot Rifle. The company sold the "High Wall," a big receiver that covered most of the breech block from the side and was intended for large, powerful cartridges, and the "Low Wall" version, which was intended for less powerful cartridges like the .22 as well as the pistol cartridges of the day.[4] "It can be furnished with or without set triggers," Winchester boasted, "with barrels of all ordinary lengths and weights, and for all standard cartridges; also with rifle and shotgun butt, plain or fancy wood, or with pistol grip." The company made 140,000 of these guns from 1885 to 1920. (Winchester would reintroduce the gun in 2005.) Browning's Winchester Model 1894, the first repeating rifle to use smokeless powder, went on to become one of the most popular and notable ever produced, remaining in continuous production from its inception until 2006, with sales of more than 7 million guns.

Browning was just getting started. In a two-year span from 1885 to 1887, the wunderkind invented eleven new guns for Winchester in a wide range of styles. Within a few years the company became the leading manufacturer of sporting firearms, most of its designs having sprung from Browning's fertile imagination. The gunsmith soon began making trips to Winchester's Connecticut factory, learning both the limits and possibilities of the impressive machinery used to build his guns. One Winchester executive noted that by the end of his first visit, "there was probably no machine in this plant that he could not operate." Browning was particularly taken with William Mason, one of the company's top mechanics, who would modify Browning's designs to make them compatible with mass production. Years later, when Browning had a falling-out with Winchester, the company claimed Mason as the true designer of their most popular early rifles. (Considering the slew of inventions Browning hatched after his break with the company, this claim seems highly unlikely.)

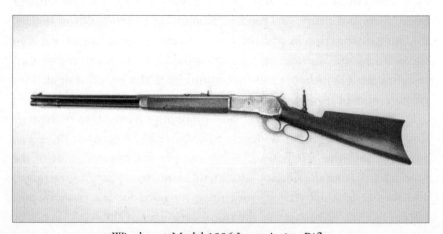

Winchester Model 1886 Lever-Action Rifle

What make this early success even more remarkable are Browning's remote western origins, his numerous personal setbacks—his second and third sons died before their first birthdays during this time—and his faith, which generated rigid hostility on the East Coast. Although there would be some debate over the depth of Browning's Mormonism—it was a topic he rarely talked about in public—there is no evidence that he was anything but a fully engaged member of his community. In 1887, at the age of thirty-two, in the midst of his burgeoning career, John "set apart" in the Mormon tradition and spent two years in Georgia proselytizing.

When John returned to Utah in 1889, the Browning brothers opened a spacious shop in Ogden, where they printed catalogs and sold everything new westerners needed to survive on the way to California or Oregon, from fishing tackle to tents to knives. But what made the shop famous were the guns. The Browning brothers purportedly owned the longest gun racks in the West. And while the brothers ran the shop, John spent most of his time inventing new models, winning two patents within two years of returning from his missionary work.

An important aspect of Browning's career to remember is that many of his greatest innovations were being created concurrently rather than sequentially. The semiautomatic shotgun, the semiautomatic handgun, and the machine gun were all percolating in his mind by 1898.

Many of these new guns, however, would not be made with Winchester. Throughout their fruitful relationship, the company bought almost every idea Browning came up with—around forty in all. Often the company purchased his designs simply to prevent them from falling into the hands of the competition. The problem with this arrangement was that Browning was increasingly annoyed that he was losing out on royalties elsewhere as Winchester shelved his ideas. His models were so successful—a conservative estimate put around two-thirds of the sporting rifles sold to Americans during this time with Winchester had been patented by Browning—the realization of his designs and the resulting royalties would have been a far more enriching and, from his perspective, fairer means of compensation.

In 1902, Browning decided to personally take a prototype automatic shotgun to show Bennett. "I want to get some action on those automatic shotguns," he told his brothers. "Those fellows down there are stalling, and we're letting the best thing I have ever made die in its sleep."[5] Browning—who had, according to his company's biography, spent more time testing this shotgun than any of his other creations—considered the gun his most innovative accomplishment to that point. It's unsurprising, then, that he demanded both production of the gun *and* royalty payments from Winchester. Bennett demurred, perhaps fearing such a precedent would be bad for the bottom line. Angered, Browning left Winchester, breaking a nearly twenty-year relationship.

Winchester's loss turned out to be a boon for competing firms. Browning not only worked with almost all of the other major firearms manufacturers but also struck out on his own with the Auto-5, the first mass-produced semiautomatic shotgun. The gun—with 12-, 16-, and 20-gauge models, still the standard today—ended up being leased to a number of manufacturers and was in continuous production until 1998, making it one of the most popular weapons in American history.

Yet it was Browning's invention of the first genuine automatic weapon that fundamentally changed the gun. As family lore has it, John formulated the idea of an automatic rifle while watching his brothers and family friends target shooting at the family's range in 1886. After witnessing the gas from one of the guns bend the grass blades, an event he had probably seen thousands of times, he blurted out to his brothers that "it might even be possible to make a fully automatic gun, one that would keep firing as long as you had ammunition." As Maxim had seen the recoil of a gun as a way to propel the next cartridge, Browning saw the wasted gas and immediately went about building a rifle that would harness it.

The next day Browning took a four-inch-square piece of five-pound iron, drilled a hole in the center to allow the bullet to pass, and placed it one inch from the muzzle. When he pulled the trigger the iron went flying across his workspace. Next he constructed a bowl-shaped steel cap with another hole in the center, but this time he connected the metal to a spring-loaded operating lever at the lock of the rifle. When the gas blew the cap, it pulled the loading lever forward, and the spring sent the lever rearward to the locked position. Another shot repeated this cycle—and so on and so on as long as he had ammunition. The energy for Browning's guns would be drawn from the breech using gas rather than blowback or recoil energy.

Browning wrote to Colt, a company founded only a few decades earlier on the exhilarating prospect of shooting five or six bullets without having to reload, that he had conceived of an automatic gas-powered machine gun that could not only be fired indefinitely but could be made cheaply enough to put in the hands of average men. Browning penned this historic dispatch with the nonchalance of a man selling office paper:

Dear Sirs:

We have just completed our new automatic machine gun & thought we would write to you to see if you are interested in that kind of a gun. We have been at work on this gun for some time & have got it in good shape. We made a small one first which shot a 44 W. C. F. chge at the rate of about 16 times per second & weight about 8 #. The one we have just completed shoots the 45 Gov't chge about 6 times per second fc with the mount weighs about 40 #. It is entirely automatic & can be made as cheaply as a common sporting rifle. If you are interested in this kind of gun we would be pleased to show you what it is & how it works as we are intending to take it down your way before long. Kindly let us hear from you in relation to it at once.

Yours Very Truly,
Browning Bros[6]

It took two years before the gun went into production, although by 1895 Browning and Colt Manufacturing quickly created prototypes that could handle various types of ammunition, including smokeless powder and popular rifle cartridges. Browning moved to Hartford for two years to supervise the manufacturing of the gun. In 1897 the Navy bought fifty Colt-made Browning machine guns, making them the first service in American history to acquire a genuine automatic machine gun. The gun saw naval action during the Spanish-American War, and the Marines brought a few along in the rescue of Europeans during the Boxer Rebellion. And just like that, the crank machine gun was rendered antiquated technology—although the Army, as is its wont to this day, kept buying less effective and expensive Gatlings for another ten years.

The American military establishment of the late 1800s and early 1900s had shown scant interest in technological advances. There was no perceptible military doctrine to utilize new weapons with effectiveness. As the century progressed, a number of American leaders would, in fact, worry about the new machine guns. They viewed their use as wasteful, undignified, and no way to fight a war. The rapid-fire gun, many thought, would strip men of their bravery and discipline. Moreover, many of the new semiautomatics were imperfect, sometimes jamming, and some leaders believed that they would cause more problems than they solved. When a number of American generals and tacticians began contemplating and forming doctrines built around rapid-fire warfare, there was big pushback from traditionalists both in the Army and out.

With some dismay, General John Pershing noted on a trip to the European front early in World War I that America's allies in Europe had "all but given up the use of the rifle." He sent a number of messages back to Washington warning that U.S. forces should remain focused on traditional weapons because "the rifle and bayonet remain the supreme weapons of the infantry soldier . . . [T]he ultimate success of the army depends on their proper use in open warfare."[7]

America, of course, still needed rifles, as they remained the standard weapon of war. In 1915 the United States military was in possession of around 600,000 Model 1903 Springfield bolt-action rifles and another 160,000 antiquated Norwegian Krags they had purchased years earlier. Once it looked like America might enter the war, the United States started manufacturing the M1917 Enfield, the "American Enfield," a knockoff of the British service rifle. This choice was made out of convenience and necessity, as a number of the American gun manufacturers were already contracted to produce weapons for their UK allies. The gun was altered to take American .30-06 Springfield ammunition. The Ordnance Department picked Winchester and Remington, and they made more than 2 million of these rifles from 1917 to 1918. More than half of these guns were manufactured at the Eddystone Rifle Works in Eddystone, Pennsylvania. (The factory is sometimes identified as an independent company, but it was actually a holding of Remington.) The Eddystone factory made 5,000 rifles a day during the war, employing as many as 10,000 people, though some of these employees were still fulfilling the contracts for arms and ammunition they had gotten from the British.[8]

The first modern war required modern weapons. In the summer of 1917 the future Army chief of staff and colonel Charles Pelot Summerall warned that artillery and rapid-fire guns were the only way to break the stalemate in Europe. That same summer a rapid-fire expert from the Army traveled to France to review the lines and wrote to Pershing that "the day of the rifleman is done. He was a good horse while he lasted, but his day is over."

These men were often dismissed as scaremongers. So it is unsurprising that by the time the United States entered World War I American soldiers were armed with antiquated machine guns, too small, too slow, and too rickety. Due to this lack of preparedness, the 14,000 U.S. Expeditionary Corps troops who landed in Europe in the summer of 1917 to fight the Central Powers were initially forced to accept donated French- and English-made models that were, in most cases, no more formidable or reliable than 1895 Colt-Browning machine guns. Oftentimes the Americans were without the right ammunition.

After contentious debate in Washington over the future of the military, a decision was made to move forward with rearmament. A call was put out to gunmakers to help fix the problem. As it happened, John Browning had been working on two new military machine guns since 1910. Both were ready by the time the U.S. Army Ordnance Department called in February 1917. One was a water-cooled machine gun and the other a shoulder-fired automatic rifle known as the Browning Machine Rifle, nicknamed the "potato digger." Browning's first official exhibition of these guns on the outskirts of Washington, DC, drew more than three hundred people, including a number of senators, congressmen, and various dignitaries from Great Britain, France, and Belgium. All went away awestruck by the jaw-dropping exhibition.

Colonel George Morgan Chinn, in a report on the history of the machine gun prepared for the Navy Department Bureau of Ordnance, noted that those who watched were blown away (in a manner of speaking) by the firepower and speed of the weapons, animated by the prospect that "a hundred men advancing with these weapons firing full automatic would literally sweep an enemy out of the way."[9] This was far too optimistic in the age of trench warfare, yet the improvement over the weapons they now had was palpable even in a field neighboring America's capital.

What excited military men most was the prospect of a gun offering "walking fire," which, as it sounds, is a military tactic of suppressive fire by infantry while moving forward. Browning would deliver. For the first time an individual American soldier could pick up and carry an automatic rifle. The M1918 Browning Automatic Rifle, called the BAR, could be carried while continuously firing twenty shots in 2.5 seconds. It could shoot nearly five hundred rounds per minute. In fact, after some modification, Browning himself took a new prototype for testing to the Springfield Armory and shot the gun at six hundred rounds per minute with not a single misfire or broken component in 40,000 shots fired. "The Colt gun is exceedingly simple in construction, and has not more than one hundred separate parts, a surprisingly small number, considering the type. It has been designed with great care and with due attention to the often conflicting requirements of lightness and strength, so that with a maximum weight of 10 pounds no part, with the single exception of the extractor, has been broken in the course of a number of very severe tests," noted the final report.[10] The weapon would be used by the American armed forces until the United States began phasing them out after the Korean War.

Browning, though always an astute businessman, saw his involvement in war as a patriotic duty. In the fall of 1917, the U.S. government negotiated a long-term contract with Browning. As his brother Matthew remembers the meeting, the government likely made an offer assuming there would be negotiations. "I supposed that John would ask for a little time to think things over and get my opinion," his brother recalled later. "But without hesitating a second, he said, 'Major, if that suits Uncle Sam, it's all right with me.'"[11] Now, a reader might be skeptical about this selfless portrayal of the gunmaker. Certainly Browning would not come out of the agreement any poorer. And, really, whom was he going to sell machine guns to if not to the military? But any delay in negotiations, though it might have made Browning richer, could have cost lives.

From the Allied perspective, Browning's gun was a lifesaver. No one in America at the time had either the technological know-how or the infrastructure to pull it off. One of the guns used by U.S. forces was the M1911. The gun's history went back to 1896, when Browning approached Colt's Manufacturing Company (formerly Colt's Patent Fire Arms Manufacturing Company) about making four semiautomatic pistols to be sold in the United States. For the European markets, Browning would start a lifelong relationship with Fabrique Nationale, located in Liège, a city with easy access to iron, coal, and lumber that had been a leading gun center in Europe since the Middle Ages. In the coming years Browning quite often visited the firm, which employed one of his sons. The Belgians were immediately taken by the man they called "Le Maître" ("the Master"). "By reputation and appearance he astonished the people of Liège," noted one contemporaneous account. "He was exceptionally tall and lean, and his head extraordinarily shiny. The features of his face, as sharp and immovable as those of a medal, seemed animated only by his regard."

Browning's patents evolved into the Model 1900, the Model 1903, the Model 1910, and the Colt Model 1911, which would possess numerous components that are still widely used in semiautomatic pistols—including, most recognizably, the detachable magazines that could be loaded in the butts of the guns. When the U.S. Army put the gun to its standard 6,000-shot test (allowing cooling every 100 rounds and cleaning every 1,000), it accomplished the task without a single failure of any kind. Its descendants would be the standard-issue sidearm of the United States armed forces from 1911 to 1986; in other words, American soldiers holstered the gun from before World War I nearly to the end of the Cold War. It would be widely embraced by American law enforcement and become a bestseller in the civilian marketplace. Colt produced more than 2.6 million military pistols based on the 1911 design and another 400,000 for civilians. All told, nearly 5 million were manufactured by various gunmakers. The design is still popular today.

The first Browning semiautomatic pistol appeared in Europe in 1899, and there would be more than 500,000 of them produced on the continent by the time Gavrilo Princip got his hands on one. The assassin's pistol was a .38-caliber, which turned out to be a problem for the American military. First used by the United States during the Philippine insurrection in 1901, the Army had gripes about the stopping power of the new gun. In one such account, a man named Antonio Caspi attempted to escape from an American prison on the island of Samar. According to the Army, Caspi "was shot four times at close range in a hand-to-hand encounter by a .38 caliber Colt's revolver loaded with U.S. Army regulation ammunition. He was finally stunned by a blow on the forehead from the butt-end of a Springfield carbine."[12] A West Point graduate named John T. Thompson, soon to invent the tommy gun, and Louis Anatole La Garde, a major in the Medical Corps, were tasked to study the inefficiencies of the .38 revolver round and figure out what caliber worked best. Thompson would shoot various calibers into animals and cadavers, while La Garde studied their medical effects. The test results, later deemed highly unscientific, were embraced by the Army. So Browning added a .45 pistol. He also added a grip frame that was made larger and sturdier, and the magazine capacity was increased from five to seven.

The 1911, like the Peacemaker or the Kentucky rifle, would take on legendary status. During World War I its reputation was buttressed by stories of American bravery. Most famous was the case of Alvin Cullum York, better known as Sergeant York, one of the most decorated American soldiers of the conflict. York famously received a Medal of Honor for leading an attack on a German machine-gun nest, killing at least 25 enemy soldiers and capturing 132. York, a Tennessean whose blacksmith father still hunted with a flintlock rifle, tamed a wild streak by joining the Church of Christ in Christian Union in his late teens. A pacifist, York petitioned for conscientious objector status but was denied. "Don't Want to Fight" was his stated reason.

York had excelled at sharpshooting contests in his home county, and once convinced that his destiny was to beat the Germans, he took to it with a single-minded gusto that few would match. In October 1918, York found himself in command of his unit after an ambush killed two of his commanding officers. He helped fight off more than a hundred Germans. After his Springfield rifle was exhausted of ammunition, York claimed to have repelled a German bayonet charge of six soldiers with nothing more than his 1911 pistol. "The American fired all of the rifle ammunition clips on the front of his belt and then three complete clips from his automatic pistol," the affidavit read. "In days past he won many a turkey shoot in the Tennessee mountains and it is believed that he wasted no ammunition on this day."[13] An investigator found twenty-three .45 rounds fired from a Colt 1911 handgun on the site.

Other well-known guns would soon follow.

General John Pershing, who had quickly come around to seeing the usefulness of rapid-fire guns, asked Browning to build an even more dynamic machine gun to deal with armored combat vehicles: Could Browning get to work inventing a machine gun that fired .50-caliber rounds? "Well," Browning is said to have answered, "the cartridge sounds pretty good, to start. As for the gun—you make up some cartridges, and we'll do some shooting."

His invention, completed in 1918, would go on to be nicknamed the

"Ma Deuce." It was too late to be used in World War I, but its progeny became part of the American armory for many decades as well. In tests, the gun fired 877 .50-caliber rounds without any malfunctions. When asked by the press how he had developed such an incredibly powerful gun, Browning replied, "One drop of genius in a barrel of sweat wrought this miracle."

Both the .30- and .50-caliber guns evolved and were widely used as antiaircraft and defensive guns at the outbreak of World War II. "Students of warfare are in general agreement that the most far-reaching single military decision made in the 20th Century was when a small group of British officers, shortly before World War II, decided to mount ten caliber .303 Brownings on their Hurricane Fighters," wrote the gun historian Colonel George Morgan Chinn. "This single act undoubtedly brought about the turning point of the war."

"I wonder from time to time," Browning is said to have confessed to one of his sons in his later years, "whether we are headed in the right direction. For instance, we are making guns that shoot farther, harder and calling it progress. If just getting farther and faster from your starting place is progress, I suppose the meaning we usually give the word is correct. But if we limit the meaning to movement toward a destination where the most pleasure and satisfaction are to be found, then this progress we're bragging about is just crazy, blind racing past the things we are looking for—and haven't the sense to recognize. And in the matter of guns that makes me crazier than most."[14]

Browning may have been conflicted about his chosen vocation in ways that Hiram Maxim and others would never be, but move forward he did. Perpetually. Many of the great American gunmakers, including Sam Colt, argued that the success of their inventions helped diminish violence among men by heightening and then equalizing their power. While this may have been true for the average person on the western plains or the immigrant living in a bustling city, the twentieth century would awaken political and ideological forces that brought death on a massive scale, escalating the authority and importance of firearms.

In late 1926, Browning died—predictably, working on the designs for a 9-millimeter semiautomatic pistol at the bench of his son Val at the

Fabrique Nationale offices. The gun he was working on would be finished by Belgian designers and finally put into production in 1935. Just as unsurprisingly, as with most of his guns, his 9-millimeter semiautomatic pistol would be popular for decades to come. Browning had created the template for the twentieth century. From now on, American inventors took his ideas and ran with them.

17

★

THE CHICAGO TYPEWRITER

"There is enough business for all of us without killing each other like animals in the street. I don't want to die in the street punctured by machine-gun fire."[1]

—Al Capone

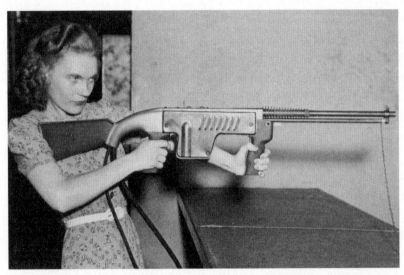

Amusements—Games and Rides—Woman shooting tommy gun

Perhaps no gun undermined the intentions of its inventor quite like the "tommy gun." And while John Browning's machine gun was the catalyst for dramatic changes in warfare, none of his weapons captured the popular imagination of the men and women at home like the Thompson submachine gun.

Aesthetically, the gun's drum magazines forever came to represent the crime, mayhem, and death of the crime-ridden Depression era. The gun was mythologized, romanticized, and misunderstood. In many ways its celebrity changed the way the average American thought about guns and the way their government conducted domestic "gun policy"—a concept they would not have understood before the 1930s. Certainly, few guns had more of an impact on the modern laws governing firearms in the twentieth century.

The tommy gun's inventor, John T. Thompson, personified many traits of nineteenth-century American entrepreneurship—passion, creativity, and practicality—but his invention was firmly entrenched in the twentieth century. It was after witnessing the force of the Gatling gun during the Spanish-American War in 1898 that Thompson, an Army man, contemplated the damage a lighter automatic gun could inflict. He wasn't the first to envision this kind of weapon, as Browning would be the first to get there. The reliance on trench warfare during the First World War had substantially changed military thinking about tactics, inducing Thompson to experiment with small, fully automatic arms—this time with an eye toward designing a weapon that troops could handle as they cleared an enemy position. They needed something lighter than any Browning gun. "We shall put aside the rifle for now and instead build a little machine gun. A one-man, hand held [sic] machine gun. A trench broom!"he told his fellow engineers. [2]

Isaac Newton Lewis, one of America's unheralded weapon makers, had been a military man as well, graduating from West Point in 1884. As an artillery officer, his initial forays into invention were modern ranging systems, rapid-firing field guns, and gas-propelled torpedoes—although, like his namesake, Lewis had wide-ranging interests in invention and mechanics and would go on to patent numerous ideas, including one of the first car-lighting systems. After the Philippine-American War, Lewis prepared a report on modernization of the United States' antiquated artillery doctrine and weaponry. He traveled to Europe to study the latest armaments and methods. What he witnessed transformed him into a sharp critic of the Army Ordnance Department—which, if perhaps not completely unrelated, had been standing in the way of the development of many of his ideas.

Frustration led Lewis not only to retire from the Army in 1913 but to leave the United States completely and move to Liège to begin manufacturing his own guns, including a light machine gun. Once the war broke out, Lewis relocated his operations to Birmingham, England, where he produced more than 100,000 "Lewis guns" for the British armed forces. A gas-operated lightweight automatic rifle that featured a top-mounted pan magazine, the Lewis gun became a vital weapon for the British during the First World War. More importantly, unlike most machine guns of the time, it did not have a water cooling system, which made the guns heavier and unwieldy, but rather drew in air to operate a mini cooling system. By 1916, 40,000 were in use with Allied forces.[3]

Thompson knew of the Lewis gun but wanted to make something even easier for soldiers to use. Convinced that automatic rifles were the future, he also soon became frustrated by the Army's insistence on single-shot rifles and retired to take a job as chief engineer of Remington Arms and manage their plant in Eddystone, Pennsylvania, then the largest in the world. By 1916 he was confident enough in his ideas to form his own engineering company, Auto-Ordnance, in Cleveland, Ohio. (He would briefly return to Springfield when America entered the war, earning a Distinguished Service Medal.)

The gun he invented packed a punch like no other light gun ever had up to that point. It hinged on the ideas of a "Blish lock."[4] The lock had been invented years earlier by John Bell Blish, a career naval officer, who had concocted a way of rapid-firing large artillery on ships a decade earlier. Although he never properly understood the physics of his invention, Blish had come to the conclusion that dissimilar metals tended to stick to each other, and he used the static friction to create a lock that discharged a spent shell and reloaded the gun in a single motion. Later, engineers would find simpler and more effective ways to create this action.

By the summer of 1918, the first prototypes of the Thompson gun, the fittingly christened "Annihilator Mark I," were being prepared for Allied troops. The delivery date on the manifest at New York Harbor read November 11, which, as luck would have it for most of the world, turned out to be the day the armistice was signed in Europe.

The guns that would have been shipped to Allied troops weighed a mere twelve pounds when fully loaded and fired like the heavier machine guns that had dominated the European theater of war. It was, as Thompson saw it, ideal for close-quarter fighting and sweeping trenches. It was also simple and elegantly constructed from limited parts that could be easily stripped down and reassembled. It could empty 20-round magazines in less than a second. Or, if one desired, it could be fitted with drums that contained 50 to 100 rounds. It used rifle-size ammunition rather than the larger calibers of bigger guns, it would be popularly called a "submachine" gun.

Because the Thompson gun had not been combat-tested, the Army remained skeptical regarding its effectiveness after the war. Thompson continued to retool the gun and attempt to sell it to police forces starting in 1919. The Colt company wanted to purchase the company for the rights to produce the gun. While Thompson resisted, he did license Colt to make 15,000 of them. Even with the efforts of Colt's impressive sales team, few bought the gun, priced at $220 (which did not include the drum magazine, which was another $20), apart from some police in larger cities. For one, a man could buy a reliable automatic pistol for a fraction of the cost. Few people needed that sort of firepower.

Early sales were sparse, and when they came to fruition, often they were from unlikely sources. One small order came from the U.S. Postal Service, one from the Marine Corps (for use by troops in the Latin American "banana wars" of the 1920s), one from the U.S. Coast Guard, and one from the Irish Republican Army. The first time the gun was used in a combat setting was in June 1921 in Dublin when an IRA member fired at British soldiers at a train station. Michael Collins, the leader of Irish independence, was impressed by the practicality of the gun. The IRA found it rather useful in surprise attacks and hit-and-runs, since the butt could be removed and the gun could be hidden under trench coats. Sympathetic Irish-Americans hatched a plan to buy hundreds and ship them to Collins. After two years of fund-raising they were able to make a large purchase, but the cargo was raided by U.S. Customs agents and the guns were impounded.

As the company, now run by John's son Marcellus, continued to struggle into the 1920s, it would again make a push to find civilian uses for the imposing gun. The company ran ads in magazines depicting the Thompson submachine gun as a perfect tool to guard farms and ranches, and even as a means of home protection. Unless a small army was invading your house, however, the tommy gun was an extravagance in both cost and potency. It was like selling a jet plane to a commuter. Most ordinary people simply didn't need it. Sales lagged.

Unordinary citizens, on the other hand, might see the possibilities. The capability of such a gun, it turns out, appealed to one particular set of discerning shopper, and their interest in the weapon portended consequences that would far outlast the tommy gun.

Many new guns that had come back from World War I ended up in civilian hands—and often in the hands of criminals. By the late 1920s, like other American business interests, gangsters began modernizing, organizing, and expanding their operations. The coming of Prohibition, which would be in effect from 1920 to 1933, only exacerbated the problem faced in larger urban areas by outgunned police forces, who typically had nothing more than shotguns and Colt revolvers.

By the mid-1920s, gang warfare became an everyday reality in the streets of Chicago. The wars were complex and rife with intrigue, but basically pitted the predominantly Irish gangsters from the North Side against the predominantly Italian South Siders, led by the infamous Al Capone. During what became known as the Beer Wars of the 1920s, turf disputes between rival gangs over gambling, prostitution, and liquor ratcheted up, and soon machine guns began making their appearance. It was during this time that the tommy gun earned a slew of nicknames from the inventive newspaper scribes of that era: "Chicago Typewriter," "Chicago Piano," "Chicago Style," "Chicago Organ Grinder," and so on.

In truth, the first gangland attacks using tommy guns were dramatic in their scope but often produced no fatalities. Perhaps gangsters meant to use the gun only as intimidation, or perhaps the thugs had yet to learn how to properly use the muscular new gun. (The latter would not have been surprising. Even soldiers had trouble aiming the Thompson because of the gun's "muzzle climb," which was the force of the recoil that raised the barrel every time it was fired.)

One infamous event transpired on September 20, 1926, when North Siders set out to avenge the assassination of their boss, Dion O'Banion. Capone, eating at the Hawthorne Inn, one of many hotels he owned in the suburb of Cicero, heard machine-gun fire open up from a car and hit the floor. Once the noise subsided, the boss of the Chicago Outfit attempted to go outside to get a glimpse of the would-be assailants as they were driving away. But the initial shooting was merely a trap meant to lure the crime boss out of the restaurant and to his death. Seven more cars drove by, teeming with gangland notables like George "Bugs" Moran, Vincent "the Schemer" Drucci, and Hymie Weiss, and they riddled the hotel with 1,000 rounds of machine-gun fire.

There wasn't a single fatality.

Soon the gangsters would improve their aim. A month later, Weiss (a Pole whose real name was Henry Wojciechowski) was ambushed on the streets of Chicago when Capone's men perched on a second-story window and unloaded their Thompson machine guns and a shotgun, killing him and another man and riddling a Catholic church with bullets. When he died, Chicago papers noted that Weiss had been carrying a .45-caliber automatic, rosary beads, and more than $5,000 in cash.

Thompson exerted much manpower and energy attempting to save the company's image from the gangsters. After the 1926 machine-gun assassination of Illinois assistant state's attorney William H. McSwiggin, Marcellus Thompson traveled to Chicago to personally attempt to track down the seller of the tommy gun. "We designed the gun for law enforcement and military usage," Marcellus told Chicago reporters. "I feel very sorry now to learn that one of them is in the hands of the lawless element. Its killing power is terrible."[5] The serial number, of course, had been filed off the discarded gun, but by this point the company was including a second secret serial number location that could be accessed only if the gun was disassembled. Marcellus drove to the North Side hardware store where the gun had been sold to mobsters. "If I tell you, I'll die," the horrified clerk reportedly explained to police later. "I sold these fellows one gun and then they said they'd kill me if I didn't get the others. Then, when they got them, they swore they'd take me for a ride if I ever squawked about them."[6] This scene played out many times over the coming years, although the gangsters became increasingly sophisticated in the smuggling of weapons.

The violence and potency of the tommy gun would be best remembered in the bloody massacre of Irish mobsters on Valentine's Day, 1929. Five members of Bugs Moran's gang and an associate were lured into a garage by gangsters posing as police officers. All of these men and a garage worker were lined up and then executed by at least two tommy guns that pumped more than seventy rounds into them. The murders became worldwide news.

It is commonly asserted that the Saint Valentine's Day Massacre immediately galvanized the American public to finally do something about gangsterism and the spread of machine-gun violence. This isn't exactly right. It is fairer to contend that the murders galvanized a cultural movement that still permeates our films and books. The truth of the matter is that the Chicago homicide rate per 100,000 residents was 9.2 in 1910 and rose, at its peak, to 14.6 in the 1930s.[7] (In the 1990s, the rate would hit 33 per 100,000 residents.) Much as they had exploited the western outlaws and their guns, movies served to glorify and mythologize the gangster and his tools.

It is a strange contradiction of American life that one could be horrified and yet consumed with the life of violent men. Yet, during the Depression, the tommy gun—without any "muzzle lift"—appeared in a slew of movies that featured criminal antiheroes, often portrayed as modern-day Robin Hoods blazing away. The silent movie *Underworld*, written by former Chicago crime reporter Ben Hecht, who claimed to have "haunted whorehouses, police stations, courtrooms, theater stages, jails, saloons, slums, madhouses, fires, murders, riots, banquet halls, and bookshops" of the city, covered the emergence of gangsters in the early 1920s. *Little Caesar* would be the first great gangster talkie in 1931, and an immediate hit. It made Edward G. Robinson a star and became a template for 1930s-era mobsters for a century to come. Other movies like *Scarface* starring Paul Muni and *The Public Enemy* starring James Cagney enjoyed similar success. All of these movies featured tommy guns. Soon there were dozens of copycat films saturating the market, and Americans loved it. Like Colts and Remingtons in western shoot-outs, tommy guns unloaded a hundredfold more on the silver screen than in real life. "No motion picture genre . . . was more incendiary than the gangster film; neither preachment yarns nor vice films so outraged the moral guardians or unnerved the city fathers as the high-caliber scenarios that made screen heroes out of stone killers," one film historian has noted.[8]

In truth, the tommy gun was rarely used even by the mob in Chicago. It was unnecessarily destructive, would bring unneeded attention, and was, even for the mob, rather expensive. The gun could cost up to $2,000 on the black market. Although the Chicago gangland wars are embedded in the nation's consciousness, it was the freelance violence of the tommy gun–wielding gangs that roamed the Midwest and elsewhere that had a far broader impact on law enforcement, which was especially shocked by the contemporary linking of motorized criminality with the machine gun.

It was men like James "Killer" Cunniffe, who in 1926 robbed a postal

196 ★   DAVID HARSANYI

office truck in Elizabeth, New Jersey, in the middle of the day, killing two and escaping with the impressive sum of $161,000, who really scared Americans.[9] The robbery was a national story, and experts quickly concluded that Cunniffe could never have pulled off such a daring criminal act without a tommy gun in his hands. "Killer" never had the chance to enjoy his bounty, as he was murdered in an argument with a gangland associate named William "Ice Wagon" Crowley. But how long before other small-time Depression-era criminals would follow his lead? newspapers wondered. The answer was not long at all.

In 1932, a gunman named Vincent "Mad Dog" Coll allegedly (and accidentally) shot four young children with a tommy gun, killing one five-year-old, in a failed kidnapping attempt in Manhattan. On October 14, 1933, the swaggering outlaw John Dillinger and his gang walked into the police headquarters of the small Indiana town of Auburn, locked up the officer on duty, and swiped all the department weapons, which included a Thompson submachine gun. The gang went on to murder three policemen using Thompsons in the coming year. The attractive Bonnie Parker (who, though present, rarely actively participated in criminality despite legend) and Clyde Barrow took it further, raiding National Guard armories across the Midwest, grabbing not only tommy guns but even a Browning automatic rifle. When thirteen officers in armored cars and armed with Thompson machine guns surrounded the gang near Kansas City, Missouri, they were outgunned by the Barrow gang's BAR. Since the guns could penetrate trees and cars, the scene resembled a minor military engagement.

Pretty Boy Floyd was particularly fond of the submachine gun, removing the front grip and butt stock and carrying it as a pistol. Baby Face Nelson died in a shoot-out involving tommy guns that claimed the lives of two FBI agents. In July 1933, "Machine Gun" Kelly (his real name was George Kelly Barnes) and his gang busted into the Oklahoma City mansion of oil tycoon Charles Urschel in a kidnapping plot. Kelly died in Leavenworth on his fifty-ninth birthday, but most public enemies met more gruesome fates.

To combat the growing violence, FBI director J. Edgar Hoover soon approved the use of Thompson submachine guns. Melvin Purvis, head of the Chicago office, insisted that every officer in his department qualify in the gun. Hoover tapped top FBI agents, national police department heads, and other experts to discuss how to combat the rising criminal behavior. In a 1934 "Memorandum for the Director," Hoover's Executive Committee considered arms that should be bought and "obtained for all purposes and should be supplied in appropriate quantities to all field offices . . ."[10] One of the guns was the Thompson submachine gun.

Marcellus Thompson's pitch to police departments had been simple. His gun was so formidable that criminals would be awed and unwilling to face the odds. It would, he argued, be the only way to effectively stop the rise of motorized criminality. The car might have been invented in Europe in the 1800s, but by the 1920s Henry Ford and the Big Three had innovated the mass-production techniques first used by gunmakers in the last century. By 1913 the United States produced some 485,000 of the world's total of 606,124 motor vehicles.[11] Everything had gotten faster, and that included criminality.

In 1922, Thompson put on an exhibition for police departments in Tenafly, New Jersey (outside New York City), in which tommy guns destroyed cars to demonstrate the stopping power of his gun. There was, of course, the small matter of practicality. Would police organizations now be equipped with military-grade weapons? Using them against civilians would undermine norms that had existed for hundreds of years. This debate resumed later. For now, a mix of genuine criminal violence and a good dose of scaremongering gave police the justification to use the gun. As we'll see later on, President Roosevelt claimed in 1934 that he was pushing the first of his two gun control bills because "Federal men are constantly facing machine-gun fire in the pursuit of gangsters."[12]

Thompson would see some success, although not in the way he had hoped. Law enforcement agencies armed themselves with the Thompson, which *Time* magazine in 1939 described as "the deadliest weapon, pound for pound, ever devised by man." Murder rates fell to historic lows by the early 1940s. By then the 1930s spasm of violence had begun to change the way many Americans thought about guns. By 1935, Auto-Ordnance was still in possession of around 4,000 of the initial order of 15,000 the United States Army had ordered at the end of World War I. Thompson's company was in near bankruptcy, its gun synonymous with crime. Thompson wrote, "I want to pay more attention now to saving human life than destroying it. May the deadly [Thompson submachine gun] only 'speak' for God and Country. It has worried me that the gun has been so *stolen* by evil men & used for purposes outside our motto, 'On the side of law and order.' "[13]

It wasn't until November 1939, when Great Britain was already at war with Germany, that large orders for the gun saved the company from bankruptcy and gangsters. The company opened a new factory in Connecticut Valley but had trouble keeping up with orders, licensing the gun to other manufacturers. The British became big believers in the tommy gun. Winston Churchill was famously photographed in a pinstriped suit and smoking a cigar while holding a short-barreled Thompson submachine gun during an inspection of invasion defenses near Hartlepool in July 1940. The Americans, too, noticed how modernization had made warfare kinetic. By this time the Germans had their own submachine guns made by Maschinenpistole. Only weeks after John Thompson passed away in 1940—his son Marcellus had died the year before from complications of a stroke—the U.S. government placed the largest orders on record for the tommy gun.

By 1942 the company had a new design that jettisoned the needlessly complex and expensive Blish lock, dropping the price from around $200 a gun to around $44. Nearly 2 million of these models were produced. The first American paratroopers were given Thompsons—and the gun went on to be used in nearly all American operations and by all services. Although the company continued to make drum magazines with 100 rounds, more soldiers carried 20-round rectangular magazines that were easy to load and carry. Unlike the criminals of the 1930s, Allied troops learned that controlled bursts of three shots were more effective than spraying entire areas with bullets. However, these soldiers would soon find themselves part of the world's largest and most powerful army. They would need guns to suit their new status.

18

★

GREAT ARSENAL OF DEMOCRACY

"In war, you win or lose, live or die—and the difference is just an eyelash."[1]

—Douglas MacArthur

You Can't Afford to Miss Either!

The young man had been infatuated with guns his entire life. By the time the First World War had broken out in Europe, the soft-spoken eighteen-year-old John Cantius Garand found himself toiling away on the Lower East Side of Manhattan in a micrometer plant. And when he wasn't reading about the newest developments in firearm technology, he was spending his spare time in the popular Coney Island and Times Square shooting booths. "One Saturday, when he was finding

out about rifles by using Coney Island as a laboratory, he shot at every target there. By nightfall, he had set up an all-time high for himself, not only
in score but in expense as well," one later profile of Garand would remark.
"He had spent $100 at the galleries in a single day!"[2]

Garand was born on New Year's Day, 1888, to a farmer in the small
town of Saint-Rémi, Québec, the seventh of eleven children. The family
settled in Connecticut in 1898. Another autodidact, Garand quit his formal education at the age of eleven to begin working in a textile mill, where
he learned everything there was about the machines that buzzed on the
floor he was tasked to sweep. When he was fourteen, Garand invented a
new jackscrew and by seventeen he was a sought-after toolmaker working
in Rhode Island before ending up in a successful if tedious manufacturing
job in downtown New York.

It was during this time that the engineer ran across a newspaper account of John Browning's development of machine guns. Apparently, to
the consternation of some in the military brass, one of Browning's new
guns had malfunctioned at a high rate. Although Garand could only de-
duce the specific technical problems in play, the article jolted the hobbyist's mind. He sat down in his apartment that day and began designing a
new automatic-firing lock to fix the problem and mailed his proposal to
the Navy's Bureau of Ordnance.

A few months later, the impressed brass invited the unknown engineer
to a conference in Washington. No doubt surprised by this slender figure
who looked to still be a teenager, the Navy soon hired Garand to consult
the government on small arms. By 1919, Garand, who would gain U.S.
citizenship in 1920, was offered a job at the Springfield Armory, which remained his professional home until retirement in 1953. Lacking the flare
or entrepreneurial instincts of America's most well-known gunmakers, the
dutiful civil service employee worked his way up to become chief ordnance designer and de facto head of the government armory over his first
decade in Springfield. It was there that he created the gun that became the
standard service rifle of the U.S. military during World War II.[3]

During his early years at Springfield, Garand was one of the few
champions of a military-grade semiautomatic rifle. Until the mid-1930s,
it was generally assumed that an automatic rifle could be utilized only
as a complementary weapon on the battlefield. Moreover, most of the

government's gunmakers thought it unrealistic to expect that such a gun could fire the potent ammunition the high command demanded.

At first it seemed that they might be right. Tests did not initially go well for Garand's new gun, although his luck began to change in 1932 when Army Chief of Staff General Douglas MacArthur insisted that any new standard rifle had to be a U.S. standard .30-caliber to match the ammunition used in the Browning automatic rifle and the Springfield. As luck would have it, Garand's competitors were working with different ammunition.

Garand spent the next decade perfecting his clip-fed, gas-operated semiautomatic rifle. The idea, patented in 1934, allowed a soldier with basic training to fire the gun at least three times faster than the .30-caliber bolt-action Springfield standard rifle the infantry had carried for over three decades. By the mid-1930s the Garand was easily outperforming its main competitor, the Pedersen rifle, in field tests, both because of its simplicity and its accuracy. "A man who has never seen the rifle can be taught its stripping and assembling within a few minutes," one ordnance tester concluded.[4] By the end of that year, plans were in place to begin manufacturing them. In January 1936, the Army officially adopted the rifle, and was soon followed by the Navy and Marines.

By the time the Army made the next switch to the M14 in 1957, it had handed out nearly 6 million M1 Garands.

Garand was surely listening to the radio on December 29, 1940, when President Franklin Roosevelt, during one of his most famous fireside chats, implored the American people to aid in the armament of Allied forces battling the Nazis in Europe. During his radio address, the president asked the nation to transform itself into "the great arsenal of democracy." The United States was, in effect, already entangled in the immense conflict against fascism. For now, it was not a matter of supplying combatants but rather the equipment to arm those who were already fighting, the president said. "The people of Europe who are defending themselves do not ask us to do their fighting," Roosevelt explained. "They ask us for the implements of war, the planes, the tanks, the guns, the freighters which will enable them to fight for their liberty and for our security."

Roosevelt went on to mention "guns" three more times in his short talk with the American people. Within a few months Congress passed the

Lend-Lease Act, allowing the United States to send implements of war to "the government of any country whose defense the President deems vital to the defense of the United States." The most well-known were the then-fraught British, but others like the Soviet Union and China also benefited greatly before it was over. The United States ended up sending $50 billion worth of material to thirty-five nations in the war effort. America, in fact, has never stopped offering foreign aid to this day.

The act was heavily debated at the time. Noninterventionists argued that the change in policy would almost surely pull the United States into the fighting. Others contended that a nation that was itself in the process of ramping up its military might could not afford to worry about producing for others. On the industrial front, critics had little to concern themselves about. The rapid and total mobilization of the manufacturing sector of the United States was an extraordinary act of national muscle flexing. Nothing like it had ever been witnessed—and America has never relinquished its place as the world's military leader.

To put this effort in some perspective, consider that the United States had virtually no war industry in 1939 and only 334,473 men serving in the armed forces. The general staff had concluded in a 1936 report that the nation would struggle to supply "airplanes, tanks, combat cars, scout cars, antiaircraft guns, searchlights, antiaircraft fire control equipment, [and] .50 caliber machine guns" for an army of even 100,000 men.[5] Yet by the middle of the war, the Willow Run plant built by Ford in Michigan was pumping out one B-24 heavy bomber per hour. By the time the war ended, more than 13 million of Garand's inventions would be produced.

When it came to small arms, thousands of men and women made this mass armament possible, but one man's ideas were its driving force. By the end of the war, Garand's gun, the M1, had been shot by more Americans than any other firearm in history. Almost as important as the gun's durability and accuracy were the speed and precision with which it could be manufactured. One of the first jobs Garand tackled when he was hired by the government was to retool the Springfield plant, which, at the time he arrived in the late 1910s, had a slew of antiquated machines, some dating back to the Civil War era.[6] By the end of 1937, Garand had the armory producing ten of his guns a day. By 1939, workers were finishing one hundred per day. By the start of 1941, Springfield was pumping out six hundred every day. By the end of the war, it could make 1,000 a day. Even that would not be enough. The government needed so many, it licensed work out to companies like Winchester, which made half a million M1s during the war. As efficiency and manufacturing increased, the price per gun began to drop precipitously, from over $200 a gun to $26.[7]

What made the Garand special? During the First World War the bolt-action rifle was standard in nearly every nation, including the United States. After every shot, a soldier had to pull back the bolt handle, unlock the breech, and eject the shell casing. The shooter then loaded a new round or cartridge into the breech and closed the bolt. The Garand was a semiautomatic—a term, despite much confusion in the modern gun debate, that merely tells us that every time a shooter pulled the trigger, the gun reloaded itself. It allowed the American soldier to fire eight shots as fast as he was able to pull the trigger eight times.

As we've seen, the concept of semiautomatic guns was not new. Others, including the French, who had created the semiautomatic Fusil Automatique Modèle 1917 rifle, already utilized the technology on the battlefield. By the start of the Second World War, the British, the Russians, and the Germans had all experimented with semiautomatic rifles. None, however, except the Americans had the technical or production capability to make the semiautomatic rifle standard for all their infantry during the war.

The decision to embrace the sturdy M1 gave the U.S. soldier a distinct advantage over his enemies in firing capacity. In truth, the M1 was somewhat unwieldy to carry, weighing just under ten pounds, and was around forty-three inches long. But it could shoot with precision and tremendous force. The MI's magazine allowed it to be reloaded quicker than any rifle used by enemy infantrymen during the Second World War. The gun was fed by an "en bloc clip"—a clip holding all the rounds together—allowing the shooter to insert the cartridge into a magazine or the gun. It used a .30-06 cartridge (known to millions of soldiers and hunters as the "30 aught 6"). The ammunition had become standard for the United States Army in 1906. The "30" signified the caliber and the "06" the year it was introduced. The bottleneck cartridge made it powerful despite its modest caliber. One of the first military cartridges to use the more powerful smokeless powder to propel a pointed bullet at higher velocities, the Americans would use the .30-06 into the 1980s in a multitude of guns, including all of Browning's World War I inventions.

The only gun that rivaled the M1 Garand's popularity was the M1 carbine. American military leaders wanted another gun that would be more substantial than a pistol but not quite as cumbersome as the M1 Garand. So a team of Springfield engineers came up with a lighter gun, partially based on Garand's design, to support troops who didn't need a full-sized rifle or were inhibited by one. Machine gunners, paratroopers, and artillery teams would all carry them. The carbine, which sometimes featured a pistol grip and folding metal stock, was adopted in May 1942 for airborne troops. It shot smaller .30-caliber ammunition and remained standard issue into the Vietnam War.

Soon the loud pinging noise that the M1's clip made when striking the back of the receiver would be recognized by both Americans and their enemies (and any kid playing *Call of Duty* on a video game console). Stories about the gun's effectiveness soon filtered home as soldiers began idealizing their M1s. "I believe in the force of a hand grenade, the power of artillery, the accuracy of a Garand," remarked Audie Murphy, one of the most decorated soldiers of the war. John R. McKinney, a private who won the Medal of Honor for his bravery in the Battle of Luzon, sang the praises of the Garand rifle he had used to storm a machine-gun nest held by ten Japanese troops—seven of whom he killed shooting at close range, three more whom he fought off using his heavy rifle as a bat. "In my opinion," General Patton wrote in a letter to the Springfield Armory at the end of the war, "the M1 rifle is the greatest battle implement ever devised."

In 1941 the *New York Times* noted that "there is every reason why John C. Garand, if he were that kind of an inventor, should put his thumbs in his armpits, puff on his cigar and say, 'I told you so ten years ago.'"[8] Garand, who passed away in 1974 at the age of eighty-six still trying to get $100,000 in back compensation, certainly wasn't that sort of inventor. As a civilian employee of the War Department earning around $6,000 a year, Garand had waived all commercial and foreign rights so that no one could use his invention but the government—literally signing away millions. Of all the famous American gunmakers, he was the one who benefited least financially from his ideas.

The ensuing wars of the twentieth century necessitated a different sort of weapon, one that was lighter and had more flexibility. At the outbreak of the Korean conflict in 1950, American soldiers were outfitted with the same weapons that they had fought with in World War II: the M1, the M1 carbine, the M1911 pistol, and the Browning automatic rifle. By the end of that war, the Americans would face the challenge of combining the advantages of all these weapons into a single lighter firearm.

The military had begun, for the first time, conducting systematic studies regarding the effectiveness of the weaponry they deployed after World War II. In 1948 the Army organized the civilian Operations Research Office and analyzed millions of battlefield and casualty reports from the two world wars to make recommendations regarding equipment and tactics. The findings didn't exactly comport with American gun lore, but they did help focus on the types of firearms that would be effective in modern combat.

What they found was that firepower mattered. This was unsurprising. Marines might have had outstanding marksmanship, but the fact was, the more a soldier fired, and the more of them who did so, the more of the enemy they killed. What *was* somewhat surprising was *how* they killed. For one thing, the vast majority of infantrymen engaged in short-range battles, skirmishes, and ambushes, often running into the enemy unexpectedly. This kind of encounter only increased during the wars in Korea and Vietnam and the later conflicts of the twentieth century. Moreover, most soldiers held their fire until the enemy was within 200 yards—the average American held it until the target was within 120 yards—even though the M1 had an effective range of more than 500 yards.[9] Perhaps the average soldier felt most comfortable hitting a target within this range, or perhaps long-range opportunities in war presented themselves far less than initially thought.

Although there is some debate over the actual percentages, despite the ease of use, many infantrymen still did not fire their weapons in combat. Early studies of the Korea conflict noted that soldiers with rapid-fire weapons were more likely to shoot. Some historians have found that it took an average of 7,000 rifle shots to achieve one combat kill during the First World War. That number would increase to 40,000 or more by the Vietnam War. (It was 92,000 bullets per enemy killed in the Iraq War. The United States now fires around 250,000 bullets for every insurgent killed in Afghanistan.) Soldiers needed to be able to fire with more ease.

It was also clear that the M1 had some serious drawbacks in modern war: it was too heavy, lacked full-automatic capability, and had only an eight-round magazine. Americans went about designing a gun that was both light (to accommodate the realities of warfare in the second half of the twentieth century) and powerful (to assuage conservative military leaders who believed bigger ammunition was necessary to put down the enemy). During World War II, the Germans also concluded that short-range warfare was the rule and began to produce the StG 44, which used a shorter cartridge that permitted controllable automatic fire from a weapon that was more compact than a battle rifle. The gun fired fully automatic like a submachine gun or semiautomatic.

Garand himself had worked on this problem at Springfield Armory as well, even before the war had ended. He had designed a selective-fire operation—semiautomatic to automatic—and a detachable magazine. It was still heavy, weighing over ten pounds. The Ordnance Department attempted to modify the design and ordered 100,000 in 1945, but the war ended before mass production could begin. Garand stayed on the case, designing what would essentially be an M1 converted into a fully automatic rifle. The new rifle carried a 20-round magazine attached at the bottom.

The new M14 would never be as beloved as other military weapons. In semiautomatic mode, the rifle was still powerful. In fully automatic mode, most soldiers had true aim only for the first shot, because the recoil made it virtually impossible to control.[10] The M14 gradually replaced the M1 rifle as the standard-issue infantry weapon, but as it was being manufactured, forward-looking engineers already had a gun in mind that was far more effective, a lot lighter, and a lot deadlier. It would make the M14's run short and herald a new age of military applications and private gun ownership.

19

★

FALL AND RISE OF THE SHARPSHOOTER

"Everyone I shot was evil. I had good cause on every shot. They all deserved to die."[1]

—Chris Kyle

A U.S. Army sniper team from the Jalalabad Provincial Reconstruction Team

On the morning of August 6, 1945, a B-29 bomber named the *Enola Gay* dropped the first atom bomb on the Japanese city of Hiroshima. Approximately 80,000 people were instantly killed and around 60,000 would soon die from the effects of the fallout. In one hundred years, mankind had gone from pouring gunpowder and ball down a barrel to incinerating cities in mere seconds. Yet the gun remained. "There would have to be a radical change in warfare to do away with the rifle," John Garand noted at the end of the war. "Even with atomic bombs, guided missiles, rockets and the rest, foot soldiers with their rifles will be needed to mop up, occupy and hold territory."

The incongruous truth of modern warfare was that even as the ham-fisted violence of atomic warfare, booming artillery, and air warfare began to dominate fighting, another, more intricate form of the gun began to emerge. World War II saw the rise of the sniper. Perhaps the most deadly of these fighters was a Finn named Simo Häyhä, who it was maintained had shot down more than five hundred Russians during the Winter War between his country and the Soviet Union in 1939–40. While modern snipers are often equipped with computerized machines measuring wind direction and speed, and even the earth's curvature—sometimes shooting in excess of a mile—Häyhä wasn't even in possession of telescopic sights. When asked whether he had any moral quandaries about the great profi-ciency he displayed in this deadly work, Häyhä simply responded that "I only did what I was told to do, as well as I could."

This would be the attitude of many of the men and women who sniped during World War II. The Soviets, quick to develop snipers and doctrines for long-range shooting, boasted of a number of skilled long-range killers, many of whom finished their careers with over 400 recorded kills—including a female Red Army sniper named Lyudmila Pavlichenko, who had 309 under her belt. The Soviets ended with 14,500 confirmed sniper kills during the war, although the number was probably far higher.[2]

Even then, until that point, for most nations sniping had been organic rather than doctrinal. The Great War had been a stalemate that created virtually motionless trench emplacements with sudden bursts of violence. It was during the long delays between fighting that the best shots in units would emerge as long-distance killing specialists. Better marksmen spent hours observing the enemy lines, waiting for a soldier, preferably an of-ficer, to forget himself and peek out over a trench. Although no army at the beginning of the war deployed units of sharpshooters for this duty, the German and Austrian Jäger battalions had a tradition of marksman-ship that went back to the 1700s. Yet even they were not equipped with any specialized weaponry to provide the necessary accuracy for precision shooting over 300 yards or so.

Within a year, however, the Germans began converting their stan-dard Mauser rifles and equipping them with excellent telescopic sights for sniper use. Nearly 20,000 of these guns were made during the war.

The Germans augmented the weapons by developing an intricate system of camouflage, building irregular parapets from material of varying composition and colors to make marksmen less conspicuous to the enemy, poking holes in metal shields and building concrete sniping posts. All of this provoked the British to act.

Hesketh Hesketh-Prichard, a British officer, adventurer, and big-game hunter, created the first Allied school for sniping in August 1916. Though his first graduating class attracted only six men, many of the ideas he implemented proved effective enough to last into World War II. One of them was having two men to work in teams, one with binoculars and the other, in the case of the British, with a Lee-Enfield bolt-action rifle with a telescopic lens and powerful precision ammunition. The English were soon matching the Germans in efficiency.

Despite their long tradition of sharpshooting, Americans came to modern sniping even later than the British. Although Morgan's Kentucky Riflemen might have been the world's first military sniper unit and both sides in the Civil War recruited sharpshooters, there was no official military policy on sharpshooting. Still, with breechloaders, percussion-lock rifles, and Minié ball, these men dramatically pushed the boundaries of both accuracy and range. The Union general John Sedgwick, for example, met an ignominious end when a bullet, reportedly fired from over 600 yards by a Confederate sharpshooter armed with a Whitworth rifle, hit him in the face just as he had finished excoriating his men: "Why are you dodging like this? They couldn't hit an elephant at this distance" were reportedly his final words. As we've seen, Hiram Berdan, an inventor and marksman, recruited his own companies of Northern sharpshooters.

Yet the tradition of sharpshooting ebbed and flowed. After the Civil War, there was widespread consternation among military officers and politicians at what they perceived as an abrupt decline in American marksmanship. Many believed that better aim might have alleviated many of the horrid injuries that accompanied the recent war. To them, it was a scandal that cost-cutting measures allowed post–Civil War infantry to practice with only ten rounds per month.[3]

One of these men, William Church, a New York journalist, editor, publisher, and war veteran, was driven to expose how a lack of marksmanship indicated a sign of a lack of patriotism and corrosion of American values. In 1870, Church tapped another concerned friend, a lawyer and former Union officer named George Wingate, to author a series of articles instructing young men on the finer points of accurate shooting. "The general ignorance concerning marksmanship which I found among the soldiers during the Civil War appalled me, and I hoped that I might better the situation," Wingate wrote.[4] The pieces were popular enough to be published as a book titled *Manuel for Target Practice*, which soon became a bestseller and ignited interest in target shooting around the country.

Church and Wingate, admirers of Germanic guns and society, looked to shooting clubs run by Central European immigrants that had recently begun popping up around the country. They used the idea as a template for their own organization. The duo launched an organization called the National Rifle Association in November 1871.

The first president of the NRA was noted Civil War general Ambrose Burnside, who had once remarked that out of "ten soldiers who are perfect in drill and the manual of arms, only one knows the purpose of the sights on his gun or can hit the broad side of a barn." The organization intended to do something about it, lobbying for $25,000 from the state of New York to help build a number of ranges in the area, the best one in Creedmoor, Long Island (when the land reverted back to New York years later it would become a famous psychiatric hospital), where they ran classes and shooting competitions.

The NRA's most notable moment in the early years occurred when a wealthy Irish lawyer named Arthur Blennerhassett Leech, who had been in charge of numerous shooting clubs in London and Dublin, decided to challenge the American club publicly to a contest of marksmanship, sending an invitation via the *New York Herald*, at the time the city's largest paper. The event generated healthy interest across the country. The British had a long history of competitive shooting, and Leech's squad had been competing in Europe for years. But, as the colorful Irishman noted, it was the first time the British could offer a "peaceful battle to their American cousins."[5] For the still-struggling NRA, the event was much-needed publicity, at the very least. Seven of the NRA's best shots were chosen to compete. Over 5,000 onlookers showed up at Creedmoor to take in the contest, which involved participants shooting fifteen times at 800, 900, and 1,000 yards. The rifles used by both teams could weigh no more than ten pounds. No telescopic sights or hair triggers were allowed. The American team—which, unlike the Irish, would clean the fouling from their rifles after every shot—won the contest 326–317.

Leech awarded the Americans a cup inscribed with the message "Presented for Competition to the riflemen of America, by Arthur Blennerhassett Leech, Captain of the International Team of Riflemen, on the occasion of their visit to New York." The cup accepted by Wingate is still competed for today, the oldest target-shooting trophy in the United States.[6] The Irishman wrote about the adventure in a book called *Irish Riflemen in New York*.[7] The contest had been a huge success, spurring many similar ones around the country in the coming years. It was a boon for the National Rifle Association and spurred a national movement for marksmanship.

While shooting became increasingly popular in America, the military did not feature specialized sharpshooters in the First World War, although it must be noted that no branch of any military places as strong an emphasis on marksmanship as the Marines. "Every Marine is a rifleman" is still a credo for a branch that requires all its servicemen to earn a marksmanship badge. Some claim that the braided quatrefoils on the top of a warrant or commissioned Marine officer's dress and service cap served as a way for musket-wielding shooters in crow's nests to recognize them while firing down during battle. Whatever its origins, the desire of Marines to tie their history to long-range shooting is indicative of the importance it plays in the branch's attitude.

Marines who landed in Europe during the First World War quickly gained a reputation as good shots. Numerous wartime accounts by the French and Germans mention their proficiency. In one such case, Herman Davis, an infantryman who had grown up refining his skills hunting small game in Arkansas, saved his platoon by taking out a number of machine gunners at Verdun from over 300 yards. For his effort, General Pershing named Davis one of the one hundred heroes of World War I. At Belleau Wood, thirty miles north of Paris, Americans suffered 10,000 casualties, including 1,800 fatalities.[8] Pershing referred to it as "the biggest battle since Appomattox and the most considerable engagement American troops had ever had with a foreign enemy."[9] One report to the German command called the Americans "vigorous, self-confident, and remarkable marksmen."[10]

After the war, Marines fielded teams in competitive marksmanship, yet still no sniper school—or countersniper strategies—existed when the Americans entered the Second World War. U.S. soldiers would soon encounter deadly enemy snipers, prompting them to act. Ernie Pyle, the great American Pulitzer Prize–winning journalist who would later be killed at Okinawa, wrote about the prevalence of German snipers during D-Day:

> Sniping, as far as I know, is recognized as a legitimate means of war-fare. And yet there is something sneaking about it that outrages the American sense of fairness. I had never sensed this before we landed in France and began pushing the Germans back. We had had snipers before—in Bezerte and Cassino and lots of other places, but always on a small scale. There in Normandy the Germans went in for sniping in a wholesale manner. There were snipers everywhere: in trees, in buildings, in piles of wreckage, in the grass. But mainly they were in the high, bushy hedge-rows that form the fences of all the Norman fields and line every roadside and lane.[11]

The Marines would be the first to formalize the training of snipers. In 1943 the branch established two schools for the purpose, one at Camp Lejeune in North Carolina and the other in Green's Farm, north of San Diego.[12] In 1944 the *War Department Basic Field Manual* defined the "sniper" as "an expert rifleman, well qualified in scouting, whose duty is to pick off key enemy personnel who expose themselves. By eliminating enemy leaders and harassing the troops, sniping softens the enemy's resistance and weakens his morale." To achieve this directive, Americans turned to the old Springfield 1903 rifles rather than the M1. The gun featured the same lock as the standard Springfield from the First World War, but the powerful gun's stock was updated and a scope mounted.[13]

Those who completed the first round of training would be designated "scout-snipers" and were used across the European theater. There was little need for sniping in the Pacific with the short-range fighting and perpetual movement—although, when a single Japanese emplacement was holding down American forward movement in Okinawa, a sharpshooting private named David Cass took it out at a range of around 1,200 yards, perhaps saving hundreds of lives.[14]

Once the war ended, so did the dedicated sniper training. The Americans again ran into snipers in Korea, most of whom were Soviet trained

U.S.M.C. Winchester M70 Sniper Rifle

and often equipped with brawny Russian-made Mosin-Nagant rifles with telescopic sights. "Constant sniper fire was the scariest part of the war," one veteran of a combat engineer battalion wrote to his hometown paper. "Snipers were in the hills; they were everywhere. And there were North Korean soldiers in civilian uniforms. On my first job of driving a grader, the sniper bullets were so close you could hear what sounded like the snapping of a whip at a circus. It was the sweetest sound in the world when you would hear that because you knew the bullet had missed you."[15]

Americans soon began developing modern-day countersniping techniques. Marine Staff Sergeant John E. Boitnott, a competitive rifleman in peacetime, helped teach a course on sharpshooting before returning to the front lines to try his own hand at scoped-rifle shooting. Boitnott noticed that Chinese snipers were targeting his regiment's trenches on Outpost Yoke, but was unable to locate their positions. Boitnott and a private named Henry Friday employed a winning though precarious countersniping strategy that entailed the latter running along the trench line as bait for the snipers. When a Chinese shooter raised his head from his position to take out Friday, Boitnott took out the wannabe shooter. The two would eliminate nine Chinese snipers before they were stopped by a commanding officer who, for good reason, found the ploy a bit too dangerous. Later, Boitnott's shots were plotted to be around 670 yards.[16]

During the Vietnam War, the Vietcong's guerrilla warfare would include not only booby traps but dedicated units of snipers. The Americans had little such formal military policy or training as snipers, even into the early years of the Vietnam War; trainers were still, in part, using H. W. McBride's 1933 book *A Rifleman Went to War: The Classic Account of Practical Marksmanship on the Battlefields of World War One* as a blueprint for their tactics. The book offered a number of sound tactical ideas and also the psychological makeup of men who would do this kind of work. McBride had worked as a cowboy in southern Colorado and northern New Mexico in the 1890s. Although he was gifted with a rifle, he said the most important part of being a sniper was "the ability to control one's own nerves and passions—in other words, never to get excited." In Vietnam, the Americans were on the lookout not merely for men with skill, but for men with extraordinary patience and the ability to withstand psychological pressure. It formed the template of the modern sniper.

By 1965, the first Marine sniper school in Vietnam opened. These snipers were armed with high-powered hunting rifles (often Winchesters) and worked in pairs—a shooter and a spotter—although both men were capable long-distance shooters. The maximum effective range at the time was somewhere around an impressive 1,100 meters. The Marine sniper course evolved into one of the most arduous courses in the military, with a failure rate of over 60 percent.

As the guns improved so did the deadliness of the sniper. One Marine, Vaughn Nickell, registered the longest confirmed kill on record until that time: 1,200 yards. A few years later Carlos Hathcock, who would go on to rack up ninety-three confirmed kills during two tours in Vietnam, shot down a Vietcong weapons carrier from 2,500 yards with a Browning M2 machine gun set for a single shot. The top-scoring American sniper of the Vietnam War, with 113 confirmed kills, was Sergeant Adelbert F. Waldron of the Army's 9th Infantry Division.[17] As world conflicts became messier and more complex, the sniper increasingly took on a bigger role in combat operations. From then on the sniper earned legendary status in American life.

20

★

PEACE DIVIDENDS

"The rifle itself has no moral stature, since it has no will of its own."
—Jeff Cooper, *The Art of the Rifle*

A U.S. Army M.P.
inspects a Chinese
AK 47

In March 1965, the first American combat troops landed in Vietnam, many of them still carrying heavy M14s. At some point the troops struggled with the powerful but ineffective fully automatic function, which became so aggravating that soldiers began jamming the select lever, making the M14 nothing more than an M1 Garand with a 20-round magazine.

To make matters even worse, at the same time American troops were encountering Vietcong equipped with a remarkably reliable and durable weapon. The Soviet AK-47, known also as the Kalashnikov, was already being used around the world. The "Avtomat Kalashnikova" went on to be one of the most produced, most durable guns in history. During the Cold War—and beyond—it would be, for practical and ideological reasons, the weapon of anti-capitalists, anti-Americans, and revolutionaries of all stripes, used by gangs, guerrilla fighters, and terrorists around the world.

Most weapons were a result of trade-offs between power and rapidity, size or range. The AK-47, as the historian Victor Davis Hanson has pointed out, managed to find the "sweet spot" between "accuracy, lethality, speed of fire, reliability, cost of production, and ease of carrying and use." More than any foreign-made gun, it would influence American attitudes about firearms.[1]

The tragic figure of Mikhail Kalashnikov was born in 1919, the seventeenth of nineteen children in a family of private farm owners in eastern Siberia. By 1930 the Kalashnikov clan was denounced by the Communist Party as "kulaks" who resisted Stalin's forced collectivization and were exiled to a penal colony. Here his father used a rifle to hunt to feed the family, and Mikhail began fiddling with it. Though he had no formal training in weapon making, Kalashnikov began an apprenticeship as a railroad engineer before being conscripted into the Red Army in 1938.

First tasked as a mechanic and then engineer, Kalashnikov rose to become a tank commander. Wounded in combat in 1941 near Moscow, the young inventor claimed to devise the idea for a durable submachine gun that would help ward off fascism while he was recovering from his wounds. "When I was lying wounded during the war, I heard the other soldiers complaining about how the German weapons were better than ours," he later said of his hospital stay in 1942. "So I was determined to invent something for the ordinary soldier—a weapon that would be simple, tough and better than any other in the world."[2]

The Russians were not new to the automatic assault rifle, producing 1,500 Fedorov Avtomats in 1915. The gun's inventor, Vladimir Fyodorov, had visited the Western Front in 1914 and witnessed the carnage generated by static machine guns. He pondered, much like John Thompson did, whether he could meld the power of the rifle with the versatility of a light machine gun. What he came up with was a recoil-operated, locked-breech weapon with a banana magazine that held 25 rounds. The gun saw limited use in World War I, although due to a lack of weapons it was used during the Soviet-Finnish war. But the weapon was simply too intricate and expensive to mass-produce, and it overheated quickly.

Kalishnikov would solve these problems. In an ironic twist of the Cold War, Kalashnikov initially benefited more from meritocracy—perhaps because he was working within the Red Army system—than his Western competitors. This is not to say he wasn't beset by roadblocks, but his gun found success far quicker. By 1944 he had designed a gas-operated carbine that applied Russian ideas to the M1 Garand rifle. Two years later, "Mikhtim," his prototype entry in the Red Army's assault rifle competition, laid the mechanical groundwork for all Russian automatic rifles moving forward.

The next year Kalashnikov designed what we now know as the AK-47. It was as the Cold War was beginning that the gun became the standard-issue assault rifle of the Soviet army. It would be mass-produced in the historic Izhevsk plant founded by Tsar Alexander I, but also in many Soviet satellite nations. There are said to be over 100 million in existence today, feeding countless revolutions in Southeast Asia, the Middle East, Latin America, and Africa.

The deceptively durable AK-47 might have looked cheap and felt rickety, but it could be disassembled, cleaned, and reassembled faster than any other military-grade rifle. While the American guns would be ergonomically superior and have far better range and accuracy, the AK-47's loose-fitting parts gave it an advantage in nearly any kind of weather or terrain. It was powerful. It seemed indestructible.

Eugene Stoner, Kalashnikov's lifelong rival, was nothing more than a gun hobbyist shooting off rounds of his strange homemade rifle on a local Southern California range during the summer, when executives for the struggling Los Angeles firm ArmaLite spotted the young man.

Stoner, an Indiana native who had grown up in Long Beach and enlisted in aviation ordnance in the U.S. Marine Corps, had just returned home after serving in the South Pacific and northern China during World War II. He would never find the fame of a Colt or a Browning, but his ideas would be implemented on a similarly grand scale. Like those gunmakers, Stoner, a tinkerer with an innate talent for mechanics, didn't benefit from any formal engineering education, but his revolutionary gun became America's standard military rifle and its civilian iterations would go on to be one of the most popular guns ever produced.

Stoner was something of an aviation technology expert when the men from ArmaLite first approached him in 1945. Stoner became the chief engineer of the small gun manufacturer. It made complete sense that the postwar start-up ArmaLite set up shop in the glitzy environs of Hollywood, California. The company, after all, embraced the kind of jet-age idealism that allowed it to break free of the constraints of traditional gun design. ArmaLite had shown early interest in hybridizing technological advances of World War II airplane design, of plastics and alloys, with their small arms. Although it took a long time for Stoner to get it right, and an even longer time to convince military leaders it could work, his creation dominates the rifle market to this day.

ArmaLite's attempts to integrate lightweight plastics into arms—it was the first gun manufacturer to have a plastics specialist on staff—led to a string of prototypes over the next few years. Most would see limited success. It wasn't until 1955, when Stoner completed the first version of his AR-10—a light, seven-pound selective-fire rifle—that the company began receiving some notice.

The gun would first be tested in trials at the Army's Aberdeen Proving Ground in Maryland in 1956. A late entry in the contest to replace the M1, the AR-10 performed admirably. It was lighter than its competition, and more accurate when fired in automatic mode. It was also perhaps a bit *too* jet-agey for the military brass, who chose to move forward with the M14, a gun they had already invested much time and effort in.

As we've seen throughout the history of American guns, men tasked with saving and taking lives were inclined to have conservative attitudes on matters of arms innovation. This is a reasonable tendency. As we've also seen, however, sometimes this inclination inhibited the adoption of advances that could save lives. The military's insistence on embracing the M14 despite all its failings likely falls in the latter category.

Despite the rejection, many military leaders who witnessed the gun were impressed enough to urge the inventor to keep improving on his design. Stoner went back to work and emerged with an even sleeker prototype, the AR-15. Only the thin barrel and a few other parts on the gun were made of steel; the rest was constructed of fiberglass and aluminum. The new model weighed only slightly over five pounds and held a magazine with 25 rounds of .22-caliber bullets. The gun was air-cooled, and the gas that escaped from a fired round would be routed back through the bolt carrier.

The AR-15 prototype was entered in 1958 trials. Although penetration favored the larger M14, it still misfired 16 rounds per 1,000 shots, or three times the rate of the better-performing AR-15.[3] Stoner later maintained that the gun had been sabotaged by forces within the Army who believed that larger, .30-caliber ammunition was a necessity for combat. (There is some evidence to back up his contention. In one test in the Arctic in Alaska, the AR-15 had performed dismally. When Stoner flew to Fort Greeley, Alaska, to investigate, he found his guns had been tampered with and rejiggered. Once fixed, the rifle performed as well as it had elsewhere.) In the final analysis, not only would the AR-15 outperform the M14 in a number of other important ways, it cost only around a third of the price to produce per unit. Despite the excellent results, in that same year Dr. Frederick Carten, head of the Ordnance Corps, reported that "the AR-15 had not demonstrated sufficient technical merit and should not be developed by the Army."

At this point Fairchild, the parent corporation of ArmaLite, had endured enough red tape and intrigue and sold off the patents for the AR-15 and AR-10 to Colt's Patent Fire Arms Manufacturing Company for the sum of $75,000 plus 4.5 percent royalty on all further production. Colt, which had been flirting with insolvency during the postwar years, saw both the civilian and military potential of the gun. The company immediately dispatched salesmen to the Far East to broker foreign deals. The gun, as it turned out, immediately impressed the officials who witnessed testing and gained many champions but precious few sales. The problem was that most of these nations had agreements in place with the United States military that allowed them to purchase officially sanctioned weapons at far cheaper rates.

It wasn't until the summer of 1960, when controversial Air Force general Curtis LeMay—the creator of the strategic bombing campaign in the Pacific theater during World War II and reportedly the model for General Buck Turgidson in Stanley Kubrick's *Dr. Strangelove*—attended an Independence Day picnic sponsored by Colt, that the gun's prospects would improve. As the tale goes, General LeMay was handed an AR-15 by Colt reps, who placed three watermelons at distances of 50, 100, and

150 yards. The general shot two of them and handed back the gun. When asked if he wanted to shoot the third, LeMay replied, "Hell, no, let's eat it." So impressed was LeMay after only two squeezes of the trigger, it seems, that he ordered 80,000 rifles on the spot.[4]

Whether LeMay was instantaneously smitten by the rifle, we will never truly know. What we do know is that, more than anyone else in government, LeMay became the champion of the AR-15. Stoner, who went on to work with Colt on the gun, needed such a sponsor, because at this point political issues, not technical ones, were holding back the gun's success, the most concerning of which was that the inferior M14 was already in production. So, after much bureaucratic wrangling, the deputy defense secretary finally approved the production of 8,500 AR-15 rifles for the Air Force in 1961. Still, Congress would not authorize funding for the new gun. So General LeMay went to the Kennedy administration directly to make his case. It took the personal intervention of President Kennedy's defense secretary, Robert McNamara, a former Ford executive whose technocratic instincts proved at times both helpful and detrimental to the AR-15, for the gun production to move forward. By 1962 the purchase was approved and plans were made for more prototypes.

At around the same time, the AR-15, through various means, had also begun showing up in the hands of American personnel in South Vietnam, where the United States now had hundreds of advisors. The reports that filtered back to military leaders and politicians extravagantly praised both the stopping power and usefulness of the guns in the jungle terrain of Southeast Asia. Finally, in 1963, McNamara was convinced that the AR-15 was superior to the M14 and met all the requirements of the universal firearm concept. After some modifications to make the rifle combat ready, production commenced, and in November of that year McNamara approved an order of 85,000 military-model AR-15s for the Army and 19,000 for the Air Force. The gun would be known as the M16.

It immediately received bad reviews. Worse, in Vietnam, serious problems emerged that threatened not only the gun's future but the lives of those who carried it. In short, the M16 would constantly jam. According to many Marines, it was costing lives. "We left with 72 men in our platoon and came back with 19. Believe it or not, you know what killed most of us? Our own rifle," one Marine told *Time* magazine in 1966.[5] Another Marine wrote a letter to war critic Senator Gaylord Nelson that was reprinted in newspapers around the country: "The weapon has failed us at crucial moments when we needed fire power most. In each case, it left Marines naked against their enemy. Often, and this is no exaggeration, we take counts after each fight, as many as 50% of the rifles fail to work."[6]

A subsequent investigation by a subcommittee of the Armed Services Committee found that "the failure on the part of officials with authority in the Army to cause caution to be taken to correct the deficiencies of the 5.56mm ammunition borders on criminal negligence."[7] For one thing, the M16 had been issued to troops without cleaning kits and a number of officers had declared the gun self-cleaning, which was simply untrue. The fouling was exacerbated because there had been orders from the Department of Defense to change the "stick powder" to "ball powder" in the ammunition. The ball powder allowed the weapon to fire at a much faster rate, but it also put more stress on the gun, causing jams. Another major glitch was that most of the guns did not feature chrome-plated chambers, which had long been known to slow corrosion and rusting and help cut down on jamming.

The Army quickly moved to retrofit the M16s, but great damage had already been done to the morale of those carrying the weapon and to the reputation of the gun. These doubts lingered. Although there was plenty of blame to go around—from the White House, which demanded the ammunition change, to the Army leadership, which failed to understand the proper maintenance of the gun—none of the problems were the fault of Stoner's design. It was the government engineers who were tasked with making the gun combat ready.

Even with all these complications, the M16 performed much better than most Americans assumed, and once the mechanical and maintenance problem had been rectified, it would become more popular than Army leadership expected. A 1968 classified report on the M16's effectiveness found that most problems with the rifle originated in the training in its use. Seventy-three percent of soldiers who were questioned had received absolutely no instruction on the gun before arriving in Vietnam. Yet, when asked, 85 percent of those soldiers still preferred the M16, or the smaller iteration of the gun, to any other rifle available.[8]

In a "President's Blue Ribbon Defense Panel" regarding the M16 in March 1970, the author, Colonel Richard Hallock, laid out both the

M14's rise and the protracted history of the M16's implementation.[9] The colonel revisited all the testing and the many trials of the M16, both before and after adoption of the weapon. He noted that the M16 had been 10 percent more lethal in Vietnam than conventional wisdom assumed—and he believed even that figure underestimated the gun's lethality. He went on to observe that 70 percent of U.S. casualties in Vietnam up until that time had been caused by small arms fire—versus the 25 to 45 percent in other American wars. Using this calculus, he concluded that the introduction of the M16 had likely saved around 20,000 American lives during the early years of the Vietnam War.

Both the Kalashnikov and the M16, two guns that epitomized the great upheavals of the second half of the twentieth century, would evolve over the decades, although the foundational ideas would remain the same. The Soviet gun was soon turned on the Russians as well, as its durability made it the gun of choice for militants of all denominations. The lives of the two inventors, on the other hand, could not have gone much differently. Stoner became a wealthy man, starting up his own company and living his final days in Florida. Kalashnikov, who claimed that he never made a penny from his famous invention, lived in a two-room apartment in Moscow on a pension, just like his neighbors. "Stoner has his own aircraft," said Kalashnikov, who was unlucky enough to be born in a communist state. "I can't even afford my own plane ticket."[10]

The professional rivalry between the guns and the men outlived the Cold War, though on a personal level on much friendlier terms. After the Soviet Union collapsed, the affable Kalashnikov was allowed to travel and talk about the gun that bore his name. He first met Eugene Stoner in 1990 at Dulles International Airport, near Washington, DC, where both participated in a documentary filmed by the Smithsonian Institution. The duo, both self-taught gunmakers whose designs had come to define small arms in the late twentieth century, spent ten days discussing their inventions, the bureaucratic roadblocks they encountered, and the technical evolution of their ideas.

In 2006, as Americans struggled against Iraq War insurgents armed with his AK-47, the eighty-six-year-old Kalashnikov noted that "even after lying in a swamp you can pick up this rifle, aim it and shoot. That's the best job description there is for a gun. Real soldiers know that and understand it.

"In Vietnam," he continued, "American soldiers threw away their M-16 rifles and used AK-47s from dead Vietnamese soldiers, with bullets they captured. That was because the climate is different to America, where M-16s may work properly."[11]

On Kalashnikov's ninetieth birthday, the Kremlin ceremony was televised live as then-president Dmitry Medvedev decorated him with the Hero of Russia, the highest award in that nation. In 2004 he would license his name to vodka and umbrella brands in Europe.

Kalashnikov, who died at the age of ninety-four in 2013—President Vladimir Putin attended the extravagant funeral—is said to have regretted what happened to his invention. The gun designer had converted to the Russian Orthodox Church and was baptized at the age of ninety-one. The year before his death, he wrote a letter to Patriarch Kirill of Moscow expressing deep regret over the success of his rifle.

My spiritual pain is unbearable.

I keep having the same unsolved question: if my rifle claimed people's lives, then can it be that I . . . a Christian and an Orthodox believer, was to blame for their deaths?

The longer I live, the more this question drills itself into my brain and the more I wonder why the Lord allowed man to have the devilish desires of envy, greed and aggression.[12]

Kalashnikov's daughter, Elena, told journalists that she believed a priest had helped her elderly father pen the letter. The spokesman for the Russian patriarch, Cyril Alexander Volkov, told the paper the religious leader had received Kalashnikov's letter and replied that "when weapons serve to protect the Fatherland," as the AK-47 had, "the Church supports both its creators and the soldiers" who use it for that purpose. "He designed this rifle to defend his country, not so terrorists could use it in Saudi Arabia."[13]

It would have been impossible for either man to know that their guns would be used by evil when they first came to their ideas. Both men were, almost surely, patriots, who fought for their countries and were driven by a desire to see less suffering, not more. A number of the most famous weapon makers—Colt, Gatling, Browning, to name just a few—believed that superior weapons made war less likely. Stoner and Kalashnikov were men of their time, and reacted accordingly. Or as the Russian inventor remarked, "Blame the Nazi Germans for making me become a gun designer . . ."[14]

In 1997, Stoner died in his garage while tinkering with guns at the age of seventy-four, a wealthy and content man. The gun he invented would not bear his name, nor would most Americans even know who he was. His AR-15 would be manufactured by dozens of American companies, including major gunmakers like Bushmaster, Remington Arms, and Smith & Wesson. The civilian AR-15, which had a military appearance if not military power, would become increasingly controversial because mass murderers would often use them. Stoner's family has claimed that the inventor never intended for his famous gun—one of the most popular in America—to fall into civilian hands. This seems unlikely, considering that both ArmaLite and Colt sold the gun directly to the civilian marketplace before they ever agreed on large military contracts. Never once during the many years the gun was sold to Americans is there any evidence that Stoner was troubled by the civilian sales—or his profession, for that matter. Perhaps the inventor had a change of heart. Whatever the case, the inventor of the AR-15 had been pulled into one of the most heated debates in American history.

21

★

THE GREAT ARGUMENT

"How many have to die before we will give up these dangerous toys?"
—Stephen King

Two men and three women of the Home Defense Unit with guns

In the early morning of January 23, 1911, an unstable Harvard graduate with the theatrical name Fitzhugh Coyle Goldsborough approached the novelist David Graham Phillips on East Twenty-First Street in Manhattan and proceeded to unload six shots from his .32-caliber semiautomatic pistol. Goldsborough, who believed the novelist had slandered his sister, then reloaded his gun, put it to his temple, and pulled the trigger.

Goldsborough died instantly, although Phillips lasted into the next day before expiring. The gruesome crime destroyed a number of lives, but none of those affected would change history quite like George Petit le Brun, the man who performed the autopsies on both bodies at the city's coroner's office. "I reasoned that the time had come to have legislation passed that would prevent the sale of pistols to irresponsible persons," he later wrote.[1] After two years of imploring local politicians to institute gun control laws, le Brun finally found an ally in Timothy D. Sullivan, the corrupt Tammany Hall operator who was known as "Big Tim" to most New Yorkers.

It is unlikely that Sullivan's attempt to take guns off the streets of New York was driven first, foremost, or, for that matter, whatsoever by concerns for the public safety. "Cynics," Sullivan's biographer Richard F. Welch noted in 2009, "suggested that Big Tim pushed through his law so Tammany could keep their gangster allies under control." This positioning would hardly be confined to Big Tim, who used the law as a means of disarming gangs that threatened his authority. Restrictionists throughout history have used gun control laws to constrain their political enemies or vulnerable populations. Whatever the case, the result was the nation's first major gun control legislation, the Sullivan Act.

Since the late 1800s a number of municipalities have attempted to control weapons in areas that featured gambling or drinking. Not one of those laws—or, most often, arbitrarily enforced set of local rules—ever challenged the notion of a law-abiding man owning a firearm. None, certainly, demanded that a man ask permission of the state to own a gun. The Sullivan Act was the first. It required New Yorkers who possessed firearms small enough to be concealed to get a license. People caught owning firearms but no license would face a misdemeanor charge, and carrying them was a felony. In addition to handguns, the law prohibited the possession or carrying of weapons such as brass knuckles, sandbags, blackjacks, bludgeons, and bombs, as well as possessing or carrying a dagger, "dangerous knife," or razor "with intent to use the same unlawfully."[2] As with almost all gun control laws that followed, criminals would ignore the strictures and, in this case, the Tammany Hall bosses enforced it only when the weapons undermined their political interests. There was no perceptible decline in gang violence or murder in New York in the ensuing decades.

So while gun control was not a wholly new idea by the time the first federal gun control policy, the National Firearms Acts of 1934 and 1938 (NFA), was passed in reaction to the gangsters, bandits, and bootleggers waving around submachine guns, both petrifying and fascinating the population at large.

In the wake of Depression-era criminality, there were calls, mostly from police departments, to do something. Because highly publicized kidnappings, murders, and robberies had sparked a scare among American law enforcement, Roosevelt mounted his "New Deal for Crime." As all "new deals" would, this one also federalized policy. Reading the debates and quotes of that time makes one imagine it was unlikely many voters understood the precedents the law was setting, or that anyone believed it would be used to challenge the individual right of American citizens to own guns. Even then, the National Rifle Association—still a hobbyist group at the time—protested the initial proposal to create a registry and fingerprint all owners. It did not oppose the idea of guns being taken from criminals.

The law instituted a tax of $200—a large amount during the Depression—on the manufacture or sale of machine guns and sawed-off shotguns, and licensing on gun manufacturers and gun dealers. Roosevelt followed this up with the passage of the National Firearms Act (NFA) of 1938, which required the licensing of interstate gun dealers, who had to record all their sales. The law prohibited sales to individuals under indictment or convicted of crimes of violence.

There were a number of versions of gun control debated by the Roosevelt administration, but Attorney General Homer Cummings supported the final bill because he believed the taxing power was the best way to ensure the constitutionality of legislation. While even fervent advocates of the NFA never openly made the case that owning a gun was anything but an individual right, Cummings had no compunctions. He admitted that the policy was meant to inhibit law-abiding citizens from owning firearms. "We certainly don't expect gangsters to come forward to register their weapons and be fingerprinted, and a $200 tax is frankly prohibitive to private citizens," Cummings contended. It wouldn't take long after the passage of the NFA for mission creep to begin.

On April 18, 1938, Arkansas and Oklahoma state police pulled over two small-time bank robbers, Jackson "Jack" Miller and Frank Layton. The 240-pound Miller had already spent the majority of his thirty-nine tumultuous years involved in criminality. In 1924, when working as a bouncer, he had killed a court reporter in a Tulsa, Oklahoma, bar. In the mid-1930s he had joined a gang that boasted of having "most of the major bank robberies in the Southwest" under their belts.[3] In 1935, Miller flipped on his own gang, helping the authorities put most of them in prison. Yet, by the time state police arrested Miller and his sidekick Layton a few years later, they were in possession of an unregistered short-barreled shotgun in the car and apparently were "making preparation for armed robbery."[4]

Miller and Layton were charged with violating the National Firearms Act. If it were up to them, the case would have ended right there, as they both pled guilty. Yet Judge Hiram Ragon, a former congressman, New Deal loyalist, and advocate of the NFA, refused to accept the pleas and assigned them a court-appointed lawyer. The duo demurred. Ragon agreed, throwing out the indictment, claiming the NFA violated the Second Amendment—something he most surely did not believe.[5] In the meantime, the two small-time crooks went on the lam. (Miller's bullet-ridden body would be found by the police in a dry Oklahoma creek later in 1939.)

The case worked its way to the Supreme Court, which many believe is exactly what Ragon had intended. Miller's lawyers didn't even file a brief or show up to make oral arguments with the court. And in May 1939 the Supreme Court of the United States issued a terse and muddled nine-page opinion—with very little actual opinion involved—that achieved what Ragon had desired: it affirmed the constitutionality of the NFA. The court found that the Second Amendment did not guarantee an individual the right to keep and bear a sawed-off double-barreled shotgun that was under eighteen inches, which was a weapon commonly used by criminals. "In the absence of any evidence tending to show that possession or use of a 'shotgun having a barrel of less than eighteen inches in length' at this time has some reasonable relationship to the preservation or efficiency of a well regulated militia," the court found, "we cannot say that the Second Amendment guarantees the right to keep and bear such an instrument."

Today's media and liberals often bring up the *Miller* case as a way of bolstering the case for a "collective" theory of gun rights. Yet the court had not offered a broad ruling regarding the Second Amendment. It had found that any person "physically capable of acting in concert for the common defense" could own weapons. The case simply decided whether the government could regulate certain kinds of guns. "*Miller* stands only for the proposition that the Second Amendment right, whatever its nature, extends only to certain types of weapons," Justice Antonin Scalia found nearly sixty years later. "It is particularly wrongheaded to read *Miller* for more than what it said, because the case did not even purport to be a thorough examination of the Second Amendment." Yet this is exactly what lower courts would do for decades. There would be no other consequential Second Amendment cases in front of the Supreme Court until 2008. In the meantime, gun control advocates gained the upper hand.

The rise of gun control in the second half of the twentieth century would have everything to do with the prevalence of crime, although the prevalence of crime had very little to do with the number of guns Americans owned. In reality, after a short spurt of gangland violence that precipitated the passage of the NFA—much of it, as we've noted, hyped by movies and mythology—there was a quick drop in the crime rate. Violent crime rates had begun falling in the mid-1930s, before the passage of the NFA, and remained historically low until the middle of the 1960s. These low crime rates were enjoyed by everyone, including those in urban centers, despite commonly held perceptions. From 1900 to the late 1950s, for instance, New York City had lower homicide rates than the national average.[6]

With millions of men returning from the war in 1945–46, there was a temporary but modest spike in violence. Yet during the entirety of the 1940s, despite the fact that millions more military men now owned and knew how to use firearms, the number of homicides using a gun remained steady at around 55 percent. Throughout the 1950s, due to the rise of the middle class, suburbanization, and the better quality of life in general, there was a further reduction of violent crime. From 1948 to 1966, the homicide rate in the United States never exceeded 5 murders per 100,000—lower than it had been in any comparable period during the twentieth century.

Unlike the scare of the 1930s, however, the violent crime spike in the mid-1960s was real, pervasive, and enduring. In 1960, 200 people per 100,000 would experience violent crime. By 1990, the number was more than 700 people per 100,000. Homicide went from fewer than 5 people per 100,000 to more than 10 people. According to the National Crime Victim Survey, there were nearly 11 million violent crimes per year in the United States from the early 1970s to the early 1990s. In many areas, an American had a better chance of experiencing a violent crime than of getting into a car accident during these years.[7]

The fear and anxiety that crime generated would have great consequences for American life and culture, among them the flight of white

Americans to the suburbs and the resulting collapse of inner cities. One yearly survey asked Americans: "Is there any area near where you live— that is, within a mile—where you would be afraid to walk alone at night?" In 1965, 34 percent of those polled answered in the affirmative. By 1982, that number had risen to 48 percent—and it would not fall back to 34 percent until the year 2000. "To millions of Americans, few things are more pervasive, more frightening, more real today than violent crime and the fear of being assaulted, mugged, robbed, or raped," one presidential commission on crime in the late 1960s noted. "The fear of being crimi- nalized has touched us all in some way."

All these tensions led to the Omnibus Crime Control and Safe Streets Act of 1968, the first federal law that overtly attempted to diminish fire- arm ownership in the United States. Among other things, the law pro- hibited convicted felons, drug users, and the mentally ill from buying firearms. It raised the age to purchase handguns from a federally licensed dealer to twenty-one. It expanded the licensing requirements of gun deal- ers and set up more detailed government tracking of guns. On the local level, municipalities would be far stricter and more invasive. It was in the aftermath of this law that the modern debate over gun control was born, with the contours of that debate remaining virtually the same ever since.

The divergence among Americans was simple. Many people— especially those who lived in places that did not have a strong tradition of firearm ownership—saw guns in the hands of criminals and believed laws helped get those guns off the streets. Others saw firearms as a way to defend themselves from the rise in lawbreaking. The anxiety of the latter group would begin to bubble up in cultural depictions of urban conflict, most famously in films like *Death Wish* and the early Dirty Harry movies, which treated vigilantism as a morally complex issue in a world of ram- pant criminality and lawlessness.

After the 1968 local gun laws began to take hold, cities began to erect bureaucratic barriers that made it increasingly difficult for law-abiding cit- izens to purchase firearms. Soon enough a problem emerged. Criminals, it turns out, did not adhere to gun laws. Law-abiding citizens, on the other hand, did. Which created a cycle: the more criminals ignored these laws, the more politicians attempted to inhibit gun ownership for everyone, and the more problematic it would become for the average citizen to purchase and own a firearm. When citizens began pointing out that they had a constitutional right to defend themselves, politicians had to reimagine what the Second Amendment meant. This was when the first pro–gun rights movement was born. A movement that had never been necessary before.

On January 6, 1968, Senator Robert Kennedy of New York, who would be assassinated later that year, spoke to a class at University of Buffalo Law School. "I think it is a terrible indictment of the National Rifle Association," he said, "that they haven't supported any legislation to try and control the misuse of rifles and pistols in this country."[8] In the March 1968 edition of the NRA magazine *American Rifleman*, an associate editor, Alan Webber, answered Kennedy's charge, listing a number of legislative efforts the organization had supported over the years, including the NFA. This piece has often been brought up by critics of the Second Amendment to claim that groups like the NRA had once had a far more pliable conception of the Second Amendment and were open to limiting individual ownership.

The truth is more complicated and, in many ways, explains the modern gun debate. For one, although the NRA had certainly been open to stricter laws concerning machine guns and dealers, the historical evidence suggests that Webber had likely overemphasized the NRA's support for gun control legislation. More importantly, however, Second Amendment advocates had indeed been forced to change their political tactics and mission by the 1970s. Gun control advocates had dramatically changed theirs.

The National Rifle Association had continued concentrating on its rifle clubs and marksmanship programs through the first half of the 1900s. With a tremendous upswing in hunting, its membership grew and it would become the premier organization for gun owners. In the 1930s, the NRA formed a legislative division to periodically update its members on goings-on in Washington. In the 1950s, the organization began teaming with law enforcement departments in shooting drills and safety lessons. The NRA did not oppose the NFA and argued that those who abused gun ownership should be fully punished. Its president, Karl Frederick, in fact, would testify in front of Congress in the middle of the crime scare of the 1930s, contending, "I have never believed in the general practice of carrying weapons. I do not believe in the general promiscuous toting of guns. I think it should be sharply restricted and only under licenses."[9]

As far as firearms went, there was precious little on the legislative front in subsequent years. In the end, the NRA did not oppose the Gun Control

Act of 1968, a law that established a system to federally license gun dealers and set restrictions on particular categories and classes of firearms. But it did successfully oppose the most invasive elements of the legislation: namely, a mandated federal registry for guns and licensing for all gun carriers. Still, many members, seeing a slippery slope, did not approve. They were soon proved right. New laws were not being enacted to punish rogue gun owners but rather to make it increasingly difficult for anyone in an urban area to own a gun. And in 1971, when the Bureau of Alcohol, Tobacco and Firearms shot and paralyzed longtime NRA member Kenyon Ballew in a Washington suburb—they claimed Ballew was suspected of possessing illegal weapons (none were found)—many co-members saw it as a portent that government agencies would abuse gun control laws to target peaceful Americans.

The NRA would have to make a choice. It could remain solely a hunting, marksmanship, and safety group, or it could embrace the growing activist wing and push back against emerging gun control regulations. By the mid-1970s it seemed as if the organization had made a choice. More than seventy of the most vociferous gun rights advocates in the organization were fired during the early part of the decade. And in 1976 the NRA board decided to move the organization headquarters from Washington to Colorado.

So at the 1977 NRA convention in Cincinnati, there was something of a coup as the politically minded advocates wrested the organization from the traditional wing. Many of today's gun control advocates like to point to the "Cincinnati revolt" as the moment when radicals took over the movement, undermining true gun owners who weren't interested in politics. More likely, the shift was merely a reflection of a growing inclination among gun owners at the time. The NRA was best positioned to take the lead on gun issues. If not, there would almost certainly have been another advocacy group—and many would emerge during these years—that would have taken its place. The gun control debate had changed, but not the gun owners. From 1977 to 1983, the NRA would more than double its membership.[10]

Two things happened as the modern gun control debate evolved in the second half of the twentieth century. The first was a renewed interest in gun ownership. Just as gun restrictionists began attaining political power, many Americans romanticized the guns of the past—and began talking about the ideals that made them important in the first place. In the 1950s, for example, there would be a huge upsurge of interest in sport hunting, target shooting, and competitive shooting. Whereas North American gun culture was born of idealism and necessity, the modern American was far more inclined to want guns for recreation and home defense. But postwar culture would also be infatuated with the Wild West, the Kentucky rifle, and America's founding—and guns were embedded in all of it.

The bigger gun manufacturers initially failed to capitalize on this opportunity to cash in on the trend, but upstarts filled the market gap. Men like Brooklynite William B. Ruger. Born in 1916, Ruger became interested in firearms at an early age. Plagued by respiratory problems, he was sent to upstate New York, where he developed a passion for mechanical devices, especially guns. "I remember seeing them in store windows and they looked so beautiful, particularly the Savage 99 and the Winchester lever action," he reminisced. "The mechanics were so artistically designed—they absolutely thrilled me. I associate them with great adventure and great art."[11]

Back in Brooklyn, the young man began disassembling these pieces of art and then rebuilding them. He was so obsessed with guns that in his spare time, he toured firearm manufacturing plants in nearby Connecticut and headed to the library and consumed engineering textbooks.

Ruger attended the University of North Carolina at Chapel Hill, but after two years he got married, had a child, and dropped out. With no real job and few prospects, the inventor began making pistol prototypes and shopping them around. Ruger's homemade inventions received a lukewarm reception from most of the big gun companies. However, in 1939, on a trip to Washington, he showed some U.S. Army engineers a homemade lever-action hunting rifle that he had converted into a gas-operated semiautomatic. Duly impressed, the U.S. Army Ordnance Corps in Springfield sent him a letter offering him a staff position as a designer.[12]

There, Ruger shined, and for the first time exhibited his independent streak by quitting to invent a light machine gun of his own design. By 1940, Ruger was working on gas-powered military-grade guns for Auto-Ordnance. "When I first learned the principles under which machine guns functioned, I was just fascinated," he explained. "I was almost like a little kid finding out how a steam engine or internal combustion engine works." But the war was coming to an end, and so was the immediate need for a light machine gun.

It was getting back to basics that would allow Ruger to compete with traditional gun giants. After the war, Ruger set up a small shop in Southport, Connecticut. Like many postwar gun manufacturers, he struggled at first, turning to the consumer products that were in great demand at the time to keep his company afloat. "One of their first big postwar projects was an automatic changing record player. I went in and made a bid on producing some of the components, and I got a big order from them," Ruger would recall.[13] Yet his virtuosity was in making guns. In the late 1940s, the budding inventor had gotten his hands on a Japanese Nambu pistol that had found its way back from the Pacific theater. Ruger used the semiautomatic pistol—which looked like the more famous German Luger: thin barrel and boxy single-piece frame—as a template for his new sporting pistol design.

While Ruger was excited about the prospects of his project, he still lacked the necessary capital to manufacture. That is, until 1949, when a Yale graduate and new friend of Ruger's named Alexander Sturm invested a modest $50,000 of his family's fortune into the newly christened Sturm, Ruger & Co. (Sturm, who had a keen interest in heraldry, would also design the company's famous Germanic eagle, a trademark that fooled many consumers who bought the Luger-like gun into thinking the company was German.)

The duo's first product—a low-cost .22-caliber recreational rimfire pistol that mirrored the aesthetics of the Nambu—was a massive hit. The "Standard" model, as it was known, would go on to become the bestselling .22 pistol of all time, spurring countless offspring and imitations that sell well to this day. The Standard model was under constant production in basically the same form for the next thirty-three years, but the new corporation expanded the basic Standard archetype into a product line of pistols over time through the introduction of a number of variant models.

Sturm died from viral hepatitis in 1951 at the age of twenty-eight, but the company he helped found saw enormous success in the recreational gun market. Ruger's considerable success was based on a knack for cost-cutting manufacturing techniques, public relations, and, perhaps most important, an innate feel for the marketplace. Unlike the men who labored under the bureaucratic constraints of government contracts, Ruger was in most ways a spiritual descendant of Colt, not Garand.

This included his consideration of aesthetics and salesmanship. Ruger would later contend that the executives at the big gun companies of the time failed because they had no real interest in the outdoors or hunting. They would take clients out golfing, not shooting, he reminded his sales staff—the CEOs' understanding of the market hinged on what consumers wanted yesterday, not tomorrow. Unlike many companies in the coming decades, Ruger would shun the new science of market research. "If I really personally like it," Ruger said in a 1981 interview, "then I can be fairly sure and positive that there will be a lot of other people who feel the same way."[14] They would. Ruger made guns for the outdoorsman, the hunter, and the hobbyist in postwar American life. His gun was priced for the average American sportsman, of whom there would be many millions.

The explosion in hunting and gun sports also led to a string of firearm and hunting magazines. Ruger and his company immediately took full advantage of this growing market, which allowed gun reviewers to disseminate opinions around the country in ways they had never been able to do before. "Firms like Winchester and Remington would loan a gun to a writer so he could write something about it, but they didn't cultivate any friendship," Ruger later noted. A piece in *American Rifleman*, the leading publication about firearms, helped spread Ruger's reputation. Through Strum, Ruger used innovative manufacturing techniques and promotion, imbuing their guns with an element of nostalgia. Most of the fundamentals of gunmaking had already been invented. And Ruger, who should not have been underestimated as an innovator himself, understood that there was a romanticism that enticed American shooters.

In many ways Ruger reinvigorated the gun market by looking to the past as much as he would the future, reintroducing guns that most other companies believed had run their course. For example, Ruger knew that Colt had discontinued making the famous single-action Army models. He also understood that there was a healthy market out there for the gun, because *he* wanted one. Ruger began reissuing a number of old models, nearly all of which were successful. The company would diversify and experience the ups and downs of any corporation. By the twenty-first century, Sturm, Ruger & Co was consistently one of the top gunmakers in the world. By this time, all the major firearm manufacturers were following his lead and taking advantage of the insatiable appetite for guns. Few industries, after all, had a historic connection to America's past like the gunmaker. Although most of the big names would also experience bumpy rides and ownership changes throughout the second half of the 1900s, by the end of the century, most of the names remained the same. Remington (founded in 1816), Smith & Wesson (1852), Colt (1855), and Winchester (1866) still dominated the marketplace. By the start of the twenty-first century there would be rekindled interest in the old guns, and technical advances would spur the industry to hundreds of millions in revenue.

The gun, it turns out, was not a faddish feature of American life. According to Gallup, gun ownership per household in 1961 was at 49 percent. In 1993 it was at 51 percent and in 2013 it was at 45 percent—despite the fact that there had been a big shift from rural to urban areas.[15] Some believe this is due to the big dip in hunting among Americans.[16] Only around 15 percent of adults lived in households in which they or their spouses were hunters. It is the lowest percentage of hunters since the highest level of 31.6 percent recorded by pollsters in 1977.

The number of guns manufactured each year in the United States, however, grew from 2.9 million in 2001 to nearly 5.5 million in 2010 to nearly 10.9 million in 2013. Around this time there was also an explosion of imported firearms. From 2001 through 2007, handgun imports nearly doubled, from 711,000 to nearly 1.4 million. By 2009, nearly 2.2 million handguns were imported into the United States. Guns from Glock, SIG Sauer, and others became wildly popular. In 2016 there would be a record 5.5 million handguns imported into the United States.[17]

Another dynamic emerged with the surge of gun ownership: crime rates fell. They fell a lot. From their peak in the early 1990s, violent crime rates, including murder, rape, and aggravated assault, would all decline. By 2014, homicide rates of 4.5 people per 100,000 were the lowest since 1963, when it was 4.6 people per 100,000. There would be a slight uptick in crime the next two years, but by the mid-2000s there was ample evidence that crime rates had far more to do with social trends and economics than they did with the level of gun ownership.

Gun control legislation had the opposite of its intended effect. In 1994 the National Institute of Justice found that 44 million people, or around 35 percent of households, owned 192 million firearms. Seventy-four percent of those who admitted to owning guns said they owned more than one firearm. Around the same time, the Bureau of Alcohol, Tobacco, Firearms and Explosives found that approximately 242 million firearms were either in the marketplace or owned by civilians in the United States. The breakdown of ownership was around 72 million handguns, 76 million rifles, and 64 million shotguns. By 2000 the ATF put the number at approximately 259 million: 92 million handguns, 92 million rifles, and 75 million shotguns. By 2007, the number of firearms had increased to approximately 294 million: 106 million handguns, 105 million rifles, and 83 million shotguns. By 2009, the estimated total number of firearms available to civilians in the United States had increased to 310 million: 114 million handguns, 110 million rifles, and 86 million shotguns.[18]

With all these guns, the originalist understanding of the Second Amendment would also regain its popularity. The politics of guns, though, would take a while to catch up.

CONCLUSION

★

Molon Labe

"The Second Amendment protects an individual right to possess a firearm unconnected with service in a militia, and to use that arm for traditionally lawful purposes, such as self-defense within the home."
—**The Supreme Court of the United States of America, 2008**

Flag raised by Texas settlers at the Battle of Gonzales in October 1835

A wide-ranging, well-funded political, cultural, and legal effort of revisionism has been undertaken to erase much of the history you've just read. Few mainstream historians looking back at the nineteenth and twentieth centuries even bother delving into the lives of men like John Hall, John Browning, Christopher Spencer, John Garand, and Eugene Stoner, much less afford them a rightful place among America's greatest innovators and manufacturers. Books about the Revolutionary era make only perfunctory mention of guns, despite their central role in the story of the nation's founding, and fewer still acknowledge the role of guns in freeing the slaves or holding back fascism or ridding the world of communism.

Worse, in contemporary America, countless historians have attempted to retroactively dismiss the ubiquitous presence of guns in American life and the role firearms played in the rise of a nation. Countless anti-gun activists have used this revisionist history to dismiss the overwhelming evidence that the founding generation believed that individual Americans had an inherent right to bear those arms. Countless politicians would lean on this fiction as a rationalization to create laws and regulations that undermined that right on both local and federal levels. Countless journalists have penned prejudiced pieces aiding the efforts of these politicians. And countless judges have latched onto this mythology in an attempt to disarm law-abiding individuals in the name of safety.

All of these forces have fostered a "collective right" theory regarding the Second Amendment that became incontestable truth in legal and political circles for many years. The singular purpose of the Second Amendment, they argued, was to arm militias, not individuals. To argue differently was an antiquated and destructive reading of the past.

As this book argues, history does not back up this contention. The notion of individual ownership of firearms was so unmistakable and so omnipresent in colonial days—and beyond—that Americans saw no more need to debate its existence than they did the right to drink water or breathe the air. Not a single Minuteman was asked to hand his musket over to the Continental Congress after chasing the British back to Boston. If they had been, the Revolution would have been short-lived, indeed. When Americans were asked to surrender their weapons, it was typically in an effort to subjugate blacks, Native Americans, or other minority populations.

As we've seen, the debate over the Second Amendment centered on who controlled the militias, the federal or state governments. Everyone understood that a militia consisted of free individuals who would almost always grab their *own* firearms—the ones they used in their everyday existence—to engage in a concerted effort to protect themselves, their community, or their country . . . sometimes from their own government. Many colonies enshrined an individual's right to bear arms in their own constitutions before the Bill of Rights was even written—most of them in much more explicit terms.

Not even the British, whose attempts to disarm Americans had sparked a rebellion, would ever challenge the underlying belief that self-defense was an individual right. "The right of self defense is the first law of nature," wrote George Tucker in the 1803 *Blackstone's Commentaries* regarding the American Second Amendment. "In most governments it has been the study of rulers to confine this right within the narrowest possible limits . . . and [when] the right of the people to keep and bear arms is, under any color or pretext whatsoever, prohibited, liberty, if not already annihilated, is on the brink of destruction."[1]

During the nineteenth century, there was still no need to debate whether the Second Amendment was an individual right. Again, before the mid-1900s the right of an individual to bear arms had been so self-evident that on the rare occasions it was mentioned it was brought up to compare American liberty with tyranny elsewhere. In an 1823 letter to John Adams, William H. Sumner, politician and general in the Massachusetts militia, noted that if the population of the United States "like that of Europe, chiefly consisted of an unarmed peasantry," it would be conquerable. "Here," he went on, "every house is a castle, and every man a soldier. Arms are in every hand, confidence in every mind, and courage in every heart. It depends upon its own will, and not upon the force of the enemy, whether such a country shall ever be conquered."[2] Adams concurred with this thinking. An armed citizenry would not be susceptible to tyranny.

"The right of the citizens to keep and bear arms has justly been considered, as the palladium of the liberties of a republic; since it offers a strong moral check against the usurpation and arbitrary power of rulers," wrote Joseph Story, an associate Supreme Court justice in the early 1800s, "and will generally, even if these are successful in the first instance, enable the people to resist and triumph over them."

Contemporary liberals often view this form of rhetoric against the government as an endorsement of treason. Of course, despite our many political fights, there is no need for armed insurrection today. What sneering contemporary critics fail to comprehend is that the founding generation believed those who would undermine the universal and inalienable liberties of the people laid out in the Constitution—whether they were in the government or not—*are* the ones committing sedition.

During the 1800s, firearm innovation and fascination allowed Americans to explore, tame, and ultimately populate the West. This project, with all its moral implications, both admirable and sometimes ugly, made the United States the most powerful economic power on earth. Meanwhile, a number of municipalities in the West passed local gun ordinances. Not one of these regulations ever challenged the idea of a man's right to own a firearm. Nor would the right to bear arms be challenged during the Civil War era, when manufacturing capacity and industrialization of the Union—spurred in part by gun innovators like Hall and Colt—helped create an infrastructure of superior armaments and technology that defeated the Confederacy.

It should be stressed that not all Americans benefited equally from the right to defend themselves—at least, not until the second half of the twentieth century. The early Americans denied both Catholics and other intolerable Christian denominations their right to self-defense. Black Americans would be denied these rights for centuries longer. Frederick Douglass reacted to the Fugitive Slave Act of 1850 by editorializing that the best remedy might be "a good revolver, a steady hand, and a determination to shoot down any man attempting to kidnap." (Would any modern gun control advocate contend his was a treasonous statement?) Even after the Civil War was won, blacks still struggled to have their liberties protected. Most of the first gun controls, in fact, were racist in intent. In 1834 the state of Tennessee revised its Constitution from "That the freemen of this State have a right to keep and to bear arms for their common defence" to "That the free white men of this State have a right to keep and to bear arms for their common defence."[3] A number of southern states followed suit.

By the first post–Civil War election in 1868, some southern blacks had begun to arm themselves. In one incident in Tennessee, a black man fought off a mob of terrorizing Klansmen who dragged him from his house by brandishing his gun. "I prevented [one of them] by my pistol, which I cocked, and he jumped back," the man explained. "I told them I would hurt them if they got away. They did not burn nor steal anything, nor hurt me." These kinds of events were the exception to the population that was often left helpless. Soon "Black Codes" were instituted that made owning guns illegal for most blacks and continued to put them at the mercy of racist governments.

When Jacob Howard, the Michigan senator, introduced the Fourteenth Amendment to ensure that blacks in the South had their constitutional rights protected, he noted that "the *personal* rights guaranteed and secured by the *first eight* amendment to the Constitution" as in the freedom of speech and of the press and "the right to bear arms," specifically (emphasis mine).[4] The late nineteenth-century civil rights leader Ida B. Wells noted that one of the lessons of post–Civil War America and "which every Afro American should ponder well, is that a Winchester rifle should have a place of honor in every black home, and it should be used for that protection which the law refuses to give."[5] T. Thomas Fortune, another black civil rights activist of the era, argued that it was with a Winchester that the black man could "defend his home and children and wife."[6] Although most of the founders certainly did not intend for the Second Amendment to protect all men, these civil rights leaders understood natural law better than most. More than a century after the Constitution was written, most discussion regarded the right to bear arms as a means to counteract internal tyranny and the threat of invasion.

As we've seen, during the 1900s—specifically in the 1930s and later 1960s—gun control advocates made headway in both gun control and rewriting history. But by the late 1970s the previously unnecessary Second Amendment activists would join social and fiscal conservatives as an emerging conservative majority in the 1980s. Congress would even pass the Firearm Owners Protection Act of 1986, which reined in the rogue ATF from harassing gun dealers and forbade the federal government from creating a national registry. (An amendment to the law, however, also banned civilian ownership of fully automatic guns manufactured after May 19, 1986. Owning one that was made before that date now requires federal registration and an extensive background check.)

Those gains proved to be short-lived. Bill Clinton would be the first president in American history to openly and actively seek to constrain gun sales to civilians and regulate ownership. He later claimed to regret this effort for political reasons, but in 1993, Clinton signed the Brady Bill—named after James Brady, the White House press secretary who was shot by John Hinckley Jr. in 1981 with a "Saturday Night Special" (popular slang for a cheap handgun) during an attempt to assassinate President Ronald Reagan. In the aftermath of the murder attempt, Brady and his wife, Sarah, would become leading gun control advocates through the Brady Campaign. (The organization had begun as the more honest National Council to Control Handguns in 1974, then Handgun Control, Inc., and finally the Brady Campaign to Prevent Gun Violence.) The Brady Bill included a slew of regulations and taxes, but its most consequential regulation would be the "waiting period." A prospective gun buyer would have to wait five business days while the authorities checked on his or her background, during which time the sale would be approved or prohibited based on an established set of criteria.[7]

As many saw it, the law, with its many procedures, had finally transformed a right guaranteed by the Constitution into a privilege, like driving. For the first time, law-abiding American citizens were impelled to ask the state for permission to buy a firearm. The NRA challenged the law on Tenth Amendment grounds. In 1997 the Supreme Court ruled that the provision of the Brady Act that forced state and local law enforcement officials to run background checks was unconstitutional. Checks would eventually occur federally through a new system called the National Instant Criminal Background Check. All the background checks would be immediately destroyed, because federal law still prohibited the creation of a national registry.

Democrats, however, weren't done. A year later they passed the Violent Crime Control and Law Enforcement Act of 1994, or what would more commonly become known as the "assault weapon ban." A truly silly law born of a campaign of scaremongering, the ten-year federal ban on the manufacture of new semiautomatic assault weapons had everything to do with the cosmetics of guns yet was ignorant of how they actually worked. Gun features that frightened non–gun owners, like collapsible stocks, pistol grips, bayonet mounts, and flash suppressors, were banned. Manufacturers found ways around these strictures, and the ban did nothing to mitigate violence, since the majority of gun homicides were executed using handguns. So when the ten-year sunset provision of the assault weapons ban ran its course, the law was not renewed by a Republican Congress—without much protest from Democrats.

Around the same time the NRA was gaining political clout, policy wonks and legal minds began laying the groundwork for reclaiming the Second Amendment. In 1983 the *Michigan Law Review* published "Handgun Prohibition and the Original Meaning of the Second Amendment" by Don Kates, a Yale Law School graduate who had worked with William Kunstler during the civil rights movement.[8] The paper, a meticulous refutation of collective rights theory, hastened a flood of new scholarship in libertarian and conservative circles. Kates's ideas even began gaining some traction with liberal academics—most notably with the highly respected Laurence Tribe—creating a momentum that resulted in a political movement, and ultimately, a challenge in the federal courts.[9]

I n 1991, former Supreme Court chief justice Warren Burger was telling reporters that the Second Amendment "has been the subject of one of the greatest pieces of fraud, I repeat the word 'fraud,' on the American public by special interest groups that I have ever seen in my lifetime." Originalism, the judicial interpretation that follows closely the original intentions of the Constitution, was anathema to many, but nothing seemed to be more grating to its opponents than the argument for the individual right of gun ownership.

Burger was correct, but not in the way he imagined. It would take one case to create an opening to prove him wrong. It came in 1998, when a doctor named Timothy Joe Emerson was in the midst of an acrimonious divorce. His wife requested a restraining order against him from a Texas court. Like many Texans, Emerson had been collecting guns for years and legally owned around thirty firearms of various types. His wife told the police that Emerson had threatened to use one of his pistols, a 9-millimeter Beretta that he kept in his office. What Emerson didn't know was that federal law forbade anyone under a domestic restraining order from possessing any firearms. He was arrested. Emerson's court-appointed lawyer argued, perhaps unaware of the dearth of Second Amendment cases or the history he was making, that without any judicial finding that his client posed a danger to his wife, Emerson still had a constitutional right to own a gun. To the surprise of many, the Fifth Circuit found that the Second Amendment "protects individual Americans in their right to keep and bear arms whether or not they are a member of a select militia or performing active military service or training."

While government lawyers looked at the panel's ruling before deciding whether to appeal to the Supreme Court (they did, although the court did not take it up), then attorney general John Ashcroft was asked to clarify his position on the Second Amendment. While not specifically mentioning the *Emerson* case, Ashcroft wrote that he "unequivocally" believed the original intent of the Second Amendment was to protect the right of individuals to arm themselves. Just as the First and Fourth Amendments secure individual rights of speech and security respectively, "the Second Amendment protects an individual right to keep and bear arms," he wrote. This was a dramatic about-face from the Clinton administration. A 2001 *Boston Globe* article noted that courts had been treating the Second Amendment as "a relic of the American Revolution."

The *Emerson* decision also sparked the interest of a number of libertarian think tank legal scholars, including Clark M. Neily, Steve Simpson, and Robert Levy (and soon a private-sector lawyer, Alan Gura). Levy, a wealthy software designer, had entered the George Mason University School of Law at the age of fifty and exited as valedictorian. After two clerkships with federal judges, he became a policy wonk at the Cato Institute in Washington. By his own admission, his interest in Second Amendment law was purely idealistic. Levy had never personally owned a gun.[10] Soon a number of other idealistic lawyers, almost none of them gun enthusiasts, began plotting their case. And everyone knew the best place to start would be in the nation's capital, where federal law not only prohibited almost every citizen from owning a handgun but compelled those who did own rifles and shotguns to keep them unloaded and disassembled or bound by a trigger lock, making them useless as a means of self-defense.

The lawsuit they were devising featured a diverse group of Americans as plaintiffs. One of the first to sign on was an African-American Capitol Hill resident named Shelly Parker. Fed up with the crime near her home, Parker attempted to clean up the neighborhood, provoking the ire of local drug dealers, who began vandalizing her property and threatening her life. In Washington, DC, however, if Parker obtained a gun to protect herself, she would be arrested. "In the event that someone does get in my home," she explained, "I would have no defense, except maybe throw my paper towels at them."

The suit—and others like it—moved slowly through the court system. Adding to the complexity of the situation was that the National Rifle Association, now the leading gun rights organization in the country, believed that bringing a Second Amendment case to higher courts could backfire and undermine gun rights by enshrining the collective rights theory. The libertarian contingent didn't believe this would be the case after *Emerson*. Moreover, hadn't lower courts already been functioning under this idea anyway? How could it get worse? The NRA attempted to consolidate cases. It sued

246 ★ DAVID HARSANYI

the more formidable Department of Justice, wrongly believing that Ashcroft's statement on the Second Amendment might dissuade it from taking the case. Levy and his team concentrated on the less formidable Washington, DC, court and a direct challenge on Second Amendment grounds.

In February 2003, the six plaintiffs filed a lawsuit in the District Court for the District of Columbia challenging the constitutionality of the Firearms Control Regulations Act of 1975. The case was first dismissed by the judge, but a three-judge panel of the U.S. Court of Appeals for the District of Columbia reversed that dismissal in a 2–1 decision. Only one of the plaintiffs had standing, and his name, Dick Heller, would become synonymous with the originalist interpretation of the Second Amendment.

Heller was a security guard at the Federal Judicial Center. While District of Columbia laws allowed "special police officers" like Heller to carry handguns to protect government employees, they were not allowed to take those guns home and protect themselves, their families, or their homes. For a long time, Heller had found this inequitable. In July 2002, at the urging of a prescient friend, Heller attempted to register his revolver with the Metropolitan Police Department. He was instantly rejected. It would, no doubt, have struck the authors of the *Federalist Papers* as outlandish, if not authoritarian, to demand a citizen get a *gun permit* to have standing in a case over his constitutional rights. Yet, due to Heller's seemingly innocuous act, the Court of Appeals was able to strike down provisions that banned citizens from owning firearms in their homes. The court held that the Second Amendment protected "an individual right to keep and bear arms," and that such a right "existed prior to the formation of the new government under the Constitution." In addition to sport shooting and self-defense, the right to own a gun, the majority wrote, should be "understood as resistance to either private lawlessness or the depredations of a tyrannical government (or a threat from abroad)."

Washington's then mayor, Adrian Fenty, immediately denounced the decision, as did a number of congressmen and law enforcement agencies, calling it "unconscionable" and claiming, "It flies in the face of laws that have helped decrease gun violence in the District of Columbia." Fenty provided no evidence for his claim, nor did it matter very much when it came to the constitutionality of Washington's ban. In April 2007, Fenty petitioned for rehearing en banc, and on November 20 of that year, the U.S. Supreme Court agreed to hear the case.

District of Columbia v. Heller was a landmark case, invalidating a federal law that prohibited owning a handgun and, at least for now, enshrining the Second Amendment as an individual right. Justice Antonin Scalia, writing for the majority, offered a historical, philosophical, and legal exposition of the history of the Second Amendment. "Putting all of these textual elements together," he wrote, "we find that they guarantee the individual right to possess and carry weapons in case of confrontation. This meaning is strongly confirmed by the historical background of the Second Amendment. We look to this because it has always been widely understood that the Second Amendment, like the First and Fourth Amendments, codified a pre-existing right."

Just as the First Amendment protects modern communication and just as the Fourth Amendment applies to modern forms of search, the Second Amendment extends to guns that "were not in existence at the time of the founding." Despite the many hyperbolic responses to the decision, Scalia did not offer a maximalist position. It is, he also wrote, "not a right to keep and carry any weapon whatsoever in any manner whatsoever and for whatever purpose."

Two years after the *Heller* decision, the Supreme Court, in *McDonald v. City of Chicago*, struck down a similar handgun ban, this one passed on a state level. Five justices concluded that the Fourteenth Amendment protects against state infringement of the same individual right that is protected from federal infringement by the Second Amendment. Although these two decisions would be extraordinarily important for gun rights advocates, they certainly didn't put all gun-related issues to bed. There would be an array of cases and tactics employed to impose gun control in the coming years. How far can the state go in banning felons and the mentally ill from owning guns? How far can they go in banning firearms in "sensitive places" such as schools and government buildings? How far can they go in banning weapons "not typically possessed by law-abiding citizens for lawful purposes"? What kind of gun is "typical"? These are just a few of the debates that would soon emerge. The fight is not ending anytime soon.

President Barack Obama might have told gun owners, "I'm not looking to disarm you," and claimed to have supported the *Heller* decision in his first campaign, but by the time he was elected in 2008, the former Illinois legislator already had a long history of supporting the most draconian gun control in the country—including a full ban on handguns in

Chicago. His initial political positioning was a reflection of how much ground Second Amendment advocates had gained over the previous decade. After every tragic mass shooting, the president renewed his commitment to more gun control, whether such controls would have stopped the murderer or not. His appeals became increasingly emotional. ("It is easier for a teenager to buy a Glock than get his hands on a computer or even a book" was a contention Obama made that no rational person could ever possibly believe.) A slew of regulations attempted to inhibit the use of ammunition and hunting. By the end of the president's second term, Democrats had ratcheted up the rhetoric, comparing Republicans to ISIS terrorists. They drafted bills to allow the state to deprive those on any government watch list of their Second Amendment right without any due process.

This was 2016, not 1968, however, and there was a slim to no chance that there would be enough support for any kind of restrictive legislation. Rather, every time Democrats engaged in a new gun control push, there was a massive counterreaction. In 2016 a trade association for firearms manufacturers found that the gun industry had gone from $19 billion in 2008 to near $50 billion by 2015. In 2008, around 160,000 Americans worked in the gun industry. By 2015 it was 288,000. During Obama's eight years as president, the FBI processed 157,233,157 firearm checks, which was 61 million more than they had the previous decade. In 2016 they ran 27,538,673. Four million more than the previous year.

Every time there is an effort to weaken the protections of the Second Amendment, there is a resurgence both in gun ownership and the idealism that surrounds it. Every time there is an effort to dismiss the vibrant and important role the gun has played in our history, a movement rises to reclaim it. There are more guns in America today than there are people. A lot more. A recent Gallup poll found that 47 percent of adults reported having a gun in their home. It is likely that even more Americans own guns and aren't inclined to tell a pollster about it. Yet, because of the divisive political realities of the age, we often hear the term "gun culture" being thrown around as invective. "Gun culture" is no less part of American life than "religious culture" or "speech culture." As our history unambiguously illustrates, gun culture is inextricably tied to American culture. One cannot exist without the other.

NOTES

★

The New Hampshire Sharp-Shooters

PROLOGUE: From Prey to Predator

1   Nicolas, Wade, *Before the Dawn: Recovering the Lost History of Our Ancestors* (Penguin, 2007), p. 151.

2   Ibid.

3   Crosby, Alfred W., *Throwing Fire: Projectile Technology Through History* (Cambridge Press, 2010), p. 15.

4   de Lazaro, Enrico, "Stone Tools Hint at 71,000-Year-Old Advanced Lethal Technology," *Science News*, Nov. 8, 2012.

5   Huley, Vic, *Arrows Against Steel: The History of the Bow and How It Forever Changed Warfare* (Cerberus Books, 2011), p. 14.

6   Morgan, Edmund S., "In Love With Guns," *New York Review of Books*, Oct. 19, 2000.

7   Hacker, Barton C., "Gunpowder and Firearms: Warfare in Medieval India, and Warfare and Weaponry in South Asia 1000–1800," *Technology and Culture* 46, no. 4 (Oct. 2005).

8   For more on the first battle to use both the longbow and the gun, see de Wailly, Henri, *Crécy, 1346: Anatomy of a Battle* (Sterling, 1987).

9   Partington, J. R., *A History of Greek Fire and Gunpowder* (Johns Hopkins University Press, 1998), p. 98.

10   Hogg, Ian V., *Artillery: Its Origin, Heyday, and Decline* (Archon, 1970), p. 41.

11   Ibid, p. 4.

12   Norris, John, *Artillery: A History* (History Press, 2012), p. 29.

13   Crosby, *Throwing Fire*, p. 113.

14   Ambrogi, Stefano, "Site of Britain's First Ever Gunbattle Revealed," Reuters, Dec. 2, 2010.

15   Pauly, Roger, *Firearms: The Life Story of a Technology* (Johns Hopkins University Press, 2008), p. 16.

1: First Contact

1   Jennings, Francis, *The Ambiguous Iroquois Empire: The Covenant Chain Confederation of Indian Tribes with English Colonies* (W. W. Norton; reprint edition, 1990), p. 41.

2   Hearn, Kelly, "First Known Gunshot Victim in Americas Discovered," National Geographic News, June 19, 2007.

3   Rose, Alexander, *American Rifle* (Delta, 2009), p. 3.

4   Champlain, Samuel de, *The Works of Samuel de Champlain* (University of Toronto, 1922), p. 129, https://archive.org/details/worksofsamueldec02 chamuoft.

5   The story is relayed in John Smith's "The Generall Historie of Virginia, New-England, and the Summer Isles," written in 1624, http://docsouth .unc.edu/southlit/smith/smith.html.

6   Champlain, *The Works of Samuel de Champlain*, p. 99.

2: Pilgrim's Progress

1   Johnson, Caleb, *Of Plymouth Plantation: Along with the Full Text of the Pilgrims' Journals* (Xlibris, 2006), p. 119.

2   For more on the Pilgrims' first meeting with the Indians, see Philbrick, Nathaniel, *Mayflower: A Story of Courage, Community, and War* (Penguin Books, 2007), pp. 56–77.

3   Bunker, Nick, *Making Haste from Babylon: The Mayflower Pilgrims and Their New World; A History* (New York: Knopf, 2010), p. 37.

4 Boorstin, Daniel J., "The Therapy Of Distance," *American Heritage* 27, no. 4 (June 1976).

5 Goldstein, Karin, "Arms & Armor of the Pilgrims," Curator of Collections, Pilgrim Society, http://www.pilgrimhall.org/pdf/Arms_Armor_of_Pilgrims.pdf.

6 Cramer, Clayton, *Armed America: The Remarkable Story of How and Why Guns Became as American as Apple Pie* (Thomas Nelson, 2009), p. 4.

7 Malcolm, Joyce, *To Keep and Bear Arms: The Origins of an Anglo-American Right* (Harvard University Press, 1996), p. 139.

8 Cramer, *Armed America*, p. 17.

9 Alden, Ebenezer, *Memorial of the Descendants of the Hon. John Alden, Member of the American Antiquarian Society, New England Historic Genealogical Society, &c.* Published for the family: 1867.

10 Peterson, Harold Leslie, *Arms and Armor in Colonial America, 1526–1783* (Bramhall House, 1956), p. 38.

11 As of this writing, the remnants of the pistol are on display at the Historic Jamestowne Museum in Jamestown, Virginia.

12 Greener, W. W., *The Gun and Its Development* (Skyhorse; 9th edition, 2013), p. 97.

13 Pauly, *Firearms*, p. 51.

14 Falkner, James, *Marlborough's War Machine, 1702–1711* (Pen and Sword Military, 2014), p. 87.

15 Johnson, Samuel, *The Sayings of Doctor Johnson,* (Duckworth Overlook, 1911), p. xvi, https://archive.org/details/sirsaiddrjohnson00john.

16 Malcolm, *To Keep and Bear Arms*, p. 12.

17 Blackstone, Sir William, *Commentaries on the Laws of England: In Four Books,* vol. 1 (J. B. Lippincott, 1886), p. 719, https://archive.org/details/commentariesonl04blacgoog.

18 Russell, Carl P., *Guns on the Early Frontiers: From Colonial Times to the Years of the Western Fur Trade* (Dover, 2005; originally published by University of California, Berkeley Press, 1957), p. 42.

19 Penn, William, *The Select Works of William Penn: In Five Volumes* (National Archives, 1726), p. 50, https://archive.org/details/collectionofwork01penn.

20 For more, see "German Settlement in Pennsylvania: Background Reading" (Historical Society of Pennsylvania and the Balch Institute for Ethnic Studies).

21 Applebaum, Herbert A., *Colonial Americans at Work* (University Press of America, 1996), p. 184.

22 Dworsky, Joel, and Dr. Timothy Trussell, "The Mylin Gun Shop Survey Project: Excavation Report for the Lancaster Colonial Settlement Project," http://www.millersville.edu/archaeology/files/mylin-gunshop-site-report .pdf.

23 Dillin, Captain John G. W., *The Kentucky Rifle* (National Rifle Association of America, 1924).

24 Greener, *The Gun and Its Development,* p. 620.

25 Grancsay, Stephen Vincent, *Craft of the Early American Gunsmith* (Metropolitan Museum of Art, 1947).

3: Powder Alarm

1 *The Works of John Adams,* vol. 1, p. 86, http://oll.libertyfund.org/titles /adams-the-works-of-john-adams-vol-1-life-of-the-author.

2 *The Laws of the State of New-Hampshire: With the Constitutions of the United States and of the State Prefixed,* published 1815, p. 460, https:// babel.hathitrust.org/cgi/pt?id=nyp.33433009057328;view=1up;seq=7.

3 Abigail Adams to John Adams, 2 September 1774, National Archives, https://founders.archives.gov/documents/Adams/04-01-02-0096.

4 Rae, Noel, *People's War: Original Voices of the American Revolution* (Lyons Press, 2011), p. 108.

5 Kopel, David B., "How the British Gun Control Program Precipitated the American Revolution," *Charleston Law Review* 6, no. 2 (Winter 2012), p. 293.

6 O'Shaughnessy, Andrew Jackson, *The Men Who Lost America: British Leadership, American Revolution, and the Fate of the Empire* (Yale University Press, 2013), p. 86.

7 Salay, David L., "The Production of Gunpowder in Pennsylvania During the American Revolution," *Pennsylvania Magazine of History and Biography* 99, no. 4 (Oct. 1975).

8 Stephenson, Orlando W., "The Supply of Gunpowder in 1776," *American Historical Review* 30, no. 2 (Jan. 1925), pp. 271–78.

9 "The Writings of George Washington from the Original Manuscript Sources, 1745–1799; prepared under the direction of the United States George Washington Bicentennial Commission and published by authority of Congress" (US Government Printing Office, 1931).

10 For more on the history of "Greek fire," see Norwich, John J., *A Short History of Byzantium* (Vintage, 1998).

11 McLachlan, Sean, *Medieval Handgonnes: The First Black Powder Infantry Weapons* (Osprey, 2010), pp. 20–23.

12   Crosby, Alfred W., *Throwing Fire: Projectile Technology Through History* (Cambridge University Press, 2002), p. 121.

13   Salay, "The Production of Gunpowder in Pennsylvania During the American Revolution," p. 425.

14   Forbes, Esther, *Paul Revere and the World He Lived In* (Mariner Books, 1999), p. 304.

15   National Park Service, National Register of Historic Places Program, "Continental Powder Works at French Creek," https://www.nps.gov/nr/feature/places/15000827.htm.

16   Russell, Carl P., *Guns on the Early Frontiers: From Colonial Times to the Years of the Western Fur Trade* (Dover, 2005; original published by University of California, Berkeley Press, 1957), p. 220.

17   "Minutes of the Provincial Council of Pennsylvania: From the organization to the termination of proprietary government," vol. 10, p. 469.

18   Kelly, Jack, *Gunpowder: Alchemy, Bombards, and Pyrotechnics: The History of the Explosive That Changed the World* (Basic Books, 2004), p. 22.

19   George Washington to Nicholas Cooke, 4 August 1775, National Archives. https://founders.archives.gov/documents/Washington/03-01-02-0149.

20   Klein, Christopher, "The Midday Ride of Paul Revere," Smithsonian.com, Dec. 12, 2011.

21   "The Parliamentary Register; Or, History of the Proceedings and Debates of the House of Commons, During the First Session of the Fourteenth Parliament of Great Britain, Volume 1," p. 106.

22   Klein, "The Midday Ride of Paul Revere."

23   Salay, "The Production of Gunpowder in Pennsylvania During the American Revolution," p. 423.

4: "Fire!"

1   Kennedy, David M., *The American Spirit: United States History as Seen by Contemporaries,* vol. 1 (Wadsworth Cengage Learning, 2006), p. 114.

2   National Archives, "The Deposition of John Robins Regarding hostilities at Lexington," https://www.docsteach.org/documents/document/deposition-of-john-robins-regarding-hostilities-at-lexington.

3   Report of the Record Commissioners of the City of Boston, vol. 16, Boston (Mass.), Registry Dept. (Rockville and Church, 1886), p. 286.

4   Halbrook, Stephen Dr., *The Founders' Second Amendment Origins of the Right to Bear* (Ivan R. Dee, 2008), p. 6.

5   Fischer, David Hackett, *Paul Revere's Ride* (Oxford University Press, 1995), p. 73.

6   Frothingham, Richard, *History of the Siege of Boston: And of the Battles of Lexington, Concord and Bunker Hill* (Little, Brown; 4th edition, 1873), p. 51.

7   Letter from Dr. Joseph Warren to Arthur Lee, Boston, April 3, 1775. http://amarch.lib.niu.edu/islandora/object/niu-amarch%3A103895.

8   Hurst, Gerald B., "The Old Colonial System," Publications. Historical Series, vol. 3 (University of Manchester, 1905), p. 182.

9   Aptheker, Herbert, *The American Revolution, 1763–1783: A History of the American People; An Interpretation* (International Publishers, 1960), p. 113.

10   Rogers, Alan, *Empire and Liberty: American Resistance to British Authority, 1755–1763* (University of California Press, 1974), p. 63.

11   Ferling, John, *Whirlwind: The American Revolution and the War That Won It* (Bloomsbury, 2015), p. 209.

12   Urban, Mark, *Fusiliers: The Saga of a British Redcoat Regiment in the American Revolution* (Bloomsbury, 2007), p. 81.

13   Johnson, Nicholas J., David B. Kopel, George A. Mocsary, and Michael P. O'Shea, *Firearms Law and the Second Amendment: Regulation, Rights, and Policy* (Aspen, 2012), p. 139.

14   "To the Speakers of the Colonial Assemblies: A Circular Letter from Franklin, William Bollan, and Arthur Lee," LS: Library of Congress—London, Feb. 5, 1775.

15   Cook, Don, *The Long Fuse: How England Lost the American Colonies, 1760–1785* (Atlantic Monthly Press, 1996), p. 81.

16   Sawyer, Charles Wintrop, *Firearms in American History: 1600 to 1800* (National Archives, 1910), p. 9.

17   Bonwick, Colin, *English Radicals and the American Revolution* (North Carolina Press, 1977), p. 124.

18   Trevelyan, Laura, *The Winchester: The Gun That Built an American Dynasty* (Yale University Press, 2016), p. 2.

19   For more on the Bellesiles, see Lindgren, James, "Fall from Grace: Arming America and the Bellesiles Scandal," *Yale University Law Journal*, vol. 111, no. 18 (2002), https://www.yalelawjournal.org/review/fall-from-grace-arming-america-and-the-bellesiles-scandal.

20   Lindgren, James, and Justin Lee Heather, "Counting Guns in Early America," *William & Mary Law Review* 43, no. 5 (2002), p. 177. Northwestern Law & Econ Research Paper No. 01-1.

21 Utter, Glenn H. (editor), *Guns and Contemporary Society: The Past, Present, and Future of Firearms and Firearm Policy* (Praeger, 2015), p. 10.

22 Ibid.

23 Lindgren and Heather, "Counting Guns in Early America," p. 177.

24 Cramer, Clayton, *Armed America: The Remarkable Story of How and Why Guns Became as American as Apple Pie* (Thomas Nelson, 2009), p. 64.

25 Goss, Elbridge Henry, *The Life of Colonel Paul Revere, Volume 1,* (Howard W. Spurr, 8th edition, 1909), p. 196.

26 For more on Paul Revere's other ride, see Fischer, *Paul Revere's Ride.*

27 For more on the battle, see Ketchum, Richard M., *Saratoga: Turning Point of America's Revolutionary War* (Henry Holt, 1999).

28 Philbrick, Nathaniel, *Bunker Hill: A City, a Siege, a Revolution* (Penguin Books, 2014), p. 221.

29 From George Washington to John Hancock, 25 September 1776, National Archives. https://founders.archives.gov/documents/Washington/03-06-02-0305.

30 Massachusetts Historical Society, *Boston Evening-Post,* 21 November 1768. http://www.masshist.org/dorr/volume/2/sequence/334.

5: The Finest Marksmen in the World

1 York, Neil L., "Pennsylvania Rifle: Revolutionary Weapon in a Conventional War?" *Pennsylvania Magazine of History and Biography* 103, no. 3 (July 1979), pp. 302–24.

2 Graham, James, *The Life of General Daniel Morgan, of the Virginia Line of the Army of the United States, with Portions of His Correspondence; Comp[iled]. from Authentic Sources* (Derby & Jackson, H. W. Derby & Co., 1856), vi, https://quod.lib.umich.edu/cgi/t/text/text-idx?c=moa;idno=ABJ2761.

3 Brandow, John H., "General Daniel Morgan's Part in the Burgoyne Campaign," *Proceedings of the New York State Historical Association* 12 (1913), pp. 119–38.

4 Graham, James, *The Life of General Daniel Morgan,* p. 39.

5 Griffith, Samuel B., *The War for American Independence: From 1760 to the Surrender at Yorktown in 1781* (University of Illinois Press, 1976), p. 182.

6 John Adams to Abigail Adams, 11–17 June 1775, Massachusetts Historical Society, http://www.masshist.org/digitaladams/archive/doc?id=L17750611ja.

7 *Virginia Gazette*, July 25, 1775, cited in Lynn Montross, *Rag, Tag and Bobtail* (Harper, 1952), pp. 49–50.

8 General Washington to the President of the Continental Congress, July 10, 1775, Library of Congress, http://www.loc.gov/teachers/classroom materials/presentationsandactivities/presentations/timeline/amrev/con tarmy/presone.html.

9 Force, Peter, American Archives, Series IV, vol. 3, p. 2, https://archive.org /details/AmericanArchives-FourthSeriesVolume3peterForce.

10 Aron, Stephen, *How the West Was Lost: The Transformation of Kentucky from Daniel Boone to Henry Clay* (Johns Hopkins University Press, 1999), p. 113.

11 Boorstin, Daniel, "The Therapy of Distance," *American Heritage* 27, no. 4 (June 1976).

12 Force, Peter, American Archives, Series IV, vol. 3, page 5; letter dated August 1, 1775, from Elbridge Gerry to General Washington.

13 *Proceedings of the Massachusetts Historical Society* 43 (Oct. 1909–June 1910), p. 574.

14 Wood, Gordon S., *The American Revolution: A History* (Modern Library, 2003), p. 62.

15 Black, Jeremy, *European Warfare, 1660–1815* (Yale University Press, 1994), p. 42.

16 *Proceedings of the Massachusetts Historical Society* 43 (Oct. 1909–June 1910), p. 574.

17 Higginbotham, Don, *Daniel Morgan: Revolutionary Rifleman* (University of North Carolina Press, 1961), p. 39.

18 Wood, *The American Revolution*, p. 62.

19 Neilson, Charles, *An Original, Compiled, and Corrected Account of Burgoyne's Campaign: And the Memorable Battle of Bemis's Heights. Sept. 19 and Oct. 7, 1777, From the Most Authentic Sources of Information; Including Many Interesting Incidents Connected with the Same: and a Map of the Battle Ground* (Albany, 1844), p. 257.

20 Ibid.

21 Higginbotham, Don, *Daniel Morgan: Revolutionary Rifleman* (University of North Carolina Press, 1979), p. 170.

22 Black, Jeremy, *European Warfare*, p. 42.

23 Plaster, Major John. *History of Sniping and Sharpshooting* (Paladin Press, 2008), p. 102.

24 Russell, Carl P., *Guns on the Early Frontiers: From Colonial Times to the Years of the Western Fur Trade* (Dover, 2005: originally published by University of California, Berkeley Press, 1957), p. 99.

25 Artemas Ward to John Adams, 23 October 1775, National Archives, https://founders.archives.gov/documents/Adams/06-03-02-0120.

6: Liberty's Teeth

1 Martin, Joseph Plumb, *A Narrative of Some of the Adventures, Dangers and Sufferings of a Revolutionary Soldier [i.e., Joseph Plumb Martin]; Interspersed with Anecdotes of Incidents That Occurred Within His Own Observation. Written by himself* (National Archives), p. 44.

2 Reid, Stuart, *The Flintlock Musket: Brown Bess and Charleville, 1715–1865* (Osprey Publishing, 2016), p. 73.

3 Chaucer, Geoffrey, *The Aldine Edition of The British Poets, The Poems of Geoffrey Chaucer In Six Volumes, Vol. V* (George Bell & Sons, York St. Covent Garden and New York, 1893), p. 259.

4 Worman, Charles, G., *Firearms in American History: A Guide for Writers, Curators, and General Readers* (Westholme, 2007), p. 113.

5 Tower, Charlemagne, *The Marquis De Lafayette in the American Revolution*, vol.1 (Cosimo Classics, 2013), p. 323.

6 Worman, Charles G., *Firearms in American History*, p. 24.

7 Ibid., p. 27.

8 Peterson, Harold Leslie, *Arms and Armor in Colonial America, 1526–1783* (Bramhall House, 1956), p. 172.

9 Martin, *A Narrative of Some of the Adventures, Dangers and Sufferings of a Revolutionary Soldier*, p. 174.

7: Freedom's Guarantee

1 Debate in Virginia Ratifying Convention, Article 1, Section 8, Clause 12.

2 Chernow, Ron, *Alexander Hamilton* (Penguin Books, 2005), p. 294.

3 Malcolm, Joyce, *To Keep and Bear Arms: The Origins of an Anglo-American Right* (Harvard University Press, 1996), p. 137.

4 *The Statutes of the Realm: Printed by Command of His Majesty King George The Third*, vol. 3, p. 123, https://catalog.hathitrust.org/Record/012297566.

5 Malcolm, Joyce, *To Keep and Bear Arms: The Origins of an Anglo-American Right*, pp. 79–83.

6 The Founders; Constitution, University of Chicago, William Blackstone, Commentaries 1:139, http://press-pubs.uchicago.edu/founders/documents/amendIIs4.html.

7   The Founders' Constitution, University of Chicago, [Volume 1, Page 90], document 4, Samuel Adams, *Boston Gazette*, 27, Feb. 1769, http://press -pubs.uchicago.edu/founders/print_documents/v1ch3s4.html.

8   Frothingham, Richard, *History of the Siege of Boston, and of the Battles of Lexington, Concord, and Bunker Hill* (Charles C. Little and James Brown, 1851), p. 25.

9   Breen, T. H., *American Insurgents, American Patriots: The Revolution of the People* (Farrar, Straus and Giroux, 2010), p. 85.

10 Simeon, Howard, "A Sermon Preached to the Ancient and Honorable Artillery-Company, in Boston, New-England, June 7th, 1773. Being the Anniversary of Their Election of Officers," p. 19, https://quod.lib.umich .edu/e/evans/N10084.0001.001/1:3?rgn=div1;view=fulltext.

11 Paine, Thomas, *The Writings of Thomas Paine* (1906), "Thoughts on Defensive War" from the *Pennsylvania Magazine*, July 1775, http://www .bartleby.com/184/112.html.

12 Halbrook, Dr. Stephen, *The Founders' Second Amendment Origins of the Right to Bear* (Ivan R. Dee, 2008), p.131.

13 Chase, Ellen, *The Beginnings of the American Revolution: Based on Contemporary Letters Diaries and Other Documents, Volume 2* (The Baker and Taylor Company, 1910), p. 182.

14 Adams, Les, *The Second Amendment Primer: A Citizen's Guidebook to the History, Sources, and Authorities for the Constitutional Guarantee of the Right to Keep and Bear Arms* (Skyhorse, 2013), p. 105.

15 "Debates and Proceedings in the Convention of the Commonwealth of Massachusetts, Held in the Year 1788, and Which Finally Ratified the Constitution of the United States" (Boston, W. White, printer to the commonwealth, 1856), p. 86.

16 Ratification of the Constitution by the State of New Hampshire; June 21, 1788 (http://avalon.law.yale.edu/18th_century/ratnh.asp).

8: Go West

1   Peterson, Harold L., *Encyclopedia of Firearms* (E. P. Dutton, 1964), p. 58.

2   Brown, Meredith M., *Frontiersman: Daniel Boone and the Making of America* (Louisiana State University Press, 2008), p. 21.

3   Carmichael, Jim, "Boone and the Bear," *Outdoor Life*, Feb. 28, 2007.

4   Cramer, Clayton, *Concealed Weapon Laws of the Early Republic: Dueling, Southern Violence, and Moral Reform* (Praeger, 1999), p. 80.

5   Rose, *American Rifle: A Biography* (Delta, 2009), p. 16.

6 Morris, Charles R., *The Dawn of Innovation: The First American Industrial Revolution* (PublicAffairs, 2012), p. 113.

7 National Historic Site Massachusetts, Springfield Armory, https://www .nps.gov/spar/faqs.htm.

8 Garavaglia, Louis A. and Charles G. Worman, *Firearms of the American West, Vol. 1, 1803–1865* (University Press of Colorado, 1998), p. 6.

9 *The Journals of the Lewis and Clark Expedition,* August 30, 1803, https://lewis andclarkjournals.unl.edu/item/lc.jrn.1803-08-30#lc.jrn.1803-08-30.01.

10 National Firearms Museum, "Treasure Gun: Girandoni Air Rifle as Used by Lewis and Clark," https://www.youtube.com/watch?v=-pqFyKh-rUI.

11 Chiaventone, Frederick J., "Lewis and Clark's Girandoni Air Rifle," December 13, 2016. http://warfarehistorynetwork.com/daily/military -history/lewis-and-clarks-girandoni-air-rifle/.

12 National Firearms Museum, "Treasure Gun: Girandoni Air Rifle as Used by Lewis and Clark," continued.

13 Morris, *The Dawn of Innovation*, p. 114.

14 Gibson, Karen Bush, *Eli Whitney: Profiles in American History* (Mitchell Lane, 2006), p. 33.

15 Bilby, Joseph G., *A Revolution in Arms: A History of the First Repeating Rifles* (Westholme Publishing, 2015), p. 31.

16 Garavaglia, Louis A. and Worman, Charles G., *Firearms of the American West, Vol. 1, 1803–1865* (University Press of Colorado, 1998), p. 11.

17 Bilby, *A Revolution in Arms*, p. 34.

18 Harpers Ferry Armory exhibit, https://www.nps.gov/hafe/learn/history culture/john-h-hall.htm.

19 Smith, Merritt R., *Harpers Ferry Armory and the New Technology: The Challenge of Change* (Cornell University Press, 1980), p. 206.

9: Peacemaker

1 Most of the information regarding Colt's family's early efforts in manufacturing were culled from Tucker, Barbara M., and Kenneth H. Tucker, *Industrializing Antebellum America: The Rise of Manufacturing Entrepreneurs in the Early Republic* (Palgrave Macmillan US, 2008).

2 Barnard, Henry, *Armsmear: The Home, the Arm, and the Armory of Samuel Colt: A Memorial* (National Archives, 1862), p. 298.

3 Barnard, *Armsmear*, p. 301.

4 Manby, Charles (ed.), *Minutes of Proceedings of the Institution of Civil Engineers*, Volume 11, Session 1851–52, p. 38. (Published by the Institution, 1852).

5   Patent USX9430 I1, Feb. 25, 1836. https://patents.google.com/patent/USX9430

6   Trumbull, Levi R., *A History of Industrial Paterson* (National Archives, 1882).

7   *Army and Navy Chronicle, and Scientific Repository*, vol. 5.

8   Andrews, Stephen P., Jan E. Dizard, and Robert Muth (eds.), *Guns in America: A Historical Reader* (NYU Press, 1999), p. 61.

9   Manby, Charles (ed.), *Minutes of the Proceedings of the Institution of Civil Engineers with Abstract of the Discussions*, vol. XI, Session 1851–52. (Published by the Institution, 1852).

10 Andrews, Dizard, and Muth, *Guns in America*, p. 65.

11 Lundeberg, Philip K., "Samuel Colt's Submarine Battery: The Secret and the Enigma," Smithsonian Research Online, https://repository.si.edu/handle/10088/2428.

12 Schiffer, Michael B., *Power Struggles: Scientific Authority and the Creation of Practical Electricity Before Edison* (MIT Press, 2008), p. 124.

13 Boorstin, Daniel J., *The Americans: The Democratic Experience* (Random House 1973), p. 35.

14 Pegler, Martin, *Colt Single-Action Revolvers* (Osprey, 2010), p. 25.

15 Barnard, *Armsmear*, p. 206

16 Andrews, Dizard, and Muth, *Guns in America*, p. 71.

17 Smith, Anthony, *Machine Gun: The Story of the Men and the Weapon That Changed the Face of War* (St. Martin Press, 2002), p. 57.

18 Lamb, Martha Joanna, *The Homes of America* (D. Appleton, 1879), p. 181.

19 Grant, Ellsworth S., "Gunmaker to the World," *American Heritage Magazine*, June, 1968, Volume 19, Issue 4.

20 Tucker and Tucker, *Industrializing Antebellum America*, p. 86.

21 Morris, Charles R., *The Dawn of Innovation*, p. 157.

22 Tucker and Tucker, *Industrializing Antebellum America*, p. 66.

23 Ibid., p. 78.

24 Trimble, Marshall, "The Peacemaker," *True West*, June 16, 2016.

25 *Punch*, Volumes 21–22 (1851), p. 11.

26 *Household Words, A Weekly Journal*, Volume 9 (1854), p. 354.

27 Dickens, Charles, No. 218 of Charles Dickens' "Household Words," May 27, 1864. It can be found in, Colt, Samuel, "On the Application of Machinery to the Manufacture of Rotating Chambered-breech Fire-arms" (National Archives, 1855), p. 354.

28 Phelps, William M., *Devil's Right Hand: The Tragic Story of the Colt Family Curse* (Lyons Press: 2013), p. 254.

10: Bullet

1   Greener, W. W., *The Gun and Its Development* (Skyhorse; 9th edition, 2013), p. 589.
2   Ibid., p. 633.
3   *Scientific American*, vol. 4, https://www.scientificamerican.com/article/the-minie-rifle-ball/
4   Leonard, Pat, "The Bullet That Changed History," *New York Times*, Aug. 31, 2012.
5   Stamp, Jimmy, "The Inventive Mind of Walter Hunt, Yankee Mechanical Genius," *Smithsonian*, Oct. 24, 2013.
6   Ibid.
7   For more on the Robbins and Lawrence factory, see Robbins & Lawrence Armory and Machine Shop/American Precision Museum, http://www.crjc.org/heritage/V09-60.htm.
8   Trevelyan, Laura, *The Winchester: The Gun That Built an American Dynasty*, p. 2.
9   Ibid., p. 10.
10 Ibid., p. 17.
11 Johnstone, William W., *Winchester 1887* (Pinnacle, 2015), p. 199.

11: Those Newfangled Gimcrackers

1   Bilby, *A Revolution in Arms*, p. 68.
2   Bartlett, Rev. W. A., "Lincoln's Seven Hits with a Rifle," *Magazine of History: With Notes and Queries* (Published by W. Abbott., 1922).
3   *The Annual of Scientific Discovery, 1865* (Gould and Lincoln), p. 98.
4   National Firearms Museum, U.S. Spencer Lever Action Repeating Carbine. http://www.nramuseum.org/guns/the-galleries/a-nation-asunder-1861-to-1865/case-14-union-carbines/us-spencer-lever-action-repeating-carbine.aspx
5   Bruce, Robert V., *Lincoln and the Tools of War* (Bobbs Merrill, 1956), p. 114.
6   Rose, *American Rifle*, p. 178.
7   Bruce, *Lincoln and the Tools of War*, p. 114.
8   Ibid.
9   American Firearm Museum exhibit, "U.S. Spencer Lever Action Repeating Carbine."
10 Bruce, *Lincoln and the Tools of War*, p. 25.

11 *Popular Science*, May 1961, p. 73.

12 Bruce, *Lincoln and the Tools of War*, p. 102.

13 Worman, *Firearms in American History*, p. 114.

14 Bruce, *Lincoln and the Tools of War*, p. 115.

15 Gettysburg National Military Park, Weapons at Gettysburg—The Spencer Repeating Rifle. https://npsgnmp.wordpress.com/2011/09/01/weapons -at-gettysburg-the-spencer-repeating-rifle/

16 Rose, *American Rifle*, p. 147.

17 Minetor, Randi, *Historical Tours Gettysburg: Trace the Path of America's Heritage* (Globe Pequot, 2015), p. 50.

18 Bruce, *Lincoln and the Tools of War*, p. 109.

19 Stevens, Captain C. A., *Berdan's United States Sharpshooters in the Army of the Potomac, 1861–1865* (Price-McGill, 1892), p. 11.

20 Trevelyan, *The Winchester*, p. 21.

21 Bilby, Joseph G., *A Revolution in Arms*, p. 22.

22 "The War of the Rebellion: A Compilation of the Official Record," series I, vol. XLV, in two parts. Part II—Correspondence, Etc. (US Government Printing Office, 1984), p. 466.

23 Leigh, Phil, "The Union's Newfangled Gimcrackers," *New York Times*, Jan. 23, 2012.

24 *Popular Science*, May 1945, p. 208.

12: Fastest Gun in the West

1 Rosa, Joseph G., *Wild Bill Hickok, Gunfighter: An Account of Hickok's Gunfights* (Red River, 2001), p. 91.

2 Holland, Barbara, *Gentlemen's Blood: A History of Dueling From Swords at Dawn to Pistols at Dusk* (Bloomsbury, 2003), p. 100.

3 Wilson, John Lyde, *The Code of Honor: Or, Rules for the Government of Principals and Seconds in Duelling*, (Thomas J. Eccles, 1838), p. 4.

4 Custer, George A., *My Life on the Plains. Or, Personal Experiences with Indians* (Sheldon, 1874), p. 34.

5 Rosa, *Wild Bill Hickok*, p. 80.

6 Garavaglia, Louis A., and Charles G. Worman, *Firearms of the American West*, vol. 2, p. vii.

7 Owens, Ron, *Oklahoma Heroes: The Oklahoma Peace Officers Memorial* (Turner, 2002), p. 72.

8 Hardin, John Wesley, *The Life of John Wesley Hardin* (Seguin, Texas: Smith & Moore, 1896), p. 14.

9 Garavaglia and Worman, *Firearms of the American West*, vol. 2, p. 253.

10 *Vie militaire dans le Dakota, notes et souvenirs (1867–1869)* (published posthumously in 1926 in English as *Army Life in Dakota*), p. 34, https://catalog.hathitrust.org/Record/000235213.

11 Worman, Charles G., *Gunsmoke and Saddle Leather: Firearms in the Nineteenth-century American West* (University of New Mexico Press, 205), p. 181.

12 Dykstra, Robert R., *The Cattle Towns* (University of Nebraska Press, 1968), p. 116.

13 Dykstra, Robert R., "Quantifying the Wild West: The Problematic Statistics of Frontier Violence," *Western Historical Quarterly*, 40, no. 3 (Autumn 2009), pp. 321–47.

14 Lee, Wayne C., *Deadly Days in Kansas*, (The Caxton Printers, 1997), p. 56.

15 Dillon, Richard, "Ben and Billy Thompson's Cow Town," April 8, 2008, HistoryNet.com.

16 Wunder, John R., "Frontier Violence," *The Encyclopedia of the Great Plains* (University of Nebraska–Lincoln, 2004), http://plainshumanities.unl.edu /encyclopedia/doc/egp.ii.026.

17 Kessler, Glenn, "Rick Santorum's Misguided View of Gun Control in the Wild West," *Washington Post*, April 29, 2014.

18 Schweikart, Larry, "The Non-Existent Frontier Bank Robbery," Foundation for Economic Education, Monday, Jan. 1, 2001.

19 FBI, Bank Crime Statistics 2015, https://www.fbi.gov/file-repository /stats-services-publications-bank-crime-statistics-2015-bank-crime-statistics -2015/view.

13: The Showman

1 Warren, Louis S., *Buffalo Bill's America: William Cody and the Wild West Show* (Vintage, 2006), p. 46.

2 Ibid., p. 47.

3 *Harpers Weekly*, December 14, 1867, pp. 792, 797–98, http://thewest .harpweek.com/Sections/Buffalo/BuffaloHunting1002.htm.

4 For more on "Beecher's Bibles," see Kansas Historical Society, https:// www.kshs.org/kansapedia/beecher-bibles/11977.

5 Shields, G. O., *Rustling in the Rockies: Hunting and Fishing by Mountain Stream* (Belford, Clarke, 1883), p. 151.

6 Ibid.

7 Spangenberger, Phil, "The 'Shoot Today, Kill Tomorrow' Gun," *True West* online, May 20, 2014, https://truewestmagazine.com/the-shoot-today -kill-tomorrow-gun/.

8 King, Gilbert, "Where the Buffalo No Longer Roamed," *Smithsonian*, July 17, 2012, https://www.smithsonianmag.com/history/where-the-buffalo -no-longer-roamed-3067904/.

9 For further reading on the decimation of the buffalo, see Drew Isenberg's *The Destruction of the Bison: An Environmental History, 1750–1920* (Cambridge University Press, 2001).

10 Robbins, Jim, "Historians Revisit Slaughter on the Plains," *New York Times*, November 16, 1999.

11 Midwest Archeological, Little Bighorn Archeological project, https://www .nps.gov/mwac/libi/firearm.html.

12 Wetmore, Helen Cody, *Last of the Great Scouts: The Life Story of Col. William F. Cody, "Buffalo Bill" as Told by His Sister* (Duluth Press, 1913), p. 204.

13 Warren, *Buffalo Bill's America*, p. 241.

14 Kasper, Shirl, *Annie Oakley* (University of Oklahoma Press, 1992), p. 215.

15 Ibid., p. 215.

16 Letter to President William McKinley from Annie Oakley, April 5, 1898, National Archives. https://www.archives.gov/research/recover/example-02 .html.

14: Hellfire

1 *Scientific American*, vol. 26, March 2, 1872, p. 2.

2 *Daily Alta California* 20, no. 6562, March 3, 1868.

3 Keller, Julia, *Mr. Gatling's Terrible Marvel: The Gun That Changed Everything and the Misunderstood Genius Who Invented It* (Penguin, 2008), p. 27.

4 Ohio State University, Exhibitions, Civil War Battlefield Medicine, https://ehistory.osu.edu/exhibitions/cwsurgeon/cwsurgeon/amputation.

5 Burns, Stanley, MD, *Behind the Lens: A History in Pictures, Surgery in the Civil War*, PBS.

6 *Maryland Medical Journal* 46, no. 5, "Medical Fame Outside of Medicine," p. xxi.

7 Ellis, John. *The Social History of the Machine Gun* (Random House, 1975), p. 11.

8 Chinn, George M. "The Machine Gun, Development During World War II and Korean Conflict by the United States and their Allies, of Full

Automatic Machine Gun Systems and High Rate of Fire Power Driven Cannons," Prepared for the Bureau of Ordnance, Department of Navy, 1951 (unclassified in July 1970), p. 36.

9 Perkins, Jacob, The American Society of Mechanical Engineers, https://www.asme.org/engineering-topics/articles/manufacturing-processing/jacob-perkins.

10 Bruce, *Lincoln and the Tools of War*, p. 138.

11 Ibid., p. 120.

12 Chivers, C. J., *The Gun* (Simon & Schuster, 2011), p. 26.

13 Cavendish, Richard, "The First Commercially Successful Machine Gun Emerged," *History Today* 62, no. 11, Nov. 2012.

14 Moss, Matthew, "The Story of the Gatling Gun: Why You Still Know the Name of a 19th Century Weapon," *Popular Mechanics*, Aug. 22, 2016.

15 Chivers, *The Gun*, p. 29.

16 *Journal of Civil War History*, Kent State University Press, 1963, p. 50.

17 Bruce, *Lincoln and the Tools of War*, p. 261.

15: An American in London

1 Maxim, Hiram Stevens. *My Life* (Methuen, 1915), p. 315.

2 Editorial board, "Terrible Automatic Engines of War," *New York Times*, March 28, 1897, http://query.nytimes.com/mem/archive-free/pdf?res=9E0DE3DF1630E132A2575BC2A9659C94669ED7CF.

3 Browne. Malcolm W., "Deadly Weapon Now 100 Machine Gun Victims Hit Untold Numbers," *New York Times*, December 15, 1985.

4 Mottelay, P. Fleury, *The Life and Work of Sir Hiram Maxim: Knight, Chevalier de la Légion d'Honneur, Etc; Etc,* (John Lane, 1920), p. xi.

5 Ibid., p. x.

6 Maxim, *My Life*, p. 163.

7 Ellis, *The Social History of the Machine Gun*, p. 13.

8 Mottelay, P. Fleury, *The Life and Work of Sir Hiram Maxim* p. 10.

9 Pauly, Roger. *Firearms: The Life Story of a Technology* (Johns Hopkins University Press, 2008), p. 123.

10 Maxim, *My Life*, p. 164.

11 Sanford, P. Gerald, *Nitro-Explosives: A Practical Treatise Concerning the Properties, Manufacture, and Analysis of Nitrated Substances, Including the Fulminates, Smokeless Powders, and Celluloid* (D. Van Nostrand, 1906), p. 351, http://www.gutenberg.org/ebooks/15308.

12 Ibid.

13 Flynn, John T., "The Merchant of Death: Basil Zaharoff," Mises Institute, Aug. 24, 2007.

14 Maxim, *My Life*, p. 213.

15 For more on German machine guns of World War I, see Bruce, Robert V., *Machine Guns of World War I: Live Firing Classic Military Weapons in Color Photographs* (Crowood Press, 2008).

16 Chivers, *The Gun*, p. 106.

16: American Genius

1 Browning, John M., and Curt Gentry, *John M Browning: American Gunmaker* (Browning Company; 10th edition, 2000), p. 47.

2 Garavaglia, Louis A., and Charles G. Worman, *Firearms of the American West*, vol. 2, p. 207.

3 Browning, and Gentry, *John M. Browning*, p. 97.

4 Campbell, Dave, "A Look Back: The Winchester Model 1885 Single-Shot Rifle," *American Rifleman*, May 2, 2016.

5 Browning, and Gentry, *John M. Browning*, p. 140.

6 Chinn, George M. *The Machine Gun, Development During World War II and Korean Conflict by the United States and Their Allies, of Full Automatic Machine Gun Systems and High Rate of Fire Power Driven Cannons*, p. 163.

7 Strohn, Matthias (ed.), *World War I Companion* (Osprey Publishing, 2013), p. 91.

8 Remington Society, "The Story of Eddystone," http://www.remington society.org/the-story-of-eddystone/.

9 Chinn, George M. "The Machine Gun, Development During World War II and Korean Conflict by the United States and their Allies, of Full Automatic Machine Gun Systems and High Rate of Fire Power Driven Cannons," p. 176.

10 Ibid., p. 164.

11 Browning, and Gentry, *John M. Browning*, p. 162.

12 La Garde, Louis Anatole, *Gunshot Injuries: How They Are Inflicted, Their Complications and Treatment* (William Wood, 1916), p. 70.

13 "Official History of the 82nd Division American Expeditionary Forces: 'All American' Division, 1917–19," p. 61.

14 Browning, and Gentry, *John M. Browning*, p. 223.

17: The Chicago Typewriter

1   Bergreen, Laurence, *Capone: The Man and the Era* (Simon & Schuster; reprint edition, 1996), p. 213.

2   Willbanks, James H., *Machine Guns: An Illustrated History of Their Impact* (ABC-CLIO, 2004), p. 86.

3   Ellis, *The Social History of the Machine Gun*, p. 13.

4   Yenne, Bill, *Tommy Gun: How General Thompson's Submachine Gun Wrote History* (Thomas Dunne, 2009), p. 31.

5   Blumenthal, Karen, *Tommy: The Gun That Changed America* (Roaring Brook Press, 2015), p. 69.

6   Ibid.

7   Northwestern, Pritzker School of Law, "Learning from the Past, Living in the Present: Patterns in Chicago Homicides, 1870 to 1930," Nov. 17, 2000, http://www.law.northwestern.edu/about/news/newsdisplay.cfm?id=463.

8   Joukowsky Institute for Archaeology & the Ancient World, Brown University, https://www.brown.edu/Departments/Joukowsky_Institute/courses/13things/7730.html.

9   Blumenthal, *Tommy*, p. 68.

10   Wack, Larry, FBI (Ret.), "FBI Firearms & the Myth of the 1934 Crime Bill," June 10, 2016, p. 5.

11   Flink, James J., *The Automobile Age* (MIT Press, 1988), p. 25.

12   Presidential Statement on Signing Crime Bill, May 18, 1934, http://www.presidency.ucsb.edu/ws/index.php?pid=14877.

13   Blumenthal, *Tommy*, p. 182.

18: Great Arsenal of Democracy

1   Hunt, Frazier, *MacArthur and the War Against Japan* (Charles Scribner's Sons, 1944), p. 71.

2   Teale, Edwin, "He Invented the World's Deadliest Rifle," *Popular Science* 137, no. 6 (Dec. 1940).

3   McCarten, John, "*The Man Behind the Gun*," *New Yorker*, February 6, 1943, p. 22.

4   Rose, *American Rifle*, p. 301.

5   Ibid.

6   Hoffman, John "A History of Innovation: U.S. Army Adaptation in War and Peace," U.S. Army Center of Military History, 2009, p. 6.

7   Ibid., p.10

8 Ibid.

9 *Modern Marvels: United States Army Weapon—M16 Assault Rifle.* Documentary, 2016, https://www.youtube.com/watch?v=d59EWOzjtSo.

10 Thompson, Leroy, *The M14 Battle Rifle* (Osprey, 2014), p. 17.

19: Fall and Rise of the Sharpshooter

1 Bailey, Sarah Pullam, "Here's the Faith in the 'American Sniper' You Won't See in the Film," *Washington Post*, Jan. 14, 2015.

2 For more on snipers of World War II, see Haskew, Michael E., *The Sniper at War: From the American Revolutionary War to the Present Day* (Amber Books, 2012).

3 Rose, *American Rifle*, p. 197.

4 Calabi, Silvio, Steve Helsley, and Roger Sanger, "The Rigby Match Rifle, Creedmoor & More," *American Rifleman*, Oct. 31, 2012.

5 Leech, Arthur Blennerhassett, *Irish Riflemen in America* (National Archives, 1875), p. 60.

6 Calabi, Silvio, Steve Helsley, and Roger Sanger, "The Rigby Match Rifle, Creedmoor & More," *American Rifleman*, Oct. 31, 2012.

7 Leech, *Irish Riflemen in America*, p. 60.

8 Moskin, J. Robert, *The U.S. Marine Corps Story* (Back Bay Books; Third edition 1992), p. 102.

9 1st Battalion, 6th Marine Regiment, Belleau Wood, official website of the United States Marines. See http://www.6thmarines.marines.mil/Units/1st-Battalion/History/.

10 Moskin, *The U.S. Marine Corps Story*, p. 121.

11 Pyle, Ernie, *Brave Men* (University of Nebraska Press, 2001), p. 394.

12 Lanning, Col. Michael Lee, *Inside the Crosshairs: Snipers in Vietnam* (Ballantine Books, 1998), p. 59.

13 For more on the history of sniping schools, see Lanning, Michael Lee, *Inside the Crosshairs: Snipers in Vietnam* (Ballantine, 2013).

14 For Cass's story, see Dockery, Kevin, *Stalkers and Shooters: A History of Snipers* (Dutton Caliber; reprint edition, 2007).

15 Haskew, *The Sniper at War*, p. 107.

16 Plaster, Major John, *History of Sniping and Sharpshooting* (Paladin Press, 2008), p. 202.

17 Distinguished Service Cross, Adelbert F. Waldron, https://valor.militarytimes.com/recipient.php?recipientid=4500.

20: Peace Dividends

1   Hanson, Victor Davis, "The World's Most Popular Gun: The Long Road to the AK-47," *New Atlantis*, no. 32 (Summer 2011), pp. 140–47.

2   Noble, Holcomb B., "Eugene Stoner, 74, Designer of M-16 Rifle and Other Arms," *New York Times*, April 27, 1997.

3   Rose, *American Rifle*, p. 267.

4   Hallahan, William H., *Misfire: The History of How America's Small Arms Have Failed Our Military* (Scribner, 1994), p. 467.

5   Coffey, Patrick, *American Arsenal: A Century of Weapon Technology and Strategy* (Oxford University Press, 2014), p. 243.

6   Gibson, James William, *The Perfect War: Technowar in Vietnam* (Atlantic Monthly, 2000), p. 130.

7   Bartocci, Christopher R., "AR-15/M16: The Rifle That Was Never Supposed to Be," *Gun Digest*, July 16, 2012.

8   "Report of the M16 Rifle Review Panel," June 1, 1968, http://www.dtic.mil/dtic/tr/fulltext/u2/a953117.pdf.

9   Hallock, Richard R. (Colonel U.S. Army (Retired), "M-16 Rifle Case Study," Prepared for the Chairman of the President's Blue Ribbon Defense Panel, March 16, 1970, http://pogoarchives.org/labyrinth/09/02.pdf.

10 Chivers, *The Gun*, p. 404.

11 Reuters, "AK-47 Inventor: U.S. Troops in Iraq Prefer My Rifle to Theirs," April 17, 2006.

12 Neuman, Scott, "Letter: Kalashnikov Suffered Remorse over Rifle He Invented," National Public Radio online, Jan. 13, 2014.

13 Ibid.

14 Heintz, Jim, "Gun Designer: 'Blame Nazis' for creation of the AK-47," Associated Press, Dec. 23, 2013.

21: The Great Argument

1   Duffy, Peter, "100 Years Ago, a Killing That Spurred a Gun Law," *New York Times*, Jan. 24, 2011, http://query.nytimes.com/gst/fullpage.html?res=9C05EED7123EF937A15752C0A9679D8B63.

2   Article 265—NY Penal Law. http://ypdcrime.com/penal.law/article265.htm.

3   Frye, Brian L., at the University of Kentucky College of Law, "The Peculiar Story of *United States v. Miller*," *NYU Journal of Liberty and Law* 3, no. 48 (2008), p. 58, http://uknowledge.uky.edu/cgi/viewcontent.cgi?article=1263&context=law_facpub.

4 Ibid.

5 Doherty, Brian, *Gun Control on Trial: Inside the Supreme Court Battle over the Second Amendment* (Cato Institute, 2009), pp. 16–17.

6 Latzer, Brian, *The Rise and Fall of Violent Crime in America* (Encounter, 2016), p. 75.

7 Ibid., p. 119.

8 *Congressional Record*, vol. 114, part 3, p. 3732.

9 Coleman, Arica, L., "When the NRA Supported Gun Control," *Time*, July 29, 2016, http://time.com/4431356/nra-gun-control-history/.

10 Doherty, Brian, *Gun Control on Trial*, p. 46.

11 Wilson, Robert L., *Ruger and His Guns: A History of the Man, the Company & Their Firearms* (Chartwell Books, 2008), p. 11.

12 National Firearm Museum, Bill Ruger Prototype Semi-Auto Rifle, https://www.youtube.com/watch?v=rXg5bWyTsVI.

13 Wilson, *Ruger and His Guns*, p. 4.

14 Brown, Aaron, "Behind America's Gun Boom: Inside the Comeback at Sturm, Ruger," *Forbes*, Nov. 5, 2012, https://www.forbes.com/sites/abrambrown/2012/10/17/behind-americas-gun-boom-inside-the-comeback-at-sturm-ruger/.

15 Gallup News Trends: Guns, http://news.gallup.com/poll/1645/Guns.aspx.

16 General Social Survey Final Report, "Trends in Gun Ownership in the United States, 1972–2014," NORC at the University of Chicago, March 2015.

17 United States Department of Justice, Bureau of Alcohol, Tobacco, Firearms and Explosives, "Firearms Commerce in the United States, 2016," https://www.atf.gov/resource-center/docs/2016-firearms-commerce-united-states/download.

18 Krouse, William J., Specialist in Domestic Security and Crime Policy, "Gun Control Legislation," Congressional Research Service, Nov. 14, 2012, https://fas.org/sgp/crs/misc/RL32842.pdf.

CONCLUSION: Molon Labe

1 Tucker, St. George. *Blackstone's Commentaries: With Notes of Reference to the Constitution and Laws of the Federal Government of the United States and of the Commonwealth of Virginia*, Amendment II Document, http://press-pubs.uchicago.edu/founders/documents/amendIIs7.html.

2 W. H. Sumner to John Adams, 3 May 1823, National Archives, https://founders.archives.gov/documents/Adams/99-02-02-7811.

3 Volokh, Eugene, UCLA Law School, "State Constitutional Rights to Keep and Bear Arms," *Texas Review of Law & Politics* 191, 2006, http://www2.law.ucla.edu/volokh/beararms/statecon.htm.

4 Curtis, Michael Kent, *No State Shall Abridge: The Fourteenth Amendment and the Bill of Rights* (Duke University Press, 1990), p. 111.

5 *Great Speeches by American Women* (Dover, 2007), p. 61.

6 Johnson, Nicholas, *Negroes and the Gun: The Black Tradition of Arms* (Prometheus, 2014), p. 132.

7 Halbrook, Stephen P., and Richard E. Gardiner, "NRA and Law Enforcement Opposition to the Brady Act: From Congress to the District Courts," *Journal of Civil Rights and Economic Development* 10, no. 1, article 2 (September 1994).

8 "Handgun Prohibition and the Original Meaning of the Second Amendment," *Michigan Law Review* 82, no. 204 (1983).

9 Neily, Clark, "*District of Columbia v. Heller*: The Second Amendment Is Back, Baby," *Cato Supreme Court Review* (2008), p. 132.

10 Liptak, Adam, "Carefully Plotted Course Propels Gun Case to Top," *New York Times*, Dec. 3, 2007, http://www.nytimes.com/2007/12/03/us/03bar.html.

GLOSSARY

★

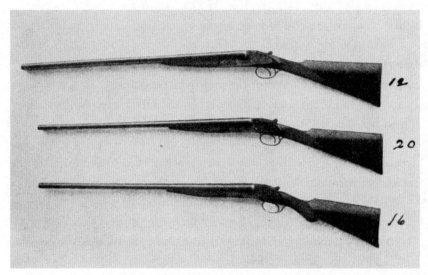

Rod and gun from Canadian Forestry Association

Automatic gun: A firearm that continuously fires as long as the trigger is pressed and there is ammunition in the magazine or clip.

Ballistics: The study of propulsion, flight, and the performance of projectiles.

Barrel: A tube, sealed at the breech of the firearm, where pressure forms from ignited propellant that forces the ball, bullet, or shell through the bore at a high velocity.

Bayonet: A knife meant for spearing that is mounted at the muzzle of a rifle or musket.

Black powder: A propellant that typically consists of 75 percent saltpeter, 15 percent charcoal, and 10 percent sulfur.

Blunderbuss: A short smoothbore gun, typically with a flared muzzle that looks something like a bell-bottom.

Bore: The interior surface of a gun's barrel.

Breech: The end of the barrel where the powder charge is ignited.

Breech-loading gun: A firearm in which the cartridge is loaded into a chamber at the rear portion of the barrel.

Brown Bess: Nickname for the Long Land Service musket, alternatively known as the King's musket and the Tower musket. It was a flintlock, .75-caliber barrel-loading musket, and it would become the standard firearm for British soldiers from 1722 to 1838.

Bullet: The projectile fired from a rifle or handgun; often confused with a "cartridge" or "round."

Butt: The rear portion of the stock.

Caliber: The measurement of the approximate diameter of the barrel or the diameter of the projectile that is placed in the barrel. A ".36-caliber" gun has a barrel diameter of 0.36 inches. A "9mm" gun has a barrel diameter of 9 millimeters.

Carbine: A long gun with a shorter barrel than a traditional musket or rifle.

Cartridge: Ammunition for a firearm that most often bundles a bullet, gunpowder, and primer in a metallic case.

Centerfire cartridge: A cartridge in which the primer is located at the center of the head. Centerfire cartridges have overtaken "rimfire" cartridges in most modern firearms.

Chamber: An area at the breech end of a barrel where the cartridge is inserted before a gun is fired.

Clip: A device that holds together rounds of ammunition, typically to prepare for insertion into a magazine.

Derringer: A small, single-shot, large-bore gun.

Double-action: Allows a revolver to be used in "single action"—cocking the hammer and then squeezing the trigger one shot at a time—or by simply squeezing the trigger to fire, thus the "double action."

Flintlock: A lock that uses a flint in the hammer to strike a spark to ignite the primer powder in the flashpan.

Frizzen: Typically an L-shaped piece of steel at the rear of a flintlock action that is hit by a flint-tipped hammer to create sparks and ignite the primer powder.

Gauge: Typically the diameter of the bore in a shotgun.

Hammer: A device that strikes the firing pin or primer.

Harquebus: The Dutch name for a widely used sixteenth-century heavy musket typically rested on a forked pole.

Lever action: A type of action that is used to load a new cartridge into the chamber of the barrel by working a lever located around (or part of) the trigger guard.

Lock: The mechanism of the gun that allows it to fire, e.g., "matchlock" and "flintlock." Referred to as a lock because the early mechanisms resembled door locks.

Long rifle: More popularly known as the Kentucky rifle or Pennsylvania rifle, one of the first widely used rifles in North America for hunting and warfare.

Magazine: A storage device that feeds ammunition into the firearm.

Magnum: A nonscientific term used to describe large cartridges.

Match: A long braided cord sometimes soaked in a solution of saltpeter that burns slowly at around four to five inches an hour, used to ignite the primer powder in a matchlock firearm.

Matchlock: One of the earliest locks where the priming powder is ignited by a slow match.

Nipple: A small protrusion in the breech end of a percussion-cap gun.

Percussion cap: A cylinder of copper or brass containing a shock-sensitive explosive that is placed over a metal "nipple" at the breech end of the gun barrel.

Pistol: A handheld gun in which the chamber is part of the barrel.

Recoil: The rearward movement of a firearm caused by the momentum of firing.

Revolver: A repeating handgun featuring a revolving cylinder with multiple chambers for cartridges.

Rifle: A long-barreled firearm featuring a pattern of grooves cut into the bore walls to allow more precise long-range shooting.

Rimfire: A cartridge that is shot after the firing pin ignites the powder when striking the rim, rather than the center, of the base.

Safety: A mechanism that prevents the inadvertent firing of the gun.

Semiautomatic gun: A type of firearm that fires one cartridge with one trigger squeeze but prepares the gun for the next shot.

Shell: A cartridge containing multiple metallic projectiles designed to be fired in a shotgun.

Shotgun: A smoothbore long gun that fires shells and is shot from the shoulder.

Single-action: A gun that can be fired only by cocking the hammer and then squeezing the trigger one shot at a time.

Smoothbore gun: A firearm, like many of the early muskets and contemporary shotguns, that features a barrel without any rifling.

Stock: Sometimes referred to as the gunstock or buttstock, it is the part of the long gun or rifle that a person holds when aiming and shooting.

Wheellock gun: A firearm with a rotating steel wheel that creates sparks, like some cigarette lighters, igniting the primer powder.

SELECTED BIBLIOGRAPHY

★

Lewis and Clark Expedition 150th anniversary issue,
designed by Charles R. Chickering

Adams, Les. *The Second Amendment Primer: A Citizen's Guidebook to the History, Sources, and Authorities for the Constitutional Guarantee of the Right to Keep and Bear Arms.* Skyhorse Publishing, 2013.

Aron, Stephen. *How the West Was Lost: The Transformation of Kentucky from Daniel Boone to Henry Clay.* Johns Hopkins University Press, 1999.

Bailyn, Bernard. *The Ideological Origins of the American Revolution.* Harvard University Press, 1967.

Barnard, Henry. *Armsmear: The Home, the Arm, and the Armory of Samuel Colt: A Memorial.* Alvord Printer, 1866.

Bilby, Joseph G. *A Revolution in Arms: A History of the First Repeating Rifles.* Westholme Publishing, 2015.

Black, Jeremy. *European Warfare, 1660–1815.* Yale University Press, 1994.

Blumenthal, Karen. *Tommy: The Gun That Changed America.* Roaring Brook Press, 2015.

Boorman, Dean K. *The History of Colt Firearms.* Lyons Press, 2001.

————. *The History of Smith & Wesson Firearms*. Lyons Press, 2002.

—————. *The History of Winchester Firearms*. Lyons Press, 2001.

Boorstin, Daniel J. *The Americans: The Democratic Experience*. Random House, 1973.

Brown, Meredith M. *Frontiersman: Daniel Boone and the Making of America*. Louisiana State University Press, 2008.

Browning, John M., and Curt Gentry. *John M. Browning: American Gunmaker*. Browning Company, 2000 (tenth edition).

Bruce, Robert V. *Lincoln and the Tools of War*. Bobbs Merrill Company, 1956.

Carman, W. Y. *A History of Firearms: From Earliest Times to 1914*. Routledge, 2015.

Chinn, George M. *The Machine Gun, Development During World War II and Korean Conflict by the United States and their Allies, of Full Automatic Machine Gun Systems and High Rate of Fire Power Driven Cannons*. Prepared for the Bureau of Ordnance, Department of Navy 1951. (Unclassified in July 1970.)

Chivers, C. J. *The Gun*. Simon & Schuster, 2010.

Clay, Oliver. *Heroes of the American Revolution*. Duffield, 1916.

Coffey, Patrick. *American Arsenal: A Century of Weapon Technology and Strategy*. Oxford University Press, 2014.

Cramer, Clayton. *Armed America: The Remarkable Story of How and Why Guns Became as American as Apple Pie*. Thomas Nelson, 2009.

Curtis, Michael Kent. *No State Shall Abridge: The Fourteenth Amendment and the Bill of Rights*. Duke University Press, 1990.

Dillin, Captain John G. W. *The Kentucky Rifle*. National Rifle Association of America, 1924.

Doherty, Brian. *Gun Control on Trial: Inside the Supreme Court Battle over the Second Amendment*. Cato Institute, 2009.

Dougherty, Glen, and Brandon Webb. *Navy SEAL Sniper: An Intimate Look at the Sniper of the 21st Century*. Skyhorse Publishing, 2013.

Dykstra, Robert R. *The Cattle Towns*. University of Nebraska Press, 1983 (reprint edition).

Edwards, William B. *Civil War Guns: The Complete Story of Federal and Confederate Small Arms; Design, Manufacture, Identification, Procurement, Issue, Employment, Effectiveness, and Postwar Disposal*. Stackpole, 1962.

Ellis, John. *The Social History of the Machine Gun*. Random House, 1975.

Elting, John T. *Amateurs, to Arms!: A Military History of the War of 1812*. Algonquin, 1991.

Fischer, David Hackett. *Paul Revere's Ride*. Oxford University Press, 1995.

Frothingham, Richard. *History of the Siege of Boston, and of the Battles of Lexington, Concord, and Bunker Hill.* Charles C. Little and James Brown, 1851.

Garavaglia, Louis A. and Charles G. Worman. *Firearms of the American West, Vol. 1, 1803–1865.* University Press of Colorado, 1998.

_____. *Firearms of the American West, Vol. 2, 1866–1894.* University Press of Colorado, 1998.

Garry, Jim. *Weapons of the Lewis & Clark Expedition.* Arthur H. Clark, 2012.

Graham, James. *The Life of General Daniel Morgan, of the Virginia Line of the Army of the United States, with Portions of His Correspondence; Comp[iled]. from Authentic Sources.* H. W. Derby, 1856.

Greener, W. W. *The Gun and Its Development.* Skyhorse, 2013 (ninth edition).

Halbrook, Dr. Stephen. *The Founders' Second Amendment Origins of the Right to Bear Arms.* Ivan R. Dee, 2008.

Hallahan, William H. *Misfire: The History of How America's Small Arms Have Failed Our Military.* Scribner, 1994.

Hardy, T. David. *Historical Basis of the Right to Keep and Bear Arms.* Report of the Subcommittee on the Constitution of the Committee on the Judiciary, United States Senate, 97th Cong., 2d Sess., 1982.

Haskew, Michael E. *The Sniper at War: From the American Revolutionary War to the Present Day.* Amber Books, 2012.

Heather, Lee Justin, and James Lindgren. *Counting Guns in Early America.* Northwestern University School of Law, Law and Economics Research Paper Series, Research Paper No. 01-1, 2002.

Hodge, Robert R. *The Browning Automatic Rifle.* Osprey, 2010.

Hoffman. Jon T. *A History of Innovation: U.S. Army Adaptation in War and Peace.* Center of Military History, United States Army, 2009.

Hogg, Ian V. *Artillery.* Macdonald, 1972.

Holland, Barbara. *Gentlemen's Blood: A History of Dueling from Swords at Dawn to Pistols at Dusk.* Bloomsbury, 2003.

Hurley, Vic. *Arrows Against Steel: The History of the Bow and How It Forever Changed Warfare.* Cerberus, 2011.

Johnson, Nicholas. *Negroes and the Gun: The Black Tradition of Arms.* Prometheus, 2014.

Johnson, Paul. *The History of the American People.* HarperCollins, 1999.

Johnstone, William W. *Winchester 1887.* Pinnacle, 2015.

Kasper, Shirl. *Annie Oakley.* University of Oklahoma Press, 1992.

Keller, Julia. *Mr. Gatling's Terrible Marvel: The Gun That Changed Everything and the Misunderstood Genius Who Invented It.* Penguin, 2008.

Kelly, Jack. *Gunpowder: Alchemy, Bombards, and Pyrotechnics: The History of the Explosive That Changed the World.* Basic Books, 2009.

Koller, Larry. *The Golden Guide to Guns.* Golden Press, 1961.

La Garde, Louis Anatole. *Gunshot Injuries: How They Are Inflicted, Their Complications and Treatment.* William Wood, 1916.

Latcher, Philip. *Sharpshooters of the Civil War.* Osprey, 2002.

Latzer, Brian. *The Rise and Fall of Violent Crime in America.* Encounter Books, 2016.

Malcolm, Joyce. *To Keep and Bear Arms: The Origins of an Anglo-American Right.* Harvard University Press, 1996.

Martin, Joseph Plumb. *A Narrative of Some of the Adventures, Dangers and Sufferings of a Revolutionary Soldier [i.e. Joseph Plumb Martin]; Interspersed with Anecdotes of Incidents That Occurred Within His Own Observation. Written by Himself.* National Archives, 1830.

Maxim, Hiram Stevens. *My Life.* Methuen, 1915.

McLachlan, Sean. *Medieval Handgonnes: The First Black Powder Infantry Weapons.* Osprey, 2010.

Morris, Charles R. *The Dawn of Innovation: The First American Industrial Revolution.* PublicAffairs, 2012.

Mottelay, P. Fleury. *The Life and Work of Sir Hiram Maxim: Knight, Chevalier de la Légion d'Honneur, Etc., Etc.* John Lane, 1920.

Pauly, Roger. *Firearms: The Life Story of a Technology.* Johns Hopkins University Press, 2008.

Pegler, Martin. *Sniper Rifles: From the 19th to the 21st Century.* Osprey, 2010.

Peterson, Harold Leslie. *Arms and Armor in Colonial America, 1526–1783.* Bramhall House, 1956.

_____. *Encyclopedia of Firearms.* E. P. Dutton, 1964.

Phelp, William M. *Devil's Right Hand: The Tragic Story of the Colt Family Curse.* Lyons, 2013.

Philbrick, Nathaniel. *Bunker Hill: A City, A Siege, A Revolution.* Penguin, 2013.

_____. *Mayflower: A Story of Courage, Community, and War.* Penguin, 2007.

Plaster, Major John. *History of Sniping and Sharpshooting.* Paladin, 2008.

Prasac, Max. *Ruger Revolvers: The Definitive History.* Gun Digest, 2013.

Reid, Stuart. *The Flintlock Musket: Brown Bess and Charleville, 1715–1865.* Osprey, 2016.

Rosa, Joseph G. *Wild Bill Hickok, Gunfighter: An Account of Hickok's Gunfights.* Red River Books, 2001.

Rose, Alexander. *American Rifle: A Biography.* Delta, 2009.

Russell, Carl P. *Guns on the Early Frontiers: From Colonial Times to the Years of the Western Fur Trade*. Dover, 2005. (Originally published by University of California, Berkley Press, 1957.)

Sawyer, Charles Winthrop. *Firearms in American History: 1600 to 1800*. National Archives, 1910.

Stevens, Captain C. A. *Berdan's United States Sharpshooters in the Army of the Potomac, 1861–1865*. Price-McGill, 1892.

Thompson, Leroy. *The Colt 1911 Pistol*. Osprey, 2011.

_____. *The M1 Carbine*. Osprey, 2011.

Trevelyan, Laura. *The Winchester: The Gun That Built an American Dynasty*. Yale University Press, 2016.

Trumbull, Levi R. *A History of Industrial Paterson*. National Archives, 1882.

Tucker, Barbara M., and Kenneth H. Tucker. *Industrializing Antebellum America: The Rise of Manufacturing Entrepreneurs in the Early Republic*. Palgrave Macmillan, 2008.

Warren, Louis S. *Buffalo Bill's America: William Cody and the Wild West Show*. Vintage, 2006.

Weir, William. *50 Weapons That Changed Warfare*. New Page, 2005.

Wexler, Brice. *Guns of the Wild West: How the West Was Won*. Skyhorse, 2013.

Wilson, John L. *The Code of Honor; or, Rules for the Government of Principals and Second in Duelling*. James Phinney, 1858.

Wilson, Robert L. *Colt: An American Legend; The Official History of Colt Firearms from 1836 to the Present*. Abbeville, 1985 (sesquicentennial edition).

_____. *Ruger and His Guns: A History of the Man, the Company & Their Firearms*. Chartwell, 2008.

Winders, Gertrude H. *Sam Colt and His Gun: The Life of the Inventor of the Revolver*. John Day, 1956.

Wood, Gordon S. *The American Revolution: A History*. Modern Library, 2003.

Worman, Charles G. *Firearms in American History: A Guide for Writers, Curators, and General Readers*. Westholme, 2007.

ACKNOWLEDGMENTS

★

The posse that attacked Christie's fort on November 3, 1892

No matter whose name appears on the front cover, writing a book is always a collaborative project. I'm grateful to my indefatigable agents, Keith Urbahn and Matt Latimer, and everyone else at Javelin, for helping me transform my passion into a book.

I doubt that anyone could have brought the project to fruition with more deftness than my editor, Natasha Simons, who showed preternatural patience while keeping me focused and helping me mold a surprisingly complicated narrative. Thanks as well to Hannah Brown, Caitlyn Reuss, Jon Karp, Al Madocs, Kristen Lemire, Lewelin Polanco, and everyone else at Threshold Editions for their support and unmatched professionalism.

Of course, though the folks above repeatedly saved me from myself, any mistakes in *First Freedom* are all my own.

Thanks, as well, to Ben Shapiro and David Limbaugh for reading the book and offering kind words. The same goes for Charles Cooke, who not only helped me ponder the role of guns in American life with his insightful writings on the Second Amendment but sparked my interest in peculiar early-nineteenth-century firearms over drinks.

My gratitude also goes out to John Ealy, Phil and Karen Myers, and Harris Vederman, and everyone else who let me bounce ideas off of them while writing *First Freedom*.

Thanks to my colleague Mollie Hemingway for her counsel and friendship. My bosses at *The Federalist*, Ben Domenech and Sean Davis, have allowed me to participate in some of the most raucous political debates of our time. For that I'm grateful. Working with them, Joy Pullmann, Madeline Osburn, Rachel Stoltzfoos, Mary Katherine Ham, Bre Payton, David Marcus, John Daniel Davidson, Mark Hemingway, and Robert Tracinski, and all the other smart people who write for *The Federalist*, has been a joy.

I also appreciate the efforts of those who edit my work elsewhere and help me be a better writer: David Yontz and Alissa Stevens at Creators Syndicate, Jason Steorts at *National Review*, and Seth Mandel at the *New York Post*.

The folks who work at the National Rifle Association's National Firearms Museum in Fairfax, Virginia, greatly enhanced my understanding of the history of the gun. (Everyone should visit if they have the chance.) Even more, the passionate amateur historians I met and overheard on my visits were equally enlightening. Thanks also to the National Archive and American Antiquarian Society for their assistance.

To Mom and Dad, who taught us about liberty (among *many* other things), your support has been invaluable. Thanks to the rest of the Harsanyi clan: Boaz, Oren, Mary Kate, Anne, Hannah, Szerena, Noah, Sadie, and Grayson. To Jim and Eva, Paul and Theresa, and Paul Jr., thank you for your support.

My greatest debt is to my family. Leah and Adira, who listened to their father prattle on about matchlock muskets and the life of Sam Colt for months, are always supportive. But I could never have written this book— or done any of the things I do—without the patience, backing, and love of my wife, Carla. Thank you.

INDEX

American Rifleman (NRA magazine), 231,
235
ammunition, 3, 29, 41, 115, 122, 248.
*See also type of ammunition or specific
model or type of weapon*
"Annihilator Mark I" (tommy gun), 191
AR-10, Stoner's, 218
AR-15, Stoner's, 218–20, 221, 224
ArmaLite Corporation, 217, 218, 219, 224
Armed Services Committee, U.S., 221
armories
centralized, 88–89
See also specific armory
Army, U.S.
and assault rifles, 218, 219, 220, 221
and Collier and Wheeler firearms, 98
Colt's relationship with, 102
creation of standing, 88
and Garand rifles, 201
and Gatling guns, 163–64, 181
M1803 rifle as official arm of, 89
and Minié bullets, 117
Operations Research Office for, 205
and Ruger guns, 233
sharpshooters in, **207**
and Spencer rifles, 127
and "30 aught 6" cartridges, 203
Thompson and, 191
and tommy guns, 192, 197
on Western frontier, 148–49
See also military, U.S.; Ordnance
Board/Department, U.S. Army;
specific person, war, or battle
Arnold, Benedict, 34, 60, 92
arrows. *See* bows and arrows; crossbows
Arrowsmith, George, 118
Ashcroft, John, 244–45, 246
assault weapons, 215–24, 243. *See also
specific weapon, war, or inventor*
Atkinson, Theodore Sr., 40
atomic bombs, 207
Austrian army, 91, 164
Auto-Ordnance (Cleveland, Ohio),
Thompson's, 191, 194, 197–98, 233

automatic weapons
air gun as precursor of, 91
and arms race, 2
benefits of, 167
and civilians, 242
cost of, 192
development of, 190
and gun control laws, 242
impact on warfare of, 167
machine guns as, 181
pistols as, 192
rifles as, 180, 184, 191
shotguns as, 179–80
and World War I, 184
See also specific weapon or inventor

background checks, 242, 243, 248
Ballew, Kenyon, 232
Barnard, Henry, 105
barrels, gun, 29, 121. *See also specific
weapon*
bayonets, 63, 93, 182
Bean, Judge Roy, 112
Beecher, Henry Ward, 145–46
Beer Wars (1920), 193
Belleau Wood, Battle at, 211
Bellesiles, Michael A., 47
Belloc, Hilaire, 166
Bennett, T. G., 177, 179–80
Berdan, Hiram, 128–29, 209
Bill of Rights, American, 71–79, 239. *See
also specific amendment*
Bill of Rights, English, 45, 73–74
Billinghurst-Requa battery gun, 161–62
Billinghurst, William, 161
Billings, Charles, 105
Billy the Kid (Henry McCarty), 137
Black Hawk War, 93
black powder. *See* gunpowder: black
blacks: and gun ownership, 239, 241–42
blacksmiths, 68
Blackstone, William, 73–74, 76
Blakeslee (Erastus) cartridge box, 125
Blish, John Bell, 191

Browning weapons (*cont.*)
  in World War II, 187
  See also specific weapon or type of weapon
Bruce, Robert V., 126, 127
Buel, James W., 136
buffalo, 87, 144–47, 150
Buffalo Bill Wild West Show, **143**, 149,
    150–51, 152
bullets
  cylindrical, 115–17
  development of, 114–18
  Minié, 116–17, 209
  "Rocket Balls" as, 117–18
Bunker Hill, Battle of, 34
Buntline, Ned (Edward Zane Carroll
    Judson Sr.), 149–50
Bureau of Alcohol, Tobacco, and
    Firearms, U.S. (ATF), 232, 237, 242
Burger, Warren, 244
Burgoyne, John, 54, 55, 59–61
Burnside, Ambrose, 210
Burton, James H., 117
Bushmaster Corporation, 224
Butler, Benjamin, 162–64
Butler, Frank, 151, 152
Byzantines, 35

Cagney, James, 195
Cakhvell, John, 96
Camp Dubois: Corps of Discovery at,
    83–84
Camp Lejeune (North Carolina):
    sharpshooter training at, 212
cannons, 2, 4, 5–7, 12, 20, 37, 40, 84
Canton, Massachusetts: gunpowder plant
    in, 38
Capone, Al, 189, 193–94
Carten, Frederick, 219
cartridges
  all-in-one, 137
  bottleneck, 203
  "center-fire," 122
  and development of breech-loading
    guns, 126

  early, 114–18
  metallic, 114–17, 130
  paper, 115
  rimfire, 121, 122
  and "Rocket Balls," 117–18
  self-contained, 84, 114–17
  and technological advances, 122
  "30 aught 6," 203
  and Western expansion, 84
  See also specific weapon
Caspi, Antonio, 185
Cass, David, 212
Catholics: and gun ownership, 21, 73, 241
Catlin, George, 109
cavalry, American: and Spencer rifles, 131
"center-fire" ammunition, 122
chambered rotating weapons, Colt's,
    97–98
Champlain, Samuel de, 11, 12, 13–16,
    17
Chappel, Alonzo, **83**
Charleville muskets, 69, **69**, 70
Chase, Anson, 97
Chaucer, Geoffrey, 67
Cheney family, 125, 126
Cheyenne Indians, 148–49
Chicago, Illinois
  gang warfare in, 193–95
  gun control laws in, 247–48
Chickamauga, Battle of, 127
China, 4, 202, 213, **215**
Chinn, George Morgan, 183, 187
Church, William, 209–10
Churchill, Winston, 198
"Cincinnati revolt," NRA, 232
cities
  gun control laws in, 230–31
  See also specific city
Civil War
  and breech-loading rifles, 126–27, 128,
    129–30, 131
  casualties in, 117, 159
  and Colt firearms, 102, 107–8, 129
  doctors in, 159–60

LIST OF ILLUSTRATIONS
AND CREDITS

★

"The Struggle on Concord Bridge." Illustration from "Life of George Washington" by Washington Irving, 1857. *The New York Public Library digital collection.*

Prologue: "A samurai shooting an early firearm in the mid-1600s." Utagawa Kuniyoshi (1797–1861).

Part I: "First Blow for Liberty." Ritchie, Alexander Hay and Darley, Felix Octavius Carr. *Library of Congress, Prints & Photographs Division*, LC-USZ62-2727.

Chapter One: "Musketeer from Jacob van Gheyn's *Wapenhandelingen van Roers. Musquetten ende Spiesen.*" (1608).

Chapter Two: "Samoset comes 'boldly' into Plymouth settlement." Woodcut designed by A. R. Waud and engraved by J. P. Davis, 1876. From the book *A Popular History of the United States* by Bryant, William Cullen and Gay, Sydney Howard (Scribner Company).
"Mayflower Gun." *Courtesy of National Rifle Association Museums.*
"Kentucky Rifle." *Courtesy of National Rifle Association Museums.*

Chapter Three: "The Method of Refining Salt-Petre" by Paul Revere, 1774. Courtesy of American Antiquarian Society.

Chapter Four: "The Battle of Lexington" by Luigi Delnoce, 1882. *The Bureau of Engraving and Printing.*

Chapter Five: "Maryland Rifleman, 1775–1776." *The New York Public Library Digital Collections.*

Chapter Six: "The Death of General Mercer at the Battle of Princeton," January 3, 1777. *Yale University Art Gallery, Trumbull Collection,* (1832.6.1).

"Brown Bess." *Courtesy of National Rifle Association Museums.*
"Charleville lock." *Courtesy of National Rifle Association Museums.*

Chapter Seven: "George Washington presiding over the Philadelphia Convention." Howard Chandler Christy, 1939. *Library of Congress, Prints & Photographs Division,* LC-USA7-34630.

Part II: "Daniel Boone Escorting Settlers through the Cumberland Gap." George Caleb Bingham, *The Bridgeman Art Library,* Object 29102.

Chapter Eight: "Daniel Boone" by Alonzo Chappel, 1862. *National Portrait Gallery of Eminent Americans,* Vol I, (Steel Engraving).
"Springfield 1795 flintlock musket." *Courtesy of National Rifle Association Museums.*

Chapter Nine: "Steel Engraving of Samuel Colt with a Colt 1851 Navy Revolver," 1855. Based on a lost daguerreotype by Philipp Graff (1814–1851) taken between 1847 and 1851.
"Colt Model 1860 Army Percussion Revolver." *Courtesy of National Rifle Association Museums.*
"Colt Second Model Dragoon Revolver." *Courtesy of National Rifle Association Museums.*

Chapter Ten: "Claude Étienne Minié." https://en.wikipedia.org/wiki/Claude-Étienne_Minié.
"Smith & Wesson Model 1." *Courtesy of National Rifle Association Museums.*

Chapter Eleven: "Frank Leslie's scenes and portraits of the Civil War," by Frank Leslie, 1894. *The Institute of Museum and Library Services.*

Chapter Twelve: "Wild Bill Hickok." *Heritage Auctions.*
"Remington New Model Army Percussion Revolver." *Courtesy of National Rifle Association Museums.*

Chapter Thirteen: "Buffalo Bill's Wild West Historical Sketches and Programme," 1896, *Missouri History Museum.*
"Sharps Rifle." *Courtesy of National Rifle Association Museums.*

Part III: "Recruits, 18th Penn. N.G., Pittsburgh." Bain News Service, 1915. *Library of Congress, Prints & Photographs Division,* LC-DIG-ggbain-22112.

Chapter Fourteen: "Battery Gun by Richard Jordan Gatling," 1865. *National Archives and Records Administration, Records of the Patent and Trademark Office.*

Chapter Fifteen: "Sir Hiram Maxim." Bain News Service, 1915. *Library of Congress, Prints & Photographs Division*, LC-DIG-ggbain-23307.

Chapter Sixteen: John M. Browning's son Lt. Val Browning with the M1918 Browning Automatic Rifle, 1918." *Army Heritage and Education Center.*
"Winchester Model 1886 Lever-Action Rifle." *Courtesy of National Rifle Association Museums.*

Chapter Seventeen: "Amusements—Games and Rides—Woman shooting tommy gun." *The New York Public Library Digital Collections.* 1935–1945.

Chapter Eighteen: "You Can't Afford to Miss Either! Buy Bonds Every Payday," 1944. *United States Department of the Treasury.*

Chapter Nineteen: "A U.S. Army sniper team from Jalalabad Provincial Reconstruction Team," U.S. Department of Defense, 2006.
"U.S.M.C. Winchester M70 Sniper Rifle." *Courtesy of National Rifle Association Museums.*

Chapter Twenty: "A U.S. Army M.P. inspects a Chinese AK-47 recovered in Vietnam," 1968. *United States Army Heritage and Education Center.*

Chapter Twenty-One: "Two men and three women of the Home Defense Unit with guns," 1935–1945. *The New York Public Library Digital Collections.*

Conclusion: "Come and Take It." Flag raised by Texas settlers at the Battle of Gonzales in October 1835. http://en.wikipedia.org/wiki/File:Texas Flag Come and Take It.svg.

Notes: "The New Hampshire Sharp-Shooters," 1861. *The New York Public Library Digital Collections.*

Glossary: "Rod and gun from Canadian Forestry Association," 1898. *University of Toronto.*

Selected Bibliography: "Lewis and Clark Expedition 150th anniversary issue, designed by Charles R. Chickering."

Acknowledgments: "The posse that attacked Christie's fort on November 3, 1892." *United States Marshals Service.*